The Place of Mediation within the Modern Civil Justice System

This book is dedicated to:
Masood's late sister, Samina ('Baji'), and his parents, Haji Maqsood Ahmed and Khurshid Begum
and
David's remarkable wife, Amy and his beautiful daughter, Evelyn Christina

The Place of Mediation within the Modern Civil Justice System

Critical Perspectives

Edited by

Masood Ahmed

Associate Professor of Law, Leicester Law School, University of Leicester, UK

David Sixsmith

Assistant Professor of Law, School of Law, Northumbria University, Newcastle upon Tyne, UK

Edward Elgar PUBLISHING

Cheltenham, UK • Northampton, MA, USA

Cover image: *Italian Landscape with Umbrella Pines*, Hendrik Voogd, 1807. Rijksmuseum, Amsterdam.

Published by

Edward Elgar Publishing Limited
The Lypiatts
15 Lansdown Road
Cheltenham
Glos GL50 2JA
UK

Edward Elgar Publishing, Inc.
William Pratt House
9 Dewey Court
Northampton
Massachusetts 01060
USA

Authorised representative in the EU for GPSR queries only: Easy Access System Europe – Mustamäe tee 50, 10621 Tallinn, Estonia, gpsr.requests@easproject.com

A catalogue record for this book is available from the British Library

Library of Congress Control Number: 2025951275

This book is available electronically in the **Elgar**online
Law subject collection
https://doi.org/10.4337/9781035341368

MIX
Paper | Supporting responsible forestry
FSC® C013604

ISBN 978 1 0353 4135 1 (cased)
ISBN 978 1 0353 4136 8 (eBook)
ISBN 978 1 0353 9527 9 (ePub)

Printed and bound by CPI Group (UK) Ltd, Croydon, CR0 4YY

Contents

List of contributors

Masood Ahmed – University of Leicester, UK

Fatma Arslan – University of Warwick, UK

Antonio Cabral – University of Rio de Janeiro State, Brazil

Peter C.H. Chan – City University of Hong Kong, China

Bryan Clark – Head of the School of Law, Lancaster University, UK

Chinwe Egbunike-Umegbolu – University of the West Indies, Jamaica

Emma van Gelder – Utrecht University, The Netherlands

Debbie De Girolamo – Queen Mary University of London, UK

Tony Guise – Director, DisputesEfiling.com Limited, UK

Viktoriia Hamaiunova – Newcastle University, UK

Victoria McCloud – retired Master of the King's Bench Division, Associate Tenant at Gatehouse Chambers, Consultant at W-Legal Solicitors, member of the Costs ADR Group, and Advisory Head of Interdisciplinary Collaboration, Euro-Expert, Paris, Sorbonne Panthéon, France

Amy Sixsmith – Sunderland University, UK

David Sixsmith – Northumbria University, Newcastle upon Tyne, UK

Marc Simon Thomas – Utrecht University, The Netherlands

Ben Wilson – University of Baltimore, USA

Foreword

When I was young and naive, I was committed to ADR and so set up an arbitration and neutral evaluation system for Personal Injury and Clinical Negligence claims called PIcArbs. Thirty QCs (as they then were) took training from a professor, and so did 30 junior barristers. The Rules were drafted, honed, edited through 33 versions and then published. Tony Guise developed brilliant e-filing software, so all claims could be issued, served, and run online. Mediation, neutral evaluation or arbitration could be chosen from the menu of ADR resolution. Fees were low. We presented to large insurers, NHS Resolution and many solicitors' firms. A pilot was set up with 10 claimant firms and five insurers who agreed to put 100 cases through. In the end, the throughput never took off. Insurers told me privately that they thought it would add to the cost of settling cases. Claimant firms told me that they thought it would reduce their legal costs. I shut the company down in 2020, having made a loss of £35,000 over 10 years.

Now, as a member of the judiciary, I remain committed to ADR. There are so many reasons why ADR is a good thing. It reduces stress, it reduces legal costs (if properly organised), it can be organised wholly in the digital domain, it will produce settlements in most cases, and it avoids the uncertainty of a court ruling or decision on the facts and it should be a lot faster than civil litigation.

ADR is like a smorgasbord. There are quite a few tasty morsels on the tray which will satisfy the litigants' hunger but, for many litigants, they all look a bit foreign. This needs to change.

Mediation has taken off in clinical negligence claims because NHS Resolution is the main defendant and has driven it, but elsewhere in litigation in England and Wales, mediation has been a bit part player with a walk-on part. Arbitration has had a firm place in commercial worlds in the last 50 years but is far from dominant. The commercial court in London is not lacking in work. Early neutral evaluation is a babe in arms in most claims but is used in building disputes.

So, this book on mediation is timely. The collection of chapters examining UK and worldwide mediation is informative, intellectual and well researched.

Let us hope that this book marks the necessary upswing in the use of mediation in England and Wales. It is not difficult to change thinking; one just has to think differently.

Sir Andrew Ritchie
Judge of the High Court, King's Bench Division
Royal Courts of Justice
London

1. Introduction to *The Place of Mediation within the Modern Civil Justice System: Critical Perspectives*

Masood Ahmed and David Sixsmith

INTRODUCTION

The fundamental human right of access to civil justice continues to be undermined by crippling litigation costs, the complex nature of the court process and severe delays. The matter has been made worse by the impact of the Covid-19 pandemic. Policy makers and the judiciary have embarked on various major reform programmes across civil justice systems in an attempt to increase access to justice. A recurring focus of reform across international jurisdictions is the formal integration of mediation within civil court processes and the gradual move towards compulsory mediation. Mediation has, at varying paces, been embraced by policy makers and the courts as a cost and time-efficient method of resolving disputes which, in turn, has the potential to ease the huge pressures on finite court resources. Mediation has also grown in international prominence with the promulgation of the Singapore Mediation Convention establishing a uniform framework for the effective recognition and enforcement of commercial mediated settlement agreements across borders.

It is the increasingly significant role that mediation is playing in domestic civil justice reform policy and in the international dispute resolution landscape that has inspired this book. Here, we bring together diverse, contemporary scholarship to examine the varying approaches to mediation's adoption and normalisation across a number of jurisdictions and on the international stage. In doing so, the book offers a critical examination of the challenges and opportunities presented by mediation and provides unique perspectives on the practices, policies, and theoretical frameworks that define its evolving role in civil justice globally. This has significant reach and relevance to policymakers, the judiciary, and scholars in the field of dispute resolution, offering key insight into how mediation has been utilised and formally integrated into civil justice systems globally and how challenges and risk may be mitigated to ensure that mediation remains an effective alternative to the court process while preserving parties' right of access to justice. By bringing together contemporary scholarship, this book enables fresh debates and perspectives on how modern civil justice systems operate more generally and provides a key reference point for those interested in, and tasked with, developing mediation's role within those justice systems for the future.

STRUCTURE OF THE BOOK

The contemporary issues discussed across the range of chapters in this book explore three core but related themes: normalisation of mediation within domestic communities who engage with civil justice systems; international and global development of mediation as a vehicle for, *inter alia*, resolving cross-border disputes; and the integration of mediation into justice systems through digital processes. This book provides a novel and contemporary reference point for debates that are currently ongoing about mediation's role in modern civil justice systems, bringing together scholars from a variety of backgrounds and jurisdictions to provide critical perspectives and conclusions reached through the application of a variety of methodologies. It is broadly acknowledged that mediation plays an enhanced role in dispute resolution processes in comparison with previously; however, this has not been without its significant challenges, many of which are explored and dissected here. It is through analysis of these challenges and difficulties that progress can be made, as mediation continues its journey towards cultural normalisation and international recognition.

The first theme to be explored by the book is the integration and cultural normalisation of mediation. In chapter 2, David Sixsmith and Amy Sixsmith make an important contribution to understanding the challenges that have arisen with the ongoing implementation of mandatory mediation into the small claims process in England and Wales. Applying Normalisation Process Theory and conducting an analysis of statistics relating to the historical performance of the Small Claims Mediation Service, they argue that there is still quite some distance to travel before cultural normalisation of mediation can be achieved. They conduct a comparative analysis with the integration of mediation into the British Columbian low value civil claim resolution process and argue that the incremental approach to normalising mediation as part of British Columbian civil justice policy for the past 30 years has enabled its successful integration into the Civil Resolution Tribunal. They draw on both this comparative analysis and the statistical evidence available to provide recommendations which, if adopted, they argue would improve both rates of party engagement with the Small Claims Mediation Service and the cultural normalisation of mediation in England and Wales more generally.

Fatma Arslan expands on the analysis of mandatory mediation and its role and effectiveness in changing domestic dispute resolution culture in chapter 3 by discussing the Turkish experience of swiftly implementing a broad 'one size fits all' mandatory mediation model across a vast range of disputes. The chapter evaluates the effectiveness of the policy in raising the profile of mediation in Turkey, particularly in the face of a European culture which typically still prefers adversarial adjudication over mediated settlement and a national dispute resolution culture which was, broadly, unaware of mediation prior to its sweeping introduction. The chapter goes on to analyse the issues that have arisen from the Turkish policy of mandatory mediation, particularly focusing on its failure to significantly impact the backlog of cases and the risk that failing to adopt a nuanced approach to its introduction will reduce mediation to simply a process that is carried out to satisfy a regulation, thus creating the perception that it is second-tier justice. The chapter concludes by discussing how a culture of settlement beyond the policy of mandatory mediation can be engendered.

Chinwe Egbunike-Umegbolu explores mediation's development as part of Nigerian dispute resolution culture in chapter 4. This chapter charts the evolution of Nigerian civil justice and highlights the role of indigenous methods of dispute resolution, alongside the post-colonial era cultural shift, in embedding alternative methods of dispute resolution to adversarial litigation. It discusses the Arbitration and Mediation Act 2023 and argues that it represents a significant step forward in its acknowledgment of mediation as a legitimate method for resolving disputes.

In chapter 5, Peter C.H. Chan evaluates the present position of judicial mediation in China, arguing that its current form, despite its efficiency and cost-effectiveness benefits, infringes on parties' right to autonomy and therefore breaches China's Civil Procedure Law. The chapter notes the important policy function played by judicial mediation, and its significant potential; however, it argues that this potential cannot be fully realised until fundamental reform of its operation is implemented, and assumptions around the suitability of mediation in every case are challenged. This chapter makes a valuable contribution to the ongoing discourse in this key and developing area of mediation scholarship.

In chapter 6, Emma van Gelder and Marc Simon Thomas consider the mediation landscape in the Netherlands, providing an overview of how mediation as a form of dispute resolution has developed within the Dutch civil justice system. The authors provide a critical analysis of government-funded initiatives, such as court-annexed mediation and the use of financial incentives to increase the use of mediation by disputants. The chapter then considers the relationship between mediation and the civil courts, before arguing in favour of increased public regulation of the mediation field, particularly with the increasing popularity of online mediation.

In chapter 7, Masood Ahmed critically considers the duty of the parties to consider and engage with mediation in light of three major developments: the Civil Justice Council's review of the pre-action protocols which, *inter alia*, places greater emphasis on mediation as a means of facilitating the early consensual settlement of disputes; the landmark decision of *Churchill v Merthyr Tydfil Borough Council* in which the Court of Appeal confirmed that the courts could compel disputing parties to engage with ADR processes provided they were permitted to revert to the court if a settlement could not be reached; and the amendments to the Civil Procedure Rules to reflect the decision in *Churchill*. Ahmed argues that, although *Churchill* and the ADR rules strictly apply to court proceedings, they also strengthen the parties' ADR duty during the pre-action stage. He also argues that the courts have the powers to compel parties to a second round of mediation even though they have engaged with mediation at the pre-action stage, which can serve as an incentive for parties to constructively engage with the protocols and, more significantly, with mediation. Ahmed explains that the courts should adopt a structured and principled approach when exercising their ADR power when considering whether to compel parties to a second round of mediation which he refers to as 'Judicial ADR Activism'.

In chapter 8, Ben Wilson provides a unique and detailed analysis of mediator neutrality in the United States, which has wider application and impact on mediation law and practice. Wilson's chapter examines the historical development of mediator neutrality by exploring the following salient questions: how did neutrality become the dominant mediator posture in the United States? How is mediator neutrality culturally defined? And is neutrality a defining principle of mediation or merely a helpful tool for mediators? Wilson explores these questions within a historical and contemporary context, drawing on the development of the law and practice of mediation and the evolution of the rich scholarly debates and discussion of the neutrality of mediators. Wilson concludes by posing salient questions and pointing to future scholarship on the topic.

Continuing the theme of legitimising and normalising mediation for both disputants and the legal community, Bryan Clark and Viktoriia Hamaiunova expand this to international commercial mediation in chapter 9. They consider the impact of the United Nations Convention on International Settlement Agreements Resulting from Mediation 2018 ('The Singapore Convention on Mediation') over the past five years. They review its principles and its objectives and evaluate the challenges associated with, amongst other things, its limited number of current ratifications and variations in domestic implementation. Building on this and using empirical data, the chapter reflects on whether the Convention will lead to a growth in international commercial mediation and concludes that, while the Convention itself is an impressive achievement, there remain some pressing issues for consideration such as the development of common mediation standards, areas of uncertainty in the Convention's drafting and the Convention's role in legitimising mediation for stakeholders.

Continuing with the international focus, in chapter 10, Debbie De Girolamo dives into the world of mediating the international art dispute. This chapter begins by exploring the suitability of mediation in resolving art disputes generally, exploring the reasons why it is felt that this particular type of dispute requires its own specific and individual process. The chapter then goes on to provide a critical evaluation of such specific art dispute mediation schemes such as the Intergovernmental Committee for Promoting the Return of Cultural Property to its Countries of Origin or its Restitution in Case of Illicit Appropriation and the specific sector ADR services offered by the World Intellectual Property Organization, and questions whether the development of more bespoke mediation schemes, responsive to the needs and requirements of the dispute itself, would be a matter to be explored and researched in the future.

The final theme explored as part of this book is the place of mediation in a digital world. Antonio Cabral's contribution at chapter 11 considers the increasing digitisation of the Brazilian civil justice system, the rise of e-mediation and the opportunities and challenges for the future integration and regulation of mediation within the online environment. He also analyses the evolution and development of mediation within the Brazilian civil justice system and considers the shift away from a purely adjudicative culture in the resolution of disputes to the integration and expansion of mediation and other forms of ADR. The chapter critically considers the innovative approaches introduced by the enactment of the Code of Civil Procedure and the Mediation Act promoting and enhancing the role of mediation before and during the court process, including the introduction of procedural agreements between the parties to engage with mediation before resorting to judicial determination of their dispute. Finally, Cabral considers the opportunities and the challenges of the future role of mediation.

In chapter 12, Tony Guise and Victoria McCloud focus on the increasing significance of mediation in the online space. The chapter commences by discussing, in more theoretical terms, the concept of justice and its complex relationship with mediation as part of a fully digitised civil justice system. It sets out a future vision of how artificial intelligence could be deployed as part of a restructured justice process and puts forward a testable hypothesis concerning the use of such technology in predicting the outcome of civil cases. The discussion is then situated against the current problems being experienced by the English civil justice system, with specific focus on and analysis of the backlog of cases causing substantial delays and expense to disputants. It concludes by discussing mediation's potential in pre-action proceedings and outlining the challenges associated with funding the digitisation of processes.

Mediation will continue to dominate the domestic and international civil justice landscape as policy makers and the judiciary continue to grapple with the perennial question of increasing access to justice. Mediation is also proving to be an effective and popular form of dispute resolution internationally, and there are unique opportunities to utilise mediation within the digital environment to improve its effectiveness for the parties, the courts and international organisations. There are also challenges in the integration of mediation which, if ignored, risk harming the parties' fundamental right of access to justice. The contributions in this book provide unique critical perspectives on the role of mediation in the resolution of disputes, and they put forward legal, practical and policy proposals for the future of mediation.

2. Achieving cultural normalisation of mediation in low value civil justice: Lessons from British Columbia

David Sixsmith and Amy Sixsmith

INTRODUCTION

In July 2023, the Ministry of Justice (MoJ) announced the introduction of mandatory mediation for all small claims issued under Part 7 of the Civil Procedure Rules in England and Wales,[1] initially for claims made on paper or traditional online systems and eventually being extended to cover all small money claims under £10,000.[2] This chapter provides an original and contemporary point of reference regarding the need to culturally normalise mediation in England and Wales. A comparative lens across England and Wales and British Columbia provides significant insight into how this could be achieved.

Viewing the implementation of mandatory mediation through the novel lens of Normalisation Process Theory (NPT), we argue that whilst compulsory mediation has the potential to add considerable value to the small claims process, mediation as a process has not yet achieved the status of being culturally normalised in England and Wales and, as such, care must be taken with the manner of its introduction and expectations should be set accordingly. While much of the rhetoric from the MoJ surrounding the introduction of mandatory mediation refers to its increasing popularity as a form of dispute resolution, this is not borne out by the statistical analysis presented in this chapter. We find that despite measures being taken to encourage parties to low value civil

1 Ministry of Justice, 'New Justice Reforms to Free up Vital Court Capacity' (gov.uk, 25 July 2023) <https://www.gov.uk/government/news/new-justice-reforms-to-free-up-vital-court-capacity>. Accessed 2 January 2024.

2 Ministry of Justice, 'Preparing for the Requirement to Mediate in Small Claims: What you Need to Know' (gov.uk, 11 April 2024) <https://insidehmcts.blog.gov.uk/2024/04/11/preparing-for-the-requirement-to-mediate-in-small-claims-what-you-need-to-know>. Accessed 26 April 2024.

claims to voluntarily engage in mediation through the Small Claims Mediation Service, a significant proportion of those parties are still opting out. We argue that this points to a wider issue with party engagement with the service, something which it is imperative to take into consideration when managing expectations of how quickly mandatory mediation can reduce the current backlog of small claims.

This is in contrast to the introduction of compulsory alternative dispute resolution (ADR) as part of the Civil Resolution Tribunal in British Columbia in 2016, a jurisdiction in which some form of ADR has been embedded into the procedure for resolving low value civil claims for nearly 30 years. Where divergences of approach are identified, solutions are proposed based on the comparative analysis of the British Columbian model. The originality of this discussion is twofold; it is the first to apply such a comparative analysis to the adoption of mandatory mediation in low value civil claims in England and Wales and it is the first to utilise NPT as a lens through which to understand the process by which the process of mediation can become embedded in cultural practices.

The chapter commences by arguing that there is a core need to look beyond the formal law and to see law in its legal cultural context. This contemporary analysis situates British Columbia as a useful comparator when considering the integration of mandatory mediation into the small claims process. This is followed by an explanation of normalisation process theory and how it has been applied and used as part of this research. The next section provides a critical exposition of the genesis of mandatory mediation in England and Wales, with an accompanying analysis of new data obtained on the historical performance of the Small Claims Mediation Service (SCMS), the vehicle through which mandatory mediation will be delivered. A rigorous and comparative examination of the evolution of mediation in British Columbia is then provided. We then set out a novel set of pragmatic recommendations for the implementation of mandatory mediation for low value civil claims in England and Wales, and advance significant proposals for enhancing the SCMS to improve rates of party engagement. In utilising the comparative approach and viewing the implementation of mandatory mediation through the lens of NPT, coupled with an in-depth analysis of the performance of the SCMS in England and Wales to date, we offer a rigorous, significant and novel perspective on the discourse surrounding mandatory mediation in low value civil claims which may resonate with both academics and practitioners across a variety of jurisdictions.

METHODOLOGY

This chapter compares England and Wales with British Columbia, with the comparator being selected from the application of a set of inclusion criteria to a range of jurisdictions in which mandatory mediation formed a part. The selection criteria were that mandatory mediation had been established as part of the formal civil justice system, not simply a pilot, that it was being used to deal with low value specified civil money claims and that there ought not to be a language barrier to overcome in accessing the source material. This was to ensure that there are no barriers to the identification of suitable data, and so that the data gathered and used for the purposes of forming conclusions is not at risk of misinterpretation or mistranslation, as it potentially would be if it were written in a language not spoken by the authors. The only jurisdiction which met all of the selection criteria was British Columbia. It is on this basis that it was selected as the natural and appropriate comparator jurisdiction for this chapter.

The basis for using a comparative analysis here is that it assists reformers with 'improving and understanding one's own domestic legal system by analysing how foreign jurisdictions have dealt with the same problem'.[3] This resonates when considering the nature of the law which governs procedure; however, this area is not and never has been devoid of context. Identically designed policies on mandatory mediation, for instance, may work perfectly in one jurisdiction but be a complete failure in another. Valid comparison, therefore, requires consideration of the wider landscape into which a particular law, policy or procedure has been, or is being, introduced, in order for the conclusions drawn and recommendations made to be both robust and useful.

Accompanying the theoretical and comparative elements of the chapter is an analysis of original data obtained through Freedom of Information Act 2000 requests submitted by the authors. The data cover the rates of engagement with the SCMS both before and after the introduction of the mediation 'opt-out' scheme, discussed in more detail below. Quantitative data analysis is carried out on those statistics, with both descriptive and inferential methods being used to present the data and to draw conclusions on what it shows when assessing the extent to which mediation has already been culturally normalised in England and Wales. Novel and original recommendations are then drawn from this on how to proceed.

NORMALISATION PROCESS THEORY

Normalisation Process Theory (NPT) is focused on 'how complex practices ... are made workable and integrated in context-dependent ways'.[4] May and

[3] Hugh Collins, 'Methods and Aims of Comparative Contract Law' (1991) 11:3 OJLS 398.

[4] May, C. and Finch, T. (2009), 'Implementing, Embedding, and Integrating Practices: An Outline of Normalization Process Theory', Sociology, Vol. 43, pp.

Finch, who developed the theory, define normalisation as 'the work that actors do as they engage with some ensemble of activities ... and by which means it becomes routinely embedded in the matrices of already existing, socially patterned, knowledge and practices'.[5] In the context of this chapter, therefore, normalisation aims to develop an understanding of the process by which mediation is not only integrated formally into the justice system but also accepted by relevant stakeholders as a routine element of the dispute resolution process in low value civil claims.

Normalisation Process Theory provides a three-stage framework through which this objective of normalisation can be assessed, which includes:

1. Material practices become routinely embedded in social contexts as a result of people working, individually or collectively, to implement them.
2. The work of implementation is operationalised through four generative mechanisms (coherence, cognitive participation, collective action, reflexive monitoring).
3. The production and reproduction of a material practice requires a continuous investment by agents in ensembles of action that carry forward in time and space.[6]

The four generative mechanisms referred to at point 2 above require additional explanation. Coherence means that the practice itself has to be held together by a logical set of ideas about its 'meaning, uses and utility'[7] and that relevant actors need to understand the practice as meaningful. Cognitive participation is the extent of the engagement and conscious commitment that the actors involved display. Collective action refers to the need of those actors to collectively invest effort in operationalising a particular practice. Reflexive monitoring is the process by which collective action is continuously evaluated by participants. When viewing the implementation of mandatory mediation through this theoretical lens, therefore, it is important to see that stakeholders understand the practice as being meaningful, that there is a collective and conscious commitment to its integration and to court users particularly understanding its value, and that there is a process of both formal and informal evaluation ongoing.

While this theory has been used extensively in the field of healthcare, this chapter represents the first time it has been used in a legal context, specifically

535–54.

[5] Ibid at 540.

[6] Ibid at 540.

[7] Ibid at 543.

in the area of mediation. Mediation has not, historically, been an integrated and mandatory part of the procedure relating to the formal resolution of low value civil claims in either England and Wales or British Columbia, and therefore its introduction represents a disruption to an existing material practice. We argue in this paper that mediation has become, over time, normalised as part of the formal dispute resolution process in British Columbia, but that it has not in England and Wales. Normalisation Process Theory may be able to provide valuable insight into why this is, as well as assisting with formulating pragmatic recommendations as to how societal normalisation of the process can be achieved in England and Wales.

MANDATORY MEDIATION IN LOW VALUE CIVIL CLAIMS IN ENGLAND AND WALES

To understand how the current model for mandatory mediation can be enhanced, we must first establish how mediation as an embedded and accepted form of dispute resolution has developed to date. We use this historical development to contextualise data obtained from the MoJ, which points to a significant issue with the extent of the cultural normalisation of mediation amongst low value court users in England and Wales to date. It could be contended that this does not matter given engagement in mediation will be mandatory anyway; however, we argue, with the assistance of normalisation process theory, that cultural normalisation leads to a much higher likelihood of increased engagement rates. Parties simply being compelled to attend does not mean that they will actually turn up, nor does it mean that they will engage in the process itself. We argue that to address this, attention needs to be given to two key matters: the first is to alter the current discourse so that focus is centred around engagement as opposed to settlement; and the second is that the introduction of mandatory mediation is accompanied by a framework of discretionary sanctions which can be applied to parties for failing to attend.

Understanding Mediation's Current Position in England and Wales

Lord Briggs stated in 2015 that one of the key objectives in reforming the procedure which governs small claims dispute resolution in England and Wales was to achieve the 'cultural normalisation' of ADR, and specifically mediation.[8] As part of his Civil Court Structure Review, Lord Briggs proposed a complete redesign of the small claims procedure, replacing the existing

---

8 Lord Justice Briggs, 'Civil Courts Structure Review: Interim Report' (2015), para 6.13.

framework with the Online Solutions Court (OSC), modelled very closely on the Civil Resolution Tribunal in British Columbia. One of the central focuses of this model was the integration of ADR into the second stage and, while Lord Briggs stopped short of recommending compulsion, he was clear that he expected many disputes to be settled by way of agreement at this stage. Briggs' approach here 'replicated Sander's under-developed appreciation that there should be an increased focus on preventive law by incorporating dispute prevention methods into the court's process'.[9]

Whilst the initial commitment[10] to adopting and developing the OSC model looks now to have been shelved,[11] Lord Briggs' report was significant as it placed ADR firmly at the centre of the reform agenda for small claims. It also recognised that one of the primary challenges facing the integration of mediation was that it was being introduced into a culture in which adversarialism was still the dominant approach.[12] Nine years on from Briggs' observations here, and in order to establish the extent of the cultural normalisation gap which mandatory mediation needs to bridge, it is therefore necessary to analyse the extent to which mediation is already embedded into the procedure for the resolution of civil claims.

Prior to the implementation of the Civil Procedure Rules (CPR) in 1999, ADR was referred to in discourse surrounding the development of the civil justice system,[13] but no formal steps were taken to elevate its status beyond being simply optional. It was only after the CPR were introduced that mediation's journey to becoming 'semi-detached'[14] to the justice system began. This was

---

9 J. Sorabji, 'The Online Solutions Court: A Multi-Door Courthouse for the 21st Century' (2017) 36(1) CJQ 51.

10 Judiciary.uk, 'Civil Court Structure Review: Joint Statement from the Lord Chief Justice and the Master of the Rolls' (judiciary.uk, 6 January 2017) <https://www.judiciary.uk/announcements/civil-courts-structure-review-joint-statement-from-the-lord-chief-justice-and-the-master-of-the-rolls/>. Accessed 1 March 2024.

11 Judiciary.uk, 'Speech by Lord Justice Colin Birss: Is a focus on data the way to improve access to justice in a multifaceted world?' (judiciary.uk, 30 November 2023) <https://www.judiciary.uk/speech-by-lord-justice-colin-birss-is-a-focus-on-data-the-way-to-improve-access-to-justice-in-a-multifaceted-world/>. Accessed 27 March 2024.

12 Lord Woolf, 'Access to Justice Interim Report' (Lord Chancellor's Department, 1995).

13 For example, see H. Heilbron and H. Hodge, 'Civil Justice on Trial – A Case for Change', Joint Report of the Bar Council and Law Society (1993).

14 Judiciary.uk, 'Speech by Lord Justice Colin Birss: Is a Focus on Data the Way to Improve Access to Justice in a Multifaceted World?' (judiciary.uk, 30 November 2023) <https://www.judiciary.uk/speech-by-lord-justice-colin-birss-is-a-focus-on-data-the

via three routes: firstly through a series of rules built into the CPR encouraging litigating parties to actively pursue methods of ADR and requiring the court to encourage it where appropriate; secondly through judicial decision-making and precedent; and thirdly via policy initiatives designed to embed mediation in dispute resolution processes. Each of these will be analysed in turn.

ADR and the Procedural Code

The overriding objective is the cornerstone of the CPR. Rule 1.4(1) requires the court to actively manage cases, with rule 1.4(2) clarifying this to mean that case management includes encouraging and facilitating parties' efforts to settle a dispute.[15] Rule 3.1(2)(m) goes slightly further, allowing the court to 'take any other step or make any other order for the purpose of managing the case and furthering the overriding objective, including hearing an Early Neutral Evaluation with the aim of helping the parties settle the case'.[16] CPR 26.4 also allows parties to request a stay, or pause, in proceedings to allow for settlement efforts to take place. This power extends to the court being able to unilaterally order a stay to allow parties to attempt some form of ADR. Finally, CPR 44 gives the court the power to impose costs sanctions on a party who has unreasonably refused to take steps to settle their dispute, even those who subsequently are successful at trial.

Achieving settlement outside of court adjudication is therefore an express objective of the CPR and, as a result, ADR has formed some part of the civil justice landscape since 1999. Although the express motivation for its inclusion at the time was to reduce costs and to further the efficiency and cost-saving agenda, driven by the expectation that more cases settling earlier would reduce the cost of running the court service,[17] this shows that the move to embed mandatory mediation into the procedure for resolving low value civil claims, and thus culturally normalise it, is not necessarily being made from a standing start.

Despite powers built into the CPR, however, voluntary uptake of mediation remained low. The DCA carried out a study in 2002 evaluating the success of Woolf's civil justice reforms, and with reference to mediation, concluded

-way-to-improve-access-to-justice-in-a-multifaceted-world/>. At para 52. Accessed 8 January 2024.

15 CPR 1.4 1(1) and (2).

16 CPR 3.1(2)(m).

17 See Simon Roberts, '"Listing Concentrates the Mind": The English Civil Court as an Arena for Structured Negotiation' (2009) Oxford J. of Legal Studies 1, Colleen M. Hanycz, 'More Access to Less Justice: Efficiency, Proportionality and Costs in Canadian Civil Justice Reform' (2008) 27 C.J.Q. 98 at 121.

as follows: 'the latest figures from CEDR (Centre for Effective Dispute Resolution) in their newsletter for Spring 2002 show that for the year ending March 2002 there was a reduction of 26% in the number of commercial mediations over the previous year. This scale of reduction was also reported by other mediation providers. The CEDR pattern is consistent with figures from the Association of Northern Mediators which delivered 214 mediations in 2000 but only 93 in 2001. The ADR Group reported a similarly large increase in the number of mediations in the year following the Woolf reforms which then subsequently levelled out'.[18] Consideration must therefore be given to how the discretion which is built into the CPR was being exercised, and how judicial attitudes to encouraging parties to engage in ADR have developed. This is key to assessing the extent to which stakeholders have *collectively* invested effort in operationalising a particular practice. Decisions from the higher courts regarding the extent to which those powers could be used to enforce that culture change have a clear impact on low value claims as a consequence of judicial precedent and pertain directly to the current relationship between ADR and its cultural normalisation in England and Wales.

Judicial Positions on ADR

From 2002 onwards, there was a noticeable rise in significant cases which dealt with the way in which the courts treated failure by a party to engage with ADR.[19] This culminated with the case of *Dunnett v Railtrack Plc*,[20] where the Court of Appeal initially ordered the parties to consider ADR and then heavily penalised the refusing party for failing to engage despite the fact they were ultimately successful in defending the claim. At this point, high-level judicial support for heavily incentivised ADR was consistent. The message of *Dunnett v Railtrack* was reinforced further by Lightman J in the case of *Hurst v Leeming*,[21] in which he stated that 'mediation is not in law compulsory, but alternative dispute resolution is at the heart of today's civil justice system'.[22] The emphasis is not on the first statement; it is on the one which qualifies it. It seemed clear that, whilst not considered compulsory, the path in that direction was being paved with every judgment.

[18] Department of Constitutional Affairs. 'Further Findings: A Continuing Evaluation of the Civil Justice Reforms' (*DCA*, August 2002) at paragraph 4.8.

[19] *Lownds v Home Office* [2002] EWCA Civ 365 at para 25; *Cowl (Frank) v Plymouth City Council* [2001] EWCA Civ 1935 at para 25.

[20] *Dunnett v Railtrack Plc* [2002] EWCA Civ 303.

[21] *Hurst v Leeming* [2001] EWHC 1051 (Ch).

[22] Ibid at para 12.

The effect of a direct judicial intervention in promoting ADR and using the cost sanctions available through the CPR was positive for the uptake of voluntary mediation. Hazel Genn, in her 2007 report on the impact of judicial pressure on the use of mediation, concluded that *Dunnett* had had a positive impact in this regard: 'Demand for the voluntary (VOL) scheme at Central London increased significantly following the case of *Dunnett v Railtrack* in 2002, which confirmed the power of the court to impose costs penalties on a successful party deemed to have acted unreasonably in refusing to mediate'.[23] Coupled with the ongoing DCA investment in court-annexed schemes, the shift towards parties using ADR, therefore increasing the chances of both swift and more cost-effective resolution, seemed to be having an impact on changing the culture.

However, this was soon to change with the decision taken by the Court of Appeal in the seminal case of *Halsey v Milton Keynes General NHS Trust*,[24] in which Lord Justice Dyson stated that 'to oblige truly unwilling parties to refer their disputes to mediation would be to impose unacceptable obstruction on their right of access to the court'.[25] This had a significant impact on the ADR agenda; Hazel Genn's view was that *Halsey* had the effect of encouraging solicitors for litigating parties to object to being referred to mediation in the knowledge that those members of the judiciary who might otherwise have tried to heavily encourage engagement with the scheme were now less secure in that position.[26] Indeed, post-*Halsey*, 80% of litigants opted out of being referred to Genn's Automatic Referral to Mediation scheme.[27] Lord Justice Dyson's

---

23 H. Genn and others, 'Twisting Arms: Court Referred and Court Linked Mediation Under Judicial Pressure' (Ministry of Justice Research Series 1/07, 2007). Available at: <https://webarchive.nationalarchives.gov.uk/+/http:/www.justice.gov.uk/docs/Twisting-arms-mediationreport-Genn-et-al.pdf>. Accessed 16 March 2021.

24 *Halsey v. Milton Keynes General NHS Trust* [2004] EWCA Civ 576.

25 Ibid per Dyson LJ at para 9.

26 H. Genn and others, 'Twisting Arms: Court Referred and Court Linked Mediation Under Judicial Pressure' (Ministry of Justice Research Series 1/07, 2007). Available at: <https://webarchive.nationalarchives.gov.uk/+/http:/www.justice.gov.uk/docs/Twisting-arms-mediationreport-Genn-et-al.pdf>. Accessed 16 March 2021 at 23.

27 Ibid 78–125.

judgment also caused inconsistency in judicial decisions which followed it,[28] leading to the overall landscape becoming both confused and unpredictable.[29]

Despite the decision being roundly criticised, an opportunity for the Court of Appeal to revisit the issue has only very recently arisen through the case of *Churchill v Merthyr Borough Council*.[30] The court made clear that the *Halsey* position on mandatory mediation was not binding and went on to say that provided a particular measure did not restrict a party's right to a fair trial, it should not be prevented, provided it sought to achieve a legitimate aim and was proportionate. It is important to recognise that this concerned parties being compelled to engage in non-court-based dispute resolution, to include mediation, by court order, as opposed to dealing with a broad brush policy; however, it is difficult to see how the introduction of mandatory mediation in small claims would not fit within the parameters laid out in *Churchill*. Importantly, the decision here represents a substantial move forward in re-establishing a unified judicial approach to compelling parties to engage in mediation, and thus evidences the collective investment of a key stakeholder in the implementation of the practice, and deals directly with many of the objections to doing so, something which also progresses mediation's journey from being an adjunct to adversarial litigation towards it being formally embedded and normalised in the culture of civil dispute resolution in England and Wales.

Development of Court-based ADR Initiatives

Finally, we must consider the initiatives implemented since the CPR were introduced which were designed to normalise mediation. Whilst there is not the capacity in this chapter to go through the schemes in depth, their evaluations revealed important empirical data on the attitudes of users when it came to considering whether to mediate. In the late 1990s, a number of court-annexed mediation schemes were set up. Evaluations were carried out by academics and reported to the DCA, a previous incarnation of HMCTS. Hazel Genn's study of the Central London County Court Mediation Pilot discovered[31] that

---

28 See, for example, *Laporte and Christian v The Commissioner of Police of the Metropolis* [2015] EWHC 371 (QB), *Burchell v Bullard* [2005] EWCA Civ 358 and *PGF II S A v OMFS Co* [2014] 1 WLR 1386.

29 M. Ahmed 'Mediation: the need for a united, clear and consistent judicial voice' (2018) 37 Civil Justice Quarterly 13.

30 [2023] EWCA Civ 1416.

31 Hazel Genn, 'The Central London County Court Pilot Mediation Scheme Evaluation Report' (Department for Constitutional Affairs 1998) at 155 <https://www.ucl.ac.uk/judicial-institute/sites/judicial-institute/files/central_london_county_court_mediation_scheme.pdf>. Accessed 3 April 2021.

for the majority of parties, their motivation to be involved came from wishing to avoid the high cost, delays and uncertainty of proceeding to a full trial, rather than a genuine desire to mediate. She also discovered that what participants actually wanted was a quick and easy adjudication of their dispute, as opposed to a negotiation.

This cautious view of mediation by litigants is borne out by the low numbers of voluntary participants who took part in that particular scheme; 'During the period of the research [May 1996 and March 1998], over 4,500 offers of mediation were dispatched by the court, but only 160 cases were mediated'.[32] Again, this is supported by the qualitative data available from other schemes, such as Birmingham, where a total of 2742 cases were allocated in the 34 months between January 2002 and October 2004, meaning that the 331 cases stayed for mediation represented approximately 11% of similar cases in Birmingham at that time.[33] There was therefore a distinct lack of appetite to engage in the process of mediation itself.

In March 2004 the Automatic Referral to Mediation (ARM) scheme was introduced at the Central London County Court. This ran for one year and operated by randomly allocating 100 cases per month to mediation upon the filing of a defence. The parties would pay £100 each, whereupon a three-hour court-based mediation would be scheduled. However, included as part of the scheme was the opportunity to 'opt-out'. An evaluation was conducted throughout the scheme's life which tracked, amongst other things, the level of engagement and percentage of 'opt-outs'. Throughout the full 12 months, the maximum percentage of cases where neither party opted out of the scheme and the case therefore proceeded without judicial intervention to mediation was 23% in August 2004.[34] The lowest percentage was 9% in December 2004, and the average overall was 16%, demonstrating a similar position to that which was found through evaluating the court-annexed mediation schemes.[35]

In 2007 the Small Claims Mediation Service was introduced, a free integrated service where civil servants would conduct consensual mediations between parties to small claims over the telephone. This is significant to the

---

32 Hazel Genn, 'The Central London County Court Pilot Mediation Scheme Evaluation Report' (Department for Constitutional Affairs 1998) at 155 <https://www.ucl.ac.uk/judicial-institute/sites/judicial-institute/files/central_london_county_court_mediation_scheme.pdf>. Accessed 3 April 2021 at p. 147, para 7.1.1.

33 L. Webley, P. Abrams and S. Bacquet 'Evaluation of the Birmingham Court-Based Civil (Non-Family) Mediation Scheme' (Department for Constitutional Affairs 2006) at p. 40. Accessed 15 March 2021.

34 Ibid at 35.

35 Ibid.

implementation of mandatory mediation in small claims, as this is the vehicle through which the mediations are going to be delivered. Following the initial success of the project, from 2012 parties to small claims litigation were automatically referred to the SCMS, but only where both parties agreed in their respective directions questionnaires. The initial referral was only made to a mediation information session where parties are given advice about the benefits of engaging in mediation and settling their dispute by consensual means. By 2013, the service had over 10,000 referrals per year and was estimated to have saved approximately 9,400 hours of judicial time.[36]

Up until May 2018, mediation was a voluntary 'opt in' process. However, in May 2018, the Online Civil Money Claims pilot introduced an 'opt out' mediation referral process.[37] This meant that parties had to actively indicate that they did not wish to be referred to the SCMS. The rationale behind the scheme was that opting litigants in automatically to taking part in mediation would lead to an increase in the low numbers of parties in low value claims who were prepared to mediate.[38] The pilot began with defended claims up to £300, which was subsequently increased to a ceiling of £500.[39] Since May 2021, all claims up to £10,000 issued using the Online Civil Money Claims pilot have been subject to the opt out scheme.[40]

It was initially anticipated that around 25% of eligible court users would opt out; however, the figures of those who actually opted out were actually significantly higher.[41] Some 73% of eligible court users actively indicated that they did not wish to participate in a free mediation appointment through the

---

[36] Sue Prince, ODR Advisory Group Working Paper on Policy Issues (July 2014) available at <https://www.judiciary.gov.uk/publications/policy-issues/>. Accessed 15 March 2021.

[37] CPR PD 51R.9(B) – Online Civil Money Claims Pilot and 111th Update: Practice Directions Amendments (2019) https://www.justice.gov.uk/courts/procedure-rules/civil/pdf/update/cpr-111th-pd-update.pdf>. Accessed 15 March 2021.

[38] Kirsty Swan, 'HMCTS Small Claims Mediation Service' (gov.uk, October 2021) <https://assets.publishing.service.gov.uk/government/uploads/system/uploads/attachment_data/file/1033969/HMCTS_small_claim_mediation_service.pdf>. Accessed 29 January 2022.

[39] The Civil Procedure (Amendment No. 3) Rules 2021 and 131st Update: Practice Directions Amendments (2021) <https://www.judiciary.uk/wp-content/uploads/2021/05/131st-PDMD-SIGNED.pdf>. Accessed 30 January 2022.

[40] CPR PD 51R.2.1(3).

[41] Civil Justice Council, 'The Resolution of Small Claims: Final Report' (January 2022) <https://www.judiciary.uk/wp-content/uploads/2022/01/20220125-CJC-Small-Claims-Report-FINAL-2.pdf>. Accessed 5 February 2022.

SCMS.[42] There is little empirical evidence which explains the basis for such low engagement; however, some commentary does exist which may advance this a little further. Personal dislike for the opposing party drives parties to engage in more expensive and time-consuming litigation;[43] Paul Randolph has argued that it is simply human nature to want to fight and win as opposed to compromise;[44] and Lord Neuberger has drawn attention to the 'credibility gap' from which mediation typically suffers in the eyes of court users.[45] This is particularly problematic as it demonstrates that attitudes towards engaging in voluntary mediation to resolve low value civil disputes have not changed significantly since the late 1990s, suggesting that it is still considered an adjunct to the civil justice system as opposed to an embedded part of it.

This is supported by the report following the Ministry of Justice's survey on dispute resolution in England and Wales during the latter part of 2021. It highlighted that lack of engagement stems from a range of different issues. Parties' lack of awareness of mediation and the lack of publicly available information to mitigate against this was identified, alongside mediation being only perceived as a 'hurdle to jump through' before applying to court, preventing parties from viewing it as a serious route to a sustainable solution and that using mediation was regarded as a 'form of capitulation'.[46] For low value claims specifically, the relatively low court fees involved in issuing a claim were cited as a deterrent for parties engaging in external mediations to settle those disputes.[47] These issues are so significant because this is not the start of the movement towards integrating mediation. As Randolph comments, campaigns have been ongoing for the past 20 years to promote awareness of mediation and its benefits, to persuade parties to engage in it voluntarily.[48] He therefore questions

---

42 Civil Justice Council, 'The Resolution of Small Claims: Final Report' (January 2022) <https://www.judiciary.uk/wp-content/uploads/2022/01/20220125-CJC-Small-Claims-Report-FINAL-2.pdf>. Accessed 5 February 2022.

43 Stewart P and Underwood A, 'Pride Comes Before a Claim – The Psychology of Dispute Resolution' (Field Fisher Waterhouse, January 2008).

44 P. Randolph, 'Compulsory Mediation' 2010, 7411 NLJ 499.

45 Lord Neuberger, 'A View from on High' (Speech at the Civil Mediation Council Conference, May 2015) <https://www.supremecourt.uk/docs/speech-150512-civil-mediation-conference-2015.pdf>. Accessed 10 May 2022.

46 Gov.uk, 'Call for Evidence on Dispute Resolution in England and Wales: Summary of Responses' (gov.uk, March 2022) <https://assets.publishing.service.gov.uk/government/uploads/system/uploads/attachment_data/file/1063691/dispute-resolution-in-england-and-wales-summary-of-responses.pdf>. Accessed 14 April 2022.

47 Ibid.

48 P. Randolph, 'Compulsory Mediation' 2010, 7411 NLJ 499.

whether it is just a matter of the public not wanting to know.[49] Viewed through the lens of NPT, this presents a significant difficulty as court users form a key stakeholder group and their commitment to accepting mediation as a formal practice is key to its normalisation.

Current Levels of Engagement with the SCMS

Establishing the current levels of engagement of court users with mediation is of key importance prior to the introduction of mandatory mediation in small claims. Underlying resistance to the process in principle will render its successful adoption in compulsory form challenging. To get a sense of whether the data published in the reports above reflects accurately the current position, it is necessary to carry out an additional and up-to-date critical analysis of the statistics. Figures provided to the authors by HMCTS and reproduced in Table 2.1 show the total number of referrals to the SCMS between April 2016 and January 2024, the numbers of mediations that actually took place and the percentage rate of settlement.

The figures demonstrate that an average of only 45.7% of cases which are referred to mediation actually make it to a mediation hearing. It is particularly concerning that in 2019, the first full year of the 'opt out' pilot conducted by HMCTS, this figure was at its lowest at 31.7%. Although settlement rates from the mediations which actually took place are good, the fact that only an average of 26.9% of cases referred to the SCMS settle and the high numbers of parties who go to the effort of actively refusing to engage do point towards an ongoing issue with cultural acceptance of mediation as a formal part of the small claims resolution process.

There are two key messages that need to be taken from this data, interlinked with each other. The first is that the primary focus needs to be on increasing engagement. Much of the rhetoric surrounds the number of cases that will settle following the introduction of mandatory mediation; however, in order to create the opportunity for settlement, parties need to be incentivised to attend mediation in the first place. Given this is the case, it is of crucial importance that the introduction of mandatory mediation is accompanied by a framework of discretionary sanctions which can be applied to parties for failing to attend. Such sanctions would need to be in line with the overriding objective and the *Churchill* guidance, and would crucially need to be consistently applied to avoid repetition of the situation that arose from the *Halsey* judgment. Without this, it is difficult to see how the policy of mandatory mediation will see levels of engagement improving beyond those outlined above.

---

49 Ibid.

Table 2.1 *Table showing engagement with Small Claims Mediation Service between 2016 and 2023*

–	April to December 2016	2017	2018	2019	2020	2021	2022	2023
Total referred	25,164	30,673	34,749	48,459	36,236	30,749	17,146	36,193
Mediations (and percentage of those referred)	11,782 (46.8%)	15,051 (49.1%)	13,842 (39.8%)	15,386 (31.7%)	18,115 (50%)	15,906 (51.7%)	8,385 (48.9%)	17,313 (47.8%)
Settled	7,618	9,477	8,296	9,448	10,345	8,805	4,304	9,024
Settlement rate (and percentage of those referred)	64.66% (30.2%)	62.97% (30.9%)	59.93% (23.9%)	61.41% (19.5%)	57.11% (28.5%)	55.36% (28.6%)	51.33% (25.1%)	52.12% (24.93%)

Source: Responses to Freedom of Information Request from authors to HMCTS dated 3 January 2022 and 28 May 2024.

That is not to say, however, that those parties who did engage with the service did not report positively on the process. Research carried out for HMCTS's Opt-Out Evaluation reported that most users were positive about their experience.[50] Where work did need to be done, however, was in managing the clear misconceptions users had around mediation itself. The mediators interviewed for the evaluation expressed frustration at the lack of understanding about how the appointment would work and, as a result, valuable time was lost from the hour session while the process was explained.[51] This then caused a discrepancy between user expectations of what the mediation could achieve and the reality. It is submitted that this ought to be treated as valuable evidence when considering how the user experience of the SCMS could be enhanced prior to mandatory mediation being formally introduced.

Therefore, considering the evaluations of mediation schemes of all forms in isolation, the challenges in introducing mandatory mediation are very clear. That said, these schemes still involved parties participating voluntarily. The focus of this chapter is on mandatory (i.e. non-voluntary) mediation and so it is useful to consider that, across the justice system more generally, compulsory engagement in some form of ADR does exist and now forms part of the fabric of dispute resolution in those areas. A good example of this can be seen in the area of family dispute resolution. Financial Dispute Resolution hearings were trialled from 1996 and formally incorporated into the Family Procedure Rules from June 2000. CPR 3.1(2)(m) expressly allows the court to order that a compulsory Early Neutral Evaluation take place which is *not* dependent on the consent of the parties. Mediation Information and Assessment Meetings (MIAMs) were trialled from April 2011, and formally incorporated into the Family Procedure Rules 2010 in April 2011. In employment cases, the ACAS Early Conciliation Scheme has been in place since April 2014. The RTA Small Claims Protocol requiring a party to make an offer to settle a claim where liability has been admitted has been permanent since May 2021. Finally, in small claims, a pilot of Dispute Resolution Hearings (DRH) was introduced in July 2020. The DRH involved a judicial early neutral evaluation and encouragement of both parties to settle. The hearing took place either over the telephone or online and was conducted by a member of the judiciary. If parties failed to attend, their statement of case was struck out. Figures obtained for the

---

50 Gov.uk, 'HMCTS Opt Out Mediation Evaluation Report' (gov.uk, 21 March 2023) <https://www.gov.uk/government/publications/hmcts-opt-out-mediation-evaluation/hmcts-opt-out-mediation-evaluation-report#:~:text=There%20are%20no%20penalties%20for,where%20they%20are%20offered%20mediation>. Accessed 8 January 2024.

51 Ibid.

Civil Justice Council report on the Resolution of Small Claims,[52] specifically in relation to the pilot scheme at Birmingham County Court, show that there are some very encouraging results from the first seven months of the scheme, with 47.5% of DRHs resulting in settlement.[53]

There are therefore pockets of the civil justice system in which compulsory ADR is operating, and that it has been for quite some time. In the areas in which permanent compulsory engagement in some form of ADR has been introduced, it has become a normalised part of the dispute resolution culture in those disciplines. It is worth noting, however, that these are instances where there has been collective and concurrent commitment and investment from policymakers, the judiciary and court users. The reason these examples are of such key significance is because they show that attitudinally England and Wales are capable of accepting ADR as a normal part of its dispute resolution culture. Parties may not always settle disputes; however, this does give reason for optimism that, if approached the correct way, formally embedding mediation into formal small claims resolution can work.

The data therefore demonstrates a mixed picture. The CPR have allowed for judicial discretion in encouraging parties to engage in mediation since their introduction. However, the lack of a consistent and unified judicial position on compelling parties to mediate, stemming from Dyson LJ's judgment in *Halsey*, has been unhelpful in driving forward the cultural normalisation of mediation as a form of dispute resolution. This uncertainty has now been clarified thanks to the decision in *Churchill*; however, given how recently this happened, it would be surprising if this had had any material impact on how mediation is generally viewed by court users when compared with litigated proceedings. The evidence from the various mediation schemes, including that available from analysing the statistics from the Small Claims Mediation Service, points to at worst a cultural resistance, at best a general apathy, to mediation as a practice. Viewed through the lens of NPT, it is therefore clear that there has been a disjointed, as opposed to a concurrent collective, investment in the integration of mediation as a practice. The points in time where the judiciary have thrown their favour behind mediation have not aligned with the times at which there has been government investment in establishing mediation schemes, which has meant that public engagement in the operationalisation of the process has remained low. There has been no continuous and collective investment in the practice of mediation, resulting in its use as part of the formal process for resolving low value civil claims being far from normalised.

---

52 Civil Justice Council, 'Resolution of Small Claims Interim Report' (2021) <https://www.judiciary.uk/wp-content/uploads/2021/06/April-2021-The-Resolution-of-Small-Claims-interim-report-FINAL.pdf>. Accessed 12 December 2023.

53 Ibid at 31, para 129.

Deprioritising focus on settlement rates and increasing attendance and engagement in the mediation process should be the key objective for the policy of mandatory mediation, and it is therefore crucial to attach discretionary sanctions, consistently applied, to reduce the risk of parties simply refusing to attend the mediation appointment. Thought needs to be given to what these sanctions would look like, with clear guidance on their application to ensure that they do not offend the principle of proportionality. Not to do so allows for the clear prospect that the policy of mandatory mediation will be rendered ineffective.

A review of the areas where some form of compulsory non-court based ADR mechanisms are operating reveals some cause for optimism, that resistance is not culturally ingrained, it is capable of being displaced provided there is a coherent approach between all invested stakeholders. We would argue that adjustments to the current model would make the transition smoother. It is the MoJ's objective that 'up to 20,000 extra cases every year could be settled away from court'[54] following the introduction of mandatory mediation. If achieving this is to be even a remote possibility, policymakers need to be led by the evidence, as opposed to simplistically viewing mandatory mediation as the silver bullet which solves the enormous pressures under which the court service is currently operating. It is here that analysis of the British Columbian experience provides a key resource. By evaluating and analysing the legal and policy framework in relation to ADR in BC and the extent to which it is, and has been, embedded into the fabric of the BC civil justice system, pragmatic recommendations can be produced which take appropriate account of the historical divergences of approach between the two jurisdictions.

THE EVOLUTION OF MEDIATION IN BRITISH COLUMBIA

Below we set out discussion on the evolution of government policy, judicial involvement and procedural reform regarding the embedding of ADR in British Columbia. In particular, we focus on what current data shows regarding public engagement with the ADR element of the Civil Resolution Tribunal. We find that, through numerous initiatives, consistent policy preference towards ADR and collective and continuous investment in operationalising mediation,

---

[54] Gov.uk, 'Government Reveals Plans to Divert Thousands of Civil Legal Disputes Away from Court' (gov.uk, 26 July 2022) <https://www.gov.uk/government/news/government-reveals-plans-to-divert-thousands-of-civil-legal-disputes-away-from-court#:~:text=If%20a%20solution%20is%20brokered,time%20and%20cost%20of%20litigation>. Accessed 20 February 2024.

this has succeeded in culturally normalising ADR as a central part of dispute resolution processes.

Mandatory Settlement Conferences for Low Value Claims

Following the Canadian Bar Association Task Force Report on Alternative Dispute Resolution,[55] British Columbia saw a significant reform of its small claims procedure in February 1991, with the introduction of the Small Claims Act.[56] This, amongst other things, increased the threshold of the small claims court to $10,000 and following recommendations proposed by the Justice Reform Committee Report in 1988, the Provincial Court introduced mandatory settlement conferences.[57] These were informal 20–30 minute meetings between the parties to small claims, facilitated by a judge who would assist the parties in reaching a satisfactory resolution to the claim. The judge could express an opinion on the strengths and weaknesses of both parties' claims and, as it was mandatory, could make a default order in the event one party failed to attend. If the matter did not settle and was referred to trial, it would be heard by a different judge. This was, for all intents and purposes, mandatory early neutral evaluation within the small claims jurisdiction in British Columbia.

After its first year in operation, its performance was formally and independently evaluated against the benchmark recommendations of the Justice Committee[58] on the instruction of the Provincial Government.[59] On settlement conferences, they found that 40.3% of cases which reached that stage were being settled and that they offered litigants a true alternative to court-imposed determination.[60] This compared to just 4.9% of disputed small claims cases settling prior to the introduction of mandatory settlement conferences.[61] When further evaluation was carried out in 2012, this figure was still holding

---

[55] Canadian Bar Association Task Force on Alternative Dispute Resolution, 'Alternative Dispute Resolution: A Canadian Perspective' (Ottawa: Canadian Bar Association, 1989) at 38.

[56] Small Claims Rules 1991.

[57] Ibid at Rule 7.

[58] Canadian Bar Association Task Force on Alternative Dispute Resolution, Alternative Dispute Resolution: A Canadian Perspective (Ottawa: Canadian Bar Association, 1989) at 120.

[59] Semmens & Adams, 'Evaluation of the Small Claims Program' (December 1992).

[60] Ibid at 21.

[61] Ibid at 32.

at 35%.[62] Additionally, the numbers of claims issued had increased by 42% within the first year of the new rules being in operation[63] and the number of replies or defences filed had increased by 89%.[64] This, the Semmens and Adams evaluation argued, was a ringing endorsement of the successful implementation of the reforms proposed by the Justice Committee and showed a genuine improvement in engagement with ADR in small claims.[65]

This must be treated with some caution, however. The introduction of mandatory settlement conferences represented a combining of judicial function,[66] essentially extending the powers of the judge at a case management conference to allow them to conduct an early neutral evaluation[67] and to mediate disputes. Judicial Dispute Resolution carries with it a range of advantages and disadvantages, discussion of which is outside the remit of this chapter;[68] however, given the historical preference for court-based, judge-led dispute resolution processes in British Columbia, the fact that ADR was being carried out by a judicial member is likely to have had some impact on the proportion of settlements.[69]

A form of mandatory ADR has now, therefore, been in existence for small claims in British Columbia since the early 1990s and that the findings of the state-endorsed evaluation were positive. Mandatory settlement conferences are still firmly embedded in the Provincial Court small claims procedure in British Columbia 30 years after their introduction. British Columbians had therefore been used to a mandatory form of ADR being embedded in their small claims resolution system for 25 years prior to the introduction of the Civil Resolution Tribunal, the model on which Lord Briggs heavily based his initial proposal for the Online Solutions Court.

---

62 BC Ministry of Justice, 'Modernizing British Columbia's Justice System' (Minister of Justice and Attorney General, February 2012) <https://www2.gov.bc.ca/assets/gov/law-crime-and-justice/about-bc-justice-system/justice-reform-initiatives/justicesystemreviewgreenpaper.pdf>. Accessed 29 December 2023.

63 Ibid.

64 Ibid at 6.

65 Ibid at 9.

66 T. Sourdin, 'Five Reasons Why Judges Should Conduct Settlement Conferences' (2011) 37(1) Monash University Law Review 145.

67 Rule 7.2.15, Small Claims Rules.

68 For a full discussion on Judicial Dispute Resolution, see T. Sourdin, 'Evaluating Mediation in the Supreme and County Courts of Victoria', Department of Justice, Victoria, Australia (April 2009) 5.

69 T. Sourdin, 'Five Reasons Why Judges Should Conduct Settlement Conferences' (2011) 37(1) Monash University Law Review 145 at 152.

Court Mediation Programme

Further moves towards the integration of mediation were made in 1996, when the British Columbia Court Mediation Program was formed. The programme itself was part of the court, although the mediators to whom disputes were referred were independent of the court service. The scheme was funded by the Ministry of the Attorney General and administered by the BC Dispute Resolution Practicum Society (now the Mediate BC Society).[70] This not-for-profit scheme provided mediators to the Court Mediation Programs in the small claims courts throughout British Columbia. Under the 1998 Practice Direction which originally governed the Small Claims Mediation Program (now Small Claims Court Rules 7.2 and 7.3), referrals to the programme were made through voluntary election by the parties, referral by a judge at a Settlement Conference or by mandatory referral in construction cases or by the date of reply (defence).[71]

By 2003, the Court Mediation Program was running 1200 small claims mediations per year across British Columbia[72] and there was evidence that the scheme was working to the satisfaction of court users: in 2002, settlement rates were 56% and 67% for mandatory and voluntary mediations respectively, 91% of the participants indicated that they would use mediation again and average satisfaction with the scheme was 4.32 out of 5.[73] As a result, in April 2003 an addition was made to Rule 7.2 Small Claims Rules which made mediation mandatory in certain classes of cases, specifically cases involving low value disputes of up to $10,000.[74] This represented an expansion of the ADR agenda in British Columbia, and the Court Mediation Program ran until May

70 Further information can be found at <https://www.mediatebc.com/about-us>.

71 Practice Direction SM CL 02 Small Claims Mediation Program.

72 S. Vander Veen, 'A Case for Mediation: The Cost Effectiveness of Civil, Family, and Workplace Mediation' (Mediate British Columbia, 2014). <https://pdfs.semanticscholar.org/c9d6/ea19a55f165d936277f372737a270eb4a301.pdf>. Accessed 15 January 2024. Also see Sarah Vander Veen and Angela Mallard, 'Three Years of Court-Connected Small Claims Mediations: The Importance of System, Program, Case, and Mediator Characteristics to the Court Mediation Program Outcomes' (Mediate BC, 7 August 2012). <www.mediatebc.com/PDFs/152Reports!and!Publications/Lessons!Learned!FINAL!VERSION_07!Aug!2012.aspx>. Accessed 15 January 2024.

73 J. Hogarth and K. Boyle, 'UBC Program on Dispute Resolution: Is Mediation a Cost-effective Alternative in Motor Vehicle Personal Injury Claims? Statistical Analyses and Observations' (Vancouver: Faculty of Law, University of British Columbia, 2002).

74 Rule 7.2 Small Claim Rules.

2016 when it was brought to a close,[75] just before the CRT was launched on 13 July 2016. During its 18 years of operation, the Court Mediation Program had conducted over 25,000 mediations,[76] an average of 1388 per year.

Notice to Mediate Scheme

The introduction of the British Columbia Small Claims Court Mediation Program added a further form of alternative dispute resolution to the small claims arsenal. This was expanded again in 2003 with the introduction of the 'notice to mediate' mechanism,[77] described by McHale as 'quasi-mandatory mediation'.[78] It introduced the option for one party to serve another with a notice to mediate. Once that notice had been served, the other party was obliged to attend a mediation with their opponent. If that party still refused, the requesting party could file an Allegation of Default notice with the court under section 33. This provides that if a participant believes that another has failed to comply with a provision of the regulation, it may (on notice to the other participant) apply for relief under section 34. Section 34 then goes on to provide that, on application, if confronted with an allegation of default that cannot be excused, the court may make various orders compelling the defaulting party's participation and, in extreme cases, dismiss a claim, strike out a defence or 'may make any order it considers appropriate with respect to costs'.[79] Section 35 states that 'the court may consider the existence of an Allegation of Default in making any order about costs, whether that order is made following final disposition of the action or otherwise'.[80] This is relevant given the discussion in the previous section surrounding the potential range of discretionary sanctions which could be available to the court to issue against parties who do not attend a mandatory mediation.

An 'opt out' system is also embedded into the procedure, meaning a party can argue exemption from mediation 'if in the court's opinion it is materially

---

75 Thomas J. Crabtree, 'Provincial Court Recognized Court Mediation Program's Contributions' (May 2016) <https://www.provincialcourt.bc.ca/downloads/announcements/Annoucement-May-05-16%20Information%20about%20CMP.pdf>. Accessed 12 January 2023.

76 Ibid.

77 Notice to Mediate (General) Regulation, see <https://www.bclaws.gov.bc.ca/civix/document/id/lc/statreg/4_2001#section34>.

78 M. Jerry McHale, 'Mediation in Civil and Family Cases in British Columbia' (*BarTalk*, June 2008) <www.cba.org/bc/bartalk_06_10/06_08/PrintHtml.aspx?DocId=31893>. Accessed 1 January 2023.

79 Section 34(1)(f) Notice to Mediate (General) Regulation.

80 Section 35 Notice to Mediate (General) Regulation.

impracticable or unfair to require a party to attend'.[81] However, since 2001, this exemption has only been claimed twice, in the cases of *Matsqui First Nation v Canada (Attorney General)*[82] and *Executive Inn Inc. v Tan.*[83] This is strong evidence to suggest that, on the whole, parties are compliant with the regulations once a notice to mediate has been served on them. In the event of non-compliance, the regulations then 'specifically contemplate uncooperative party behaviour in relation to ADR and confer a jurisdiction to penalize that behaviour in costs'.[84] A judge can compel a party who has refused to engage without reasonable excuse and, in extreme situations, strike their statement of case out on the basis of this failure. Finally, if the case does proceed to final adjudication, the court has the power to impose costs penalties on the non-compliant party. The scheme therefore represents a well-structured series of procedural steps centred on a heavily pro-ADR agenda.

The notice to mediate scheme has been described as the catalyst for a wider culture change in attitudes towards ADR[85] in British Columbia. Swanson argues that, as a consequence of its structure, it has succeeded in normalising the use of mediation in settling disputes[86] as 'the Notice to Mediate can be served without court interference and that this means parties take responsibility for mediation themselves and are then encouraged to use mediation in future'.[87]

The differences between the process adopted in the Notice to Mediate Regulations and that of the CPR are clear. The only area of overlap comes at the end: the way in which parties can be penalised by the court for failing to engage in ADR. However, whereas the Notice to Mediate Regulations follow a clearly articulated process, the CPR confers a general expectation that parties will engage in ADR, followed by affording judges the power to encourage this at case management stage, with a potential but by no means guaranteed risk that a party may face a costs penalty for refusing to engage.

---

81 Section 23(c) Notice to Mediate (General) Regulation.

82 *Matsqui First Nation v Canada (Attorney General)*, 2015 BCSC 1409.

83 *Executive Inn Inc. v Tan* 2008 BCCA 93.

84 Thomas S. Woods, 'Costs Sanctions for Unreasonable Refusal to Mediate: Coming to a Courthouse Near You' (2006) 31 Advoc Q 393.

85 Swanson, D. Creative Mediation System in British Columbia: A Model for us All (*mediatbankry.com*, 2018) <https://mediatbankry.com/2018/01/09/creative-mediation-system-in-british-columbia-a-model-for-us-all/>. Accessed 13 February 2024.

86 Ibid.

87 Scottish Government: 'An International Evidence Review of Mediation in Civil Justice' (June 2019) <https://www.gov.scot/publications/international-evidence-review-mediation-civil-justice/pages/9/>. Accessed 10 January 2023.

As was demonstrated in the discussion earlier in this chapter, this has led to a significant amount of inconsistency and, thus, a failure to encourage any more than a 'semi-detached' relationship between ADR and the justice system in England and Wales to date.

The question which follows, therefore, is whether the British Columbian approach has led to the same level of judicial involvement in enforcing regulations and rules relating to ADR. Upon review of the case law, cases involving unreasonable refusal to engage in ADR are conspicuous by their absence. While the judiciary in England and Wales was considering the position on how the provisions of the CPR should be used to encourage CDR or penalise those litigants who refused to engage in it, there is a noticeable lack of such jurisprudence across the same period in British Columbia.[88]

This leads to two key findings. The first point to note is that the adoption of a structured, compulsory ADR approach is more likely to lead to cultural normalisation of ADR than the use of judicial discretionary encouragement and penalty costs alone and secondly, it suggests that Swanson was correct in his view that the Notice to Mediate scheme succeeded in achieving a culture change regarding the use of ADR in British Columbia. As Ross comments, 'the effectiveness of the British Columbia approach stemmed in part from decisive implementation but is also surrounded by a range of approaches to dispute resolution that are top-down and more diverse … change there was driven by government'.[89] When viewed through the lens of NPT, it is clear that relevant stakeholders in Canada collectively and concurrently invested meaning in and demonstrated commitment to the normalisation of mediation within the civil justice system over a significant period of time. This coherence has enabled normalisation of the process within court users themselves.

Civil Resolution Tribunal

This leads to consideration of the way in which ADR is used, and has been received, as part of the Civil Resolution Tribunal (CRT). It is important to note that there are some key differences between the CRT and the current model for the integration of mandatory mediation in England and Wales. The first key difference is that the CRT is an online tribunal with jurisdiction to decide, inter alia, low value civil disputes. However, it runs alongside the court system and is not a replacement for it. The second is that the collaborative dispute resolution process, and therefore the CRT's equivalent of the mediation stage

---

88 Woods (n 84).

89 M.L. Ross, 'Embedding Mediation in Scottish Civil Justice: Riding the Tide for a Cultural Shift?' (2021) 40.1 Civil Justice Quarterly 41.

in England and Wales, is in fact split into two phases: phase 2 is negotiation and phase 3 is facilitation.[90] Phase 1 is focused on parties using a Solution Explorer online tool to receive free legal information and assist them with either making or defending a claim without the assistance of a legal representative. The negotiation stage at phase 2 does not involve any third-party representative from the CRT, only the parties to the dispute. In the event that parties are unable to settle their dispute at phase 2, they move on to phase 3 where the level of CRT involvement increases, with a CRT case manager, or facilitator, being allocated to the case.

The range of statutory powers the case manager has at phase 3 to facilitate consensual dispute resolution is considerable. They can perform early neutral evaluation, assist with negotiation and mediate the dispute between the parties.[91] It is also particularly interesting that under section 25 of the Civil Resolution Tribunal Act 2012, the case manager has the power to require parties to take part in the ADR process. This does not, of course, mean that parties are forced into settlement. It simply means that they must engage in the process of facilitated ADR at the relevant stage of proceedings and that the case manager has the statutory authority to enforce this. This represents a significantly wider remit than that undertaken by the mediator within the Small Claims Mediation Service.

The final key difference is the notable distinction between the ways in which the parties communicate during the process and how the early stages of the facilitation are dealt with. The facilitation stage of the CRT is mostly carried out asynchronously via electronic communication channels with the option, where necessary or appropriate, for the facilitator to communicate with the parties by phone or video.[92] The facilitator also speaks to the parties on a preliminary basis to ensure they understand the process itself before efforts to facilitate settlement of the dispute commence – in essence a pre-mediation meeting. The SCMS is limited to a one-hour telephone appointment with no such prior communication. These differences are of interest when it comes to considering how the SCMS could potentially be enhanced in the future – something which will be looked at in more depth in the conclusions and recommendations section.

---

[90] Shannon Salter and Darin Thompson, 'Public-Centered Civil Justice Redesign: A Case Study of the British Columbia Civil Resolution Tribunal' (2017) 3 McGill J Disp Resol 113 at 131.

[91] Ibid.

[92] CivilResolutionBC.ca, 'What is Facilitation' (Civil Resolution Tribunal, British Columbia) <https://civilresolutionbc.ca/help/what-is-facilitation/>. Accessed 16 February 2024.

Analysis of the CRT is valuable as it demonstrates the extent to which parties in British Columbia are content to engage in dispute resolution methods outside of judicial determination, thus serving as evidence of the level to which ADR has been culturally normalised. Firstly, regarding general satisfaction, data are available from a survey-based study of 49 tribunal users.[93] The study found as follows:

> Sixteen survey respondents were involved in a CRT dispute that was resolved in the Case Management Phase at the CRT, either at the negotiation stage or at the facilitation stage. Of these, almost all (14, or 88%) said that they were either very satisfied or somewhat satisfied. Six of these 16 (38%) were also in the group of respondents who had been to court before. All of the survey respondents who had prior experience in court and who had resolved their disputes at one of the collaborative stages reported that the CRT was easier than court, and that they were more satisfied with the experience at the CRT than with their court experience.[94]

While the sample size is small, this suggests that there is a general feeling of satisfaction with the service which is being provided by the CRT, specifically concerning its facilitated resolution stage. However, it is also important to consider what the available statistics say. Table 2.2 collates the statistics published by the CRT on an annual basis regarding the number of small claims applications and the number of those applications that are resolved by consent.

It is significant that there is a fall in the percentage of claims that resulted in default or non-compliance from one or both parties, reducing from 27.6% in 2017/18 and 41.5% in 2018/19 to 17.7% in 2022/2023. It is worth noting here that this statistic not only covers the number of users who have failed to attend stage 2, but also non-compliance or failure to participate at any stage; however, it is still very useful data. It demonstrates that participation levels are increasing year on year, and the most recent CRT annual report specifically refers to their focus on increasing levels of engagement.[95] This serves to underscore the need for policymakers in England and Wales to alter the rhetoric to zone in on using mandatory mediation to address historically low levels of participation in small claims cases.

The statistics also demonstrate another important point for England and Wales, which relates to expectations and the importance of managing them in

---

93 Sykes K., Dickson R., Ewart S., Foulkes C., and Landry M., 'Civil Revolution: User Experiences with British Columbia's Online Court' (2020) 37(1) Windsor Y B Access Just 161.

94 Ibid at 178.

95 CivilResolutionBC.ca (Civil Resolution Tribunal Annual Report, 2022/23) <https://civilresolutionbc.ca/wp-content/uploads/CRT-Annual-Report-2022–2023.pdf> at page 32. Accessed 2 January 2024.

Table 2.2 *Table showing number of small claims applications and the number of those application which are resolved by consent in the Civil Resolution Tribunal*

Year (1 April to 31 March)	Number of small claims applications	Number of small claims resolved by consent/ withdrawn	Number of small claims resulting in default/ non-compliance	Number of small claims resolved by consent	Number of small claims to adjudication
2016/2017		–	–	–	–
2017/2018	3668	661 (18%)	1,012 (27.6%)	947 (25.8%)	100 (0.27%)
2018/2019	4821	1,665 (34.5%)	2,001 (41.5%)	1,953 (40.5%)	1,074 (22.3%)
2019/2020	4926	1,927 (39.1%)	1,692 (34.3%)	1,927 (39.1%)	889 (18%)
2020/2021	4238	1,737 (41%)	1,048 (24.7%)	1,737 (41%)	1,026 (24.2%)
2021/2022	4175	1,637 (39.2%)	988 (23.7%)	1,637 (39.2%)	892 (21.3%)
2022/2023	4733	1,595 (33.7%)	837 (17.7%)	1,795 (37.9%)	883 (18.6%)

Note: Civil Resolution Tribunal Annual Reports available here: https://civilresolutionbc.ca/about-the-crt/reports-and-publications/
Source: Civil Resolution Tribunal Annual Reports 2016–2023.

relation to settlement. As this chapter has set out, ADR and particularly mediation have been a compulsory part of the civil claim resolution process in British Columbia in some form or another since the early 1990s. There is agreement across commentators that it has achieved cultural normalisation, yet the settlement rate is still only around 40%. This needs to be taken into consideration when the MoJ is referring to targets for the number of claims that are likely to be removed from the court system following mandatory mediation being introduced, particularly given the evidence which shows that mediation has some distance to go before it is culturally normalised in England and Wales.

CONCLUSION AND RECOMMENDATIONS

Cultural normalisation of ADR lies at the heart of the policy of mandatory mediation in low value civil claims achieving its potential in England and Wales. From our underpinning analysis and critique of the challenges faced by policymakers, our application of normalisation process theory and our quantitative analysis of original data sourced from the MoJ, we have identified that there is a significant distance to travel before this point is reached in England and Wales. The rigorous and contemporary comparative analysis provided in this chapter has, however, enabled us to make a number of novel and pragmatic recommendations concerning what can be done now to ease the journey. Policy discourse focusing on rates of engagement as opposed to rates of settlement through mediation, the development of a discretionary set of penalties to be imposed on parties who fail to attend mediation alongside guidance on how these are to be used, increasing the range of mediums through which parties engage with the Small Claims Mediation Service and introducing pre-mediation meetings as standard are matters which ought to be given urgent consideration.

Viewing developments in England and Wales through the lens of NPT, it is clear the cultural normalisation of ADR in civil claims has simply not happened to date. There has not been a collective commitment amongst relevant stakeholders to operationalise and embed mediation into formal dispute resolution processes. This, in turn, has led to low levels of engagement by court users, demonstrated by the reports carried out on the court-annexed mediation schemes during the 2000s, the CEDR study carried out in the same time period and the uptake and percentage engagement and settlement rates of the Small Claims Mediation Service. On the other hand, in British Columbia, some form of compulsion to engage in ADR has been in place for over 30 years, through settlement conferences, mandatory mediation schemes in small claims and quasi-mandatory external mediation through the notice to mediate scheme. The CRT brought these already widely used variants of ADR together and incorporated them as normalised methods of resolving disputes in phases

2 and 3. This, coupled with the statistical data available, suggests that ADR is viewed as an integrated part of the procedure to resolve small claims by tribunal users in British Columbia, and it has thus achieved cultural normalisation.

That is not to say that there are not reasons for optimism in England and Wales. Integration of mandatory ADR in family and employment cases, and the permanent adoption of it in small claims matters through Dispute Resolution Hearings in Birmingham County Court demonstrate that there is not an ingrained cultural resistance to it. However, the fact that mediation has not reached the point where it is normalised cannot be ignored by policymakers; it must be taken into account when managing the integration of mandatory mediation. The culture change sought in England and Wales is not an overnight process; indeed this is made more challenging by the fact that mediation is simply being added on to an existing dispute resolution structure with deep roots in adversarial culture. No meaningful steps appear to have been taken to invest in revising the format of the SCMS, nor has there been any direct attempt to present the small claims dispute resolution system to court users as anything other than an adversarial process with an element of consensual dispute resolution embedded.

Changing this will therefore require leadership and consistency in approach from those who develop and implement policy, and it will take time. This has to be taken into consideration when both targets and expectations are set. One of the core recommendations of this chapter is that the discourse surrounding the mandatory mediation policy needs to shift from focusing on increasing the rates of settlement through mediation to increasing the current rate of engagement in mediation.

Interlinked with this, urgent attention ought to be turned to the development of a framework of discretionary penalties which can be used by the court against parties who fail to attend without good reason, accompanied by clear guidelines on how and in what circumstances these sanctions should be applied to avoid the same inconsistency as followed the decision in *Halsey* from reoccurring. In British Columbia, directions on how parties who refuse to engage in ADR at stage 2 will be dealt with are set out in the Civil Resolution Tribunal Act. The Notice to Mediate Regulations allow the court to make various orders which compel parties to participate where no good reason not to do so has been put forward, including making costs orders or in extreme circumstances, dismissing a claim or striking out a defence. Analysis needs to be conducted on the range of sanctions which would fall within the parameters of the overriding objective and the *Churchill* guidelines. Given the Small Claims Mediation Service statistics demonstrate a significant percentage of parties who are referred to mediation actively not engaging with the service currently, it is likely that failure to adopt a similar approach in England and Wales risks that trend continuing and essentially rendering the term ‘mandatory’ illusory.

This in turn would undermine once again mediation's journey to being culturally normalised in England and Wales.

This chapter has also highlighted ways in which the format of the Small Claims Mediation Service could potentially be adapted in the future. Consideration should be given to expanding the ways in which mediators engage with parties. The CRT exhibits good practice here; case officers are able to use a variety of media to communicate with parties engaged in the dispute resolution process. This is to recognise the myriad ways people in society communicate with each other, to make the process as inclusive as possible and to not place unnecessary barriers in the way of disputants engaging with the service.[96] There does not seem to be a good reason not to extend this good practice to England and Wales, allowing mediations to take place via both video and telephone depending on party preference and enabling parties to communicate with the mediation service via email or, as investment in digitising the civil justice system develops, through a designated platform. This leads to the final core recommendation, and that is for the formal integration of a pre-mediation meeting. This is standard practice in private mediations and is considered a very effective tool to draw parties into the process and overcome any resistance to mediation those parties may have before the mediation itself took place.[97] It would also enable the mediator to answer any questions regarding the process prior to the mediation taking place which may address at least some of the concerns cited by mediators in the Opt-Out Mediation Evaluation Report. Its inclusion would enhance the chances of increasing party participation and engagement with the SCMS.

The introduction of mandatory mediation represents a crucial phase in the evolution and development of this area, finally giving mediation a central role in the resolution of civil disputes. However, the historical lack of stakeholders' concurrent collective and continuous investment in normalising mediation cannot be overlooked simply because it appears to exist now. It must also be recognised that mediation is not being integrated as part of a newly reformed system, but rather being added on to an existing one of which it was not designed to be a part. As can be seen from this novel discussion, the success of the model of mandatory mediation proposed here is dependent on taking into account the wider landscape into which it is being introduced and

96 Shannon Salter and Darin Thompson, 'Public-Centered Civil Justice Redesign: A Case Study of the British Columbia Civil Resolution Tribunal' (2017) 3 McGill J Disp Resol 113 at 131.

97 Sixsmith, D., 'The COVID-19 Response as a Mediation Blueprint for the Future? Mediators' Perspectives on the Shift to Remote Mediation in Civil Disputes' (2023) Journal of Mediation, Theory and Practice 1.

by studying the lessons from jurisdictions such as BC, where the application of NPT suggests that normalisation of mediation has been achieved, it is possible to manage its integration appropriately. The more carefully this is done, the more likely it is that cultural normalisation of mediation in low value civil claims in England and Wales will finally be achieved.

3. Can mandatory mediation cure it all? The Turkish experience

Fatma Arslan

INTRODUCTION

Since the late 2010s, mediation as a pre-action (i.e. pre-court) requirement has become an integral part of the Turkish civil justice system following its wholesale introduction for labour, consumer, and commercial disputes. Prior to these ambitious reforms, both society and the judiciary were largely unfamiliar with the concept of amicable settlement and alternative methods of dispute resolution (ADR), including mediation. Historically, the Turkish legal system has been considered to be one of the most extreme examples of legal transplants.[1] It has been a long-standing preference of Turkish lawmakers to choose and adapt foreign laws that are seen to be the 'best-fit' for various reasons. With respect to the mediation reforms, Turkey's willingness to become a European Union (EU) member has provided the context as part of other extensive legal reforms since the early 2000s.[2] EU progress reports have mentioned 'the need to raise awareness'[3] on mediation for the first time in 2009, with subsequent reports increasingly advocating for its greater use, leading to the introduction of first Turkish mediation regulations in 2012.[4]

---

[1] Esin Orücü, 'A General View of Legal Families and of Mixing Systems', in Esin Orücü, David Nelken (eds), *Comparative Law: A Handbook* (Oxford: Hart, 2007), 164.

[2] For a detailed analysis on the EU's influence on Turkish judicial reform, see Meltem Müftüler-Baç, 'Judicial Reform in Turkey and the EU's Political Conditionality (Mis)Fit between Domestic Preferences and EU Demands', MAXCAP Working Paper, No 18 (January 2016), available at http://userpage.fu-berlin.de/kfgeu/maxcap/system/files/maxcap_wp_18.pdf.

[3] Turkey 2009 Progress Report, Commission Staff Working Paper (14 October 2009), p 69, available at https://www.ab.gov.tr/files/AB_Iliskileri/Tur_En_Realitons/Progress/turkey_progress_report_2009.pdf.

[4] Law on Mediation in Civil Disputes, No 6325.

Although Turkey's EU accession process lost its momentum towards the mid-2010s,[5] Turkish policymakers were, nevertheless, increasingly desperate to address the chronic paralysis in civil courts owing to excessive workload and delay.[6] This crisis has worsened after the failed coup attempt in 2016, which resulted in the suspension of thousands of judges.[7] The years that followed the coup, up until today,[8] can be described as the era of mandatory mediation in Turkey, as it was introduced for one category of civil dispute after another in an attempt to alleviate the congested courts.

While mandatory mediation has long been a widely adopted civil justice reform tool globally, as a continental European jurisdiction,[9] Turkey's implementation of it has been notably ambitious. Turkish policymakers seem to have excelled in their efforts, surpassing even Italy, which is renowned for initiating a 'mediation explosion'[10] in continental Europe following its introduction of mandatory mediation. The unique circumstances surrounding the incorporation of mandatory mediation in Turkey make it an intriguing subject of study for those looking for insights into the challenges and opportunities associated with implementing ADR practices in jurisdictions that have historically relied heavily on adjudication with roots entrenched in the civil continental legal tradition.

To this end, this chapter is structured as follows. It begins with an overview of the mandatory mediation framework across three categories of civil disputes: employment, commercial, and consumer. It then provides a critical analysis of how these reforms have fared in terms of achieving their objectives of reducing backlog and delay. The analysis reflects on the problems that have arisen, primarily due to the hasty and wholesale transplantation of mandatory

---

[5] Müftüler-Baç (n 2), p 13.

[6] This problem has long been a major point of criticism. For instance, see the following Progress Reports produced by the European Commission in the early 2010s: Turkey 2011 Progress Report, Commission Staff Working Paper (12 October 2011) at p 49, https://neighbourhood-enlargement.ec.europa.eu/system/files/2018-12/tr_rapport_2011_en.pdf; Turkey 2012 Progress Report, Commission Staff Working Paper (10 October 2012) at p 70, https://neighbourhood-enlargement.ec.europa.eu/system/files/2018-12/tr_rapport_2012_en.pdf.

[7] Harry Cockburn, 'Turkey Coup: 2,700 Judges Removed from Duty Following Failed Overthrow Attempt', Independent (16 July 2016), available at https://www.independent.co.uk/news/world/europe/turkey-coup-latest-news-erdogan-istanbul-judges-removed-from-duty-failed-government-overthrow-a7140661.html.

[8] July 2025.

[9] Derya Tarman, 'Turkey', in Jan M Smits, Jaakko Husa, Catherine Valcke, Madalena Narciso, *Elgar Encyclopaedia of Comparative Law* (Elgar 2023) 535.

[10] Giuseppe De Palo, 'The Italian Mediation Explosion: Lessons in Realpolitik' (2012) 28(2), Negotiation Journal, 181.

mediation without adequate consideration for the different categories of civil disputes. Additionally, the chapter offers insights into how these problems could be addressed. The chapter concludes that while mandatory mediation reforms have significantly raised the profile of ADR in Turkey, their impact on alleviating the backlog appears limited. Ultimately, the chapter advocates for a more nuanced and holistic approach to ADR reform.

MANDATORY MEDIATION AS THE MAIN ADR METHOD IN CIVIL DISPUTES

Turkey's first significant step towards mediation was marked by the enactment of the Law on Mediation in Civil Disputes (hereinafter, Law on Mediation) in 2012, which governs voluntary mediations for the resolution of civil disputes, including those with a foreign element.[11] As mentioned above, the harmonisation with EU laws was a key driving force in Turkish policymaking.[12] The Law on Mediation was developed drawing from the regulations of European jurisdictions such as Austria, Germany and Hungary,[13] international instruments such as the UNCITRAL Model Law on International Commercial Conciliation,[14] and the Green Paper on alternative dispute resolution in civil and commercial law,[15] as well as the EU Mediation Directive.[16] The new law has prompted a modest increase in the number of mediations taking place in

---

11 Law on Mediation in Civil Disputes, No 6325, Full text available in English: https://rm.coe.int/turkish-law-on-mediation-in-civil-disputes/1680a72d94; a secondary legislation titled 'Regulation of Law on Mediation in Civil Disputes' was also published on 26 January 2013, in order to regulate the procedures and principles on mediation. Available in English: https://rm.coe.int/turkish-regulation-of-law-on-mediation-in-civil-disputes/1680a72d95 accessed 13 August 2023.

12 Deniz Ilter, Attila Dikbas, 'Construction Mediation in Turkey and an Overview of the Draft Mediation Law' (2008), https://www.irbnet.de/daten/iconda/CIB14509.pdf.

13 Mustafa Serdar Ozbek, 'Law on Mediation in Civil Disputes no 6325 with Comparisons' (24 January 2014), http://www.arabulucu.com/arabuluculuk-mevzuati/law-on-mediation-in-civil-disputes-no-6325-with-comparisons.

14 UNCITRAL Model Law on International Commercial Conciliation 2002, https://uncitral.un.org/sites/uncitral.un.org/files/media-documents/uncitral/en/03-90953_ebook.pdf.

15 Green Paper on alternative dispute resolution in civil and commercial law (2002), https://op.europa.eu/en/publication-detail/-/publication/61c3379d-bc12-431f-a051-d82fefc20a04.

16 Directive 2008/52/EC of the European Parliament and of the Council of 21 May 2008 on certain aspects of mediation in civil and commercial matters [2008] OJ L 136/3.

Turkey, with a significant portion of them being related to labour disputes.[17] The policymakers were encouraged by the high settlement rates in the limited number of voluntary mediations taking place[18] and there was an ever-growing pressure due to backlog. These developments have ignited a series of civil justice reforms centred around mandatory mediation. This new approach was again inspired by European models, particularly the Italian pre-action mandatory mediation.[19]

Before moving on to the specifics of dispute categories, it is essential to provide an overview of how Turkish mandatory mediation operates in general. While the framework for mandatory mediation is almost identical across the three sectors, there are minor adaptations, primarily regarding the duration of the mediation process, to reflect sector-specific characteristics. The mediation procedure is not integrated into the litigation process. Instead, parties involved in disputes subject to mandatory mediation must apply to the mediation bureaus that are located within the same territorial jurisdiction of the competent court.[20] The mediator can be appointed by the competent mediation bureau from a roster published by the Ministry of Justice[21] or parties can agree on a mediator from the roster themselves.[22] The bureau then provides the appointed mediator with the parties' details so they can initiate contact and arrange the first meeting.[23] Parties may attend mediation meetings in person or be represented by their lawyers.[24]

To ensure parties can proceed with litigation if mediation fails, it is essential for mediation activities to be documented with a record by the mediator.[25] If the claimant fails to include the original copy of the final mediation minutes when filing a lawsuit, the case will be dismissed on procedural grounds. Moreover, if mediation negotiations do not result in an agreement, the mediator's fee

---

[17] According to the official statistics for 2016, over 85% of mediation that has taken place was related to labour disputes. See Judicial Statistics 2016, 208, https://adlisicil.adalet.gov.tr/Resimler/SayfaDokuman/27820191126572016.pdf.

[18] Accordingly, the success rate was almost 95%, see the official statistics, ibid, at p 206.

[19] Giuseppe De Palo, 'Mediating Mediation Itself: The Easy Opt-Out Model Settles the Perennial Dispute Between Voluntary and Mandatory Mediation' (2021) 22 Cardozo Journal of Dispute Resolution 543, 560.

[20] Law on Mediation in Civil Disputes, Art 18/A (4).

[21] ibid Art 18/A (5).

[22] ibid.

[23] ibid Art 18/A (7).

[24] Law on Mediation in Civil Disputes, Art 15 (6).

[25] ibid Art 3 (11).

for the first two hours is paid from the budget of the Ministry of Justice.[26] In the case of a successful settlement, the remaining fee is paid equally by the parties unless otherwise agreed,[27] and all fees are calculated according to the minimum tariff.[28] Additionally, the law ensures that a settlement agreement reached through mediation is automatically enforceable without needing a court order.[29] Once signed by the parties, their lawyers, and the mediator, the agreement has the same legal effect as a court judgment[30] and cannot be contested in court later.[31] If a party fails to comply with the agreed-upon actions, the other party can seek an enforcement order, with the court only being able to review the suitability of the dispute for mediation and the appropriateness of the agreement for enforcement.

The law initially granted the courts the authority to impose cost sanctions on parties who unreasonably refuse to participate in mandatory mediation, requiring them to cover legal costs in full even if they ultimately win the lawsuit.[32] Although similar provisions are commonly found in civil procedure rules across both common law and civil law jurisdictions to incentivise early settlement,[33] it has sparked considerable controversy in Turkey and was eventually annulled by the Turkish Constitutional Court in 2024.[34] This development, among others, can be seen as a consequence of a hasty approach to ADR reform which overlooks broader systemic and cultural issues, as will be discussed in detail below.

The following sections will now critically explore the regulatory framework for each category of civil disputes subjected to mandatory mediation: labour, commercial and consumer disputes.

---

26 ibid Art 3(14).

27 ibid Art 3(13).

28 ibid.

29 Law on Mediation in Civil Disputes Art 18/A.

30 Law on Mediation in Civil Disputes, No 6325, Art 18(4).

31 ibid Art 18(5).

32 ibid Art 18/A.

33 In England, adverse costs orders can be imposed on parties unreasonably refusing mediation by virtue of Civil Procedure Rules 44.2. In Italy, according to Legislative Decree 28/2010, section 13, if mediation is not attempted without a valid justification, the court can order the uncooperative party to pay an administrative fee which would in effect double their court fees.

34 For a detailed analysis, see the section titled 'Consumer Disputes' below.

LABOUR DISPUTES

The Labour Courts, which operate under the Law on Civil Procedure[35] and the Law on Labour Courts,[36] have been considered to be one of the primary contributors to the state of crisis in the Turkish civil court system. The problem of backlog and delay reached its peak in the mid-2010s, with over half a million pending labour lawsuits and approximately 300,000 of them remaining unresolved from one year to the next. [37] In order to address this chronic problem, in 2017, mandatory mediation was introduced through amendments made to the law on Labour Courts and entered into force in January 2018. The new regulations were implemented without a previous pilot project as policymakers were increasingly desperate for immediate solutions to aid the overburdened system.

Accordingly, the regulations require parties to attempt mediation before initiating a lawsuit for disputes arising from individual or collective labour agreements, specifically in cases involving labour receivables, indemnities, or reinstatement to work.[38] Once the initial mediation meeting has taken place, the mediation process must be completed within three weeks.[39] However, mediators have the discretion to extend the process for an additional week in exceptional circumstances. The law does not specify which circumstances warrant an extension, nor does it outline the consequences if mediation is not completed within the given time limits. With respect to the mediator's fee, in practice, the employers seem to frequently pay the entire mediation fee.[40]

The new regulations have ignited a wave of strong opposition, particularly from the legal profession and labour unions. For instance, the chair of the Confederation of Progressive Trade Unions of Turkey asserted that the mandatory mediation requirement would effectively serve as a 'barrier to access to justice' for workers, coercing them to accept less favourable terms than they

---

[35] Law on Civil Procedure, No 6100.

[36] Law on Labour Courts, No 7036.

[37] Judicial Statistics 2016, p 186 (in Turkish), https://adlisicil.adalet.gov.tr/Resimler/SayfaDokuman/27820191126572016.pdf.

[38] Law on Labour Courts, No 7036, Art 3(1). Also note that according to Art 3(3), claims for pecuniary and non-pecuniary damages that may arise from workplace accidents or occupational diseases, as well as any declaratory lawsuits, actions, objections, or revocation lawsuits regarding these damages, are not subject to mandatory mediation.

[39] ibid Art 3(10).

[40] Official website of the Department of Mediation, 'Frequently asked questions on mandatory mediation' (in Turkish), https://adb.adalet.gov.tr/Home/SSSorularDetay/2.

rightfully deserve.[41] The Union of Turkish Bar Associations has also voiced its disapproval in their statement[42] considering the new law at odds with the Constitution of the Republic of Turkey and underlined the fact that the purpose of the regulations in labour law is the protection of the workers who are often in an economically disadvantaged position.[43]

Shortly after the introduction of mandatory mediation, opposition MPs in the Turkish parliament sought the annulment of both the mandatory mediation provision and the provision imposing cost sanctions on uncooperative parties before the Turkish Constitutional Court. The application was dismissed, with the judgment emphasising the following points:[44] Firstly, the court recognised that mediation offers benefits to both parties by providing a faster, less expensive, and mutually satisfactory dispute resolution method, and to the overburdened courts by reducing caseloads. Additionally, the court determined that the cost sanction was intended to enhance mediation's effectiveness and align with the constitutional principle of conducting trials efficiently and at minimum cost. The decision also offers some insight into the status of mediation within the Turkish civil justice system. Accordingly, in the court's view, 'it is not possible to characterise mediation, … as a judicial activity or a method in competition with the judiciary, [but] as a unique dispute resolution method that takes place next to judicial remedies and operates without interfering with judicial authority'.[45] In essence, the court's rationale for upholding mandatory mediation primarily relies on the efficiency concerns raised by the government. The court acknowledges that although it is essential for disputes to be resolved by the state through the courts, expecting courts to handle every dispute could increase their workload and prolong case durations unreasonably.[46]

More than five years after the introduction of mandatory pre-action mediation for labour disputes, statistics indicate a significant increase in mediation activity. However, inconsistencies in the data published by the Ministry of Justice make it difficult to assess trends with precision. The 2021 figures suggest that over 300,000 mandatory pre-action mediations took place in

---

41 DISK basin aciklamasi (29 May 2017), https://disk.org.tr/2017/05/zorunlu-arabuluculuk-isciye-zararlidir-yargi-erkinin-ozellestirilmesine-hayir/.

42 Turkiye Barolar Birligi, 'Duyuru No 2017:61' (26 October 2017), http://d.barobirlik.org.tr/2017/20171026160906238.pdf.

43 ibid.

44 Turkish Constitutional Court, 11.07.2018, E: 2017/178, K: 2018/82, https://normkararlarbilgibankasi.anayasa.gov.tr/Dosyalar/Kararlar/KararPDF/2018-82-nrm.pdf.

45 ibid para 21.

46 ibid para 16.

labour disputes, with more than half resulting in settlement.[47] However, the 2022 statistics only report the total number of mandatory mediations across all sectors, i.e. labour and commercial combined, indicating that over 500,000 such mediations occurred that year.[48] These discrepancies were attributed to a 'change in the counting technique'[49] by the Mediation Department of the Ministry of Justice, although the specifics of this change remain unclear. Since 2023, the Ministry has resumed publishing sector-specific figures. However, it now reports only a single combined figure for both voluntary and mandatory mediations in labour disputes, making it impossible to isolate data for mandatory mediation alone. Despite these limitations, the 2024 statistics show that mediation activity in labour disputes exceeded one million cases, with a settlement rate of approximately 66%.[50]

Despite the lack of transparency in these statistics, it is evident that the Ministry of Justice's proactive approach has effectively normalised pre-action mediation for resolving labour disputes. Nevertheless, with respect to achieving the goal of easing the pressure on overburdened courts, mandatory mediation seems to have had a modest effect. In fact, over the years, the volume of unresolved cases carried over to subsequent years has continued to grow, despite a slight improvement in case clearance rates.[51] The potential reasons behind this persistent problem will be examined below.

COMMERCIAL DISPUTES

The Commercial Courts in Turkey have also been under a heavy burden of backlog and delay. Due to an increasing caseload each year and unresolved cases from previous years, the average time to handle a case rose from

---

47 Judicial Statistics 2021, p 215 (in Turkish), https://adlisicil.adalet.gov.tr/Resimler/SayfaDokuman/310520221416422021HİZMETEÖZELKİTAP.pdf.

48 Judicial Statistics 2022, p 55.

49 Ministry of Justice, Announcement on the 2023 Judicial Statistics, available at (in Turkish) https://adlisicil.adalet.gov.tr/Home/SayfaDetay/2023-adalet-istatistikleri-yayininda-yer-alan-hukuk-mahkemeleri-idare-ve-vergi-mahkemeleri-ve-arabuluculuk-istatistiklerine-iliskin-2015-2022-yillarina-ait-tablolar-revize-edilmistir26032024094153.

50 Judicial Statistics 2024, p 33, available in English at https://adlisicil.adalet.gov.tr/Resimler/SayfaDokuman/7042025092455Adalet_İstatistikleri_2024%20Türkçe_Ingilizce.pdf.

51 In 2017, over 350,000 cases passed unresolved to the next year. This figure has not improved at all, with almost 390,000 passing unresolved to the following year in 2024. Ibid. p 28.

approximately 311 days in 2013 to an all-time high of 586 days in 2020.[52] Encouraged by the 'success'[53] of mandatory mediation for labour disputes, in January 2019, Turkey expanded mandatory mediation into commercial disputes regarding receivables and compensation claims by amending the Turkish Commercial Code with the Law no 7155.[54]

The process is fairly similar to the one for the labour disputes: mandatory mediation is a pre-requisite for filing a lawsuit before the Commercial Courts. If a party fails to initiate mediation and files a lawsuit, the case will be dismissed on procedural grounds.[55] Legislators have recognised the distinct nature of commercial disputes by extending the timeframe in which the mediation needs to be finalised. Accordingly, once a commercial dispute is assigned to a mediator, the mediator must complete the process within 6 weeks and, under exceptional circumstances, this period can be extended up to 2 more weeks.[56]

According to the annual statistics, the number of cases before commercial courts, which was approximately 127,000 in 2011, with a constant increase, exceeded 240,000 at the end of 2018. After the introduction of mandatory mediation in 2019, this number has gone down significantly to 194,000 in 2020,[57] and the disposition time has slightly improved.[58] However, perhaps due to the effects of Covid-19 pandemic, the backlog has increased since then.[59] It is not easy to isolate the impact mandatory mediation had on these figures. What is clearer, however, is that in terms of settlement rates, mediation in commercial

---

52 Judicial Statistics 2021, p 142, available at (in Turkish) https://adlisicil.adalet.gov.tr/Resimler/SayfaDokuman/310520221416422021HİZMETEÖZELKİTAP.pdf.

53 Department of Mediation, *Compulsory Mediation for the Resolution of Commercial Disputes*, Information booklet, p V. https://adb.adalet.gov.tr/Resimler/SayfaDokuman/1512021090954Ticari%20Uyuşmazlıklarda%20Dava%20Şartı%20Arabuluculuk.pdf.

54 The law No 7155 has incorporated Art 5(A) into the Turkish Commercial Code. Accordingly, the assessment of admissibility for mandatory mediation and the duration of mandatory mediation for the resolution of commercial disputes is governed by Art 5(A) of the Turkish Commercial Code. Other issues relating to mandatory mediation are governed by the Law on Mediation in Civil Disputes (Law No 6325).

55 Turkish Commercial Code, No 6102, Art 5(A).

56 ibid.

57 Judicial Statistics 2020, p 186, available (in English) https://adlisicil.adalet.gov.tr/Resimler/SayfaDokuman/1692021162011adalet_ist-2020.pdf accessed 18 August 2023.

58 Disposition time has gone down from 443 days in 2019 to 419 days in 2024. Judicial Statistics 2023, p 25.

59 Judicial Statistics 2023, p 27 (in English).

disputes has been significantly less successful compared with labour disputes, with a noticeable downward trend. According to 2021 statistics, over 136,000 commercial disputes were referred to mandatory mediation, with a success rate of approximately 48%.[60] By 2023, the success rate for both voluntary and mandatory mediation in commercial cases had declined to around 35%[61] and further dropped to 26% in 2024.[62] Despite this striking decline, the issue receives little attention from the stakeholders. It remains unclear what is driving this trend on the ground, and there seems to be no sign of intention to investigate the underlying causes.

CONSUMER DISPUTES

In Turkey, specialised consumer courts have jurisdiction over disputes stemming from 'consumer transactions and consumer-oriented practices'.[63] While the degree of backlog and delay is not as severe as that experienced in generalised civil courts or labour courts, the consumer court system still faces considerable pressure. According to the 2020 statistics, over 130,000 cases were pending before the consumer courts, with more than 50% postponed to the following year without a resolution.[64] Thus, consumer disputes are the most recent category of civil disputes to benefit from the ambitious mediation reforms instigated by the Turkish policymakers, intended to, once more, relieve pressure on the overburdened courts.

Prior to the introduction of mandatory mediation for consumer claims, which was introduced in July 2020,[65] Turkey employed a two-tiered CDR system: disputes below a certain monetary threshold were handled by Consumer Arbitration Boards (CABs), while those exceeding the threshold were within the jurisdiction of the Consumer Courts. Since July 2020, a pre-action mandatory mediation step has been enforced as a prerequisite for court proceedings in disputes exceeding TRY 149,000 (~GBP 2,742).[66] Meanwhile, disputes

---

[60] Judicial Statistics 2021 p 216.

[61] Judicial Statistics 2023, p 33.

[62] Judicial Statistics 2024, p 33.

[63] Law on Consumer Protection, No 6502, Art 73/1. Available in English at https://ticaret.gov.tr/data/5d42a9b313b87632542a2dae/LAW%20ON%20CONSUMER%20PROTECTION.pdf.

[64] Judicial Statistics 2023, p 28.

[65] Law on Consumer Protection, No 6502, Art 73/A (Amendment Law No 7521, which was enacted on 28 July 2020, has made the amendment for the mandatory mediation provision for the resolution of consumer disputes).

[66] Exchange rate as of 4 July 2025, see the bylaw declaring the annual monetary threshold for 2025: https://www.resmigazete.gov.tr/eskiler/2024/12/20241220

falling below this monetary threshold remain within the jurisdiction of the CABs, without a mandatory mediation obligation. The mandatory mediation process in Turkey for resolving consumer disputes closely mirrors the procedure introduced for commercial and labour disputes. Without delving into the identical details, it is noteworthy that the legislative framework has incorporated some measures to recognise the typically disadvantaged position of the consumer in these disputes. To this end, firstly, consumers were not subject to the pre-existing cost penalties for failing to attend the initial mediation meeting without a valid excuse.[67] Secondly, if a lawsuit resulting from the mediation process ends in the consumer's favour, the mediation fee is collected from the defendant.[68] The timeframe for mandatory mediation, on the other hand, is the same as that for labour disputes.

Before turning to the statistics on mandatory mediation in consumer disputes, it is important to highlight a significant development that signals the ongoing resistance to the integration of mediation within the litigation process. The provision imposing cost sanctions on the party who refuses to attend the first mandatory mediation meeting was brought before the Turkish Constitutional Court by a consumer court of first instance, seeking its annulment. Despite a similar application being dismissed when the provision was first introduced for employment disputes, as mentioned above, the court has found the rule to be unconstitutional this time and annulled it in March 2024.[69] In essence, the court considered that the cost sanction provision places a disproportionate burden on the party who did not attend the mandatory mediation meeting but later succeeded in court as the regulations do not provide any exceptions or a threshold with respect to the extent of the winning party's success in their claims at the end of litigation.[70] It is clear that, in their decision to annul the cost sanctions provision, the Constitutional Court contradicted its reasoning in the 2018 decision mentioned above. However, the court's reference to exceptions or a threshold in their judgment brings to one's mind the offers to settle mechanism which is widely adopted in common law jurisdictions like England and Wales.[71] Accordingly, if the offeree refuses a formal settlement offer under the Civil Procedure Rules Part 36, the case proceeds to judgment, resulting in a less favourable outcome than the offer, the offeree must pay the offeror's

---

-2.htm.

67 Law on Consumer Protection, No 6502, Art 73/A.

68 ibid.

69 Turkish Constitutional Court, 14.03.2024, E: 2023/160, K: 2024/77, available at https://normkararlarbilgibankasi.anayasa.gov.tr/Dosyalar/Kararlar/KararPDF/2024-77-nrm.pdf; the annulment of the cost sanctions provision took effect in January 2025.

70 ibid para 32.

71 Civil Procedure Rules (England and Wales) 1998 (CPR) r.36.15.

legal costs from the moment the offer was made.[72] Turkish policymakers have not yet responded to the annulment by introducing a replacement provision and it remains unclear if they intend to draw on the English model.

According to the statistics from 2021, among over 84,000 mandatory mediations that took place as a pre-condition for lodging a claim with the consumer courts, almost half have been successfully settled.[73] The 2023 statistics, on the other hand, indicate that the success rates went down to around 34% in 2023[74] and picked up to around 40% in 2024.[75] It is still early days to observe the impact of mandatory mediation on consumer court workload. However, the average length of trial in consumer courts seems to have dropped considerably since the introduction of mandatory mediation[76] along with some modest reductions in the number of cases that are postponed to the following year.[77]

LESSONS LEARNED AND THE CHALLENGES AHEAD

The analysis above reveals that mandatory mediation has been fairly successful, particularly in labour disputes, by resolving a significant number of cases that would otherwise have gone to litigation. This has undoubtedly saved time and money for both the parties involved and the civil justice system. Nevertheless, the success in the settlement rates has not been translated into a significant reduction in disposition times or the backlog of cases except for consumer disputes. The fact that the backlog continues to be a significant problem was also highlighted in the European Commission's 2024 assessment report on Turkey.[78] While the Covid-19 pandemic has undeniably impacted the figures on backlog and delay, it is also crucial to recognise that mandatory mediation is a relatively recent development and it is still evolving, which means its potential in improving court congestion has not fully realised. Given the above, Turkish policymakers continue to show a growing enthusiasm for

---

72 For a detailed analysis on this mechanism, see, Pablo Cortes, 'A Comparative Review of Offers to Settle – Would an Emerging Settlement Culture Pave the Way for Their Adoption in Continental Europe?' (2012) 32(1) CJQ 42.

73 Judicial Statistics 2021, p 217, https://adlisicil.adalet.gov.tr/Resimler/SayfaDokuman/310520221416422021HİZMETEÖZELKİTAP.pdf.

74 Judicial Statistics 2023, p 33.

75 Judicial Statistics 2024, p 33.

76 From 454 days in 2020 to 320 days in 2024, Judicial Statistics 2024, p 25.

77 ibid p 28.

78 European Commission, 'Turkiye 2024 Report' (Commission Staff Working Document, 30.10.2024) at p 27, https://enlargement.ec.europa.eu/document/download/8010c4db-6ef8-4c85-aa06-814408921c89_en?filename=Türkiye%20Report%202024.pdf.

expanding the use of mandatory mediation. The most recent example is Law No 7445, which amends the Execution and Bankruptcy Law and certain other laws. Published in the Official Gazette on April 5, 2023, this law further extends mandatory mediation to disputes related to immovable properties and lease agreements.

As previously mentioned, Turkey did not conduct any pilot projects before introducing mandatory pre-action mediation across various sectors.[79] As a result, the implementation process has faced numerous obstacles which could have been mitigated, stemming from ambiguities in the law, the judiciary's unfamiliarity with mediation, and the incompetence of some mediators. It is clear that the urgency to address the overburdened court system has driven policymakers to hastily introduce mandatory mediation as a one-size-fits-all solution. Therefore, the approach towards addressing the problems with implementation has been reactive rather than proactive, with solutions improvised on an ad hoc basis as they arise. The following sections will discuss some of these problems and provide insights with respect to mediator quality and training, confusion regarding mediators' roles, the one-size-fits-all approach that overlooks sector-specific characteristics of civil disputes, and the challenge of fostering a culture of settlement among stakeholders, particularly within the judiciary. Overall, these practical challenges highlight the need for a more systematic and nuanced approach to using mediation as a civil justice reform tool.

ISSUES WITH MEDIATOR QUALITY AND TRAINING

Improving the qualifications of mediators has been among the most significant challenges since the introduction of mandatory mediation. In practice, many mediators do not seem to conduct the process with utmost care and do very little towards encouraging creative solutions between the parties. This is also acknowledged by the Department of Mediation, which issued an announcement in 2020, urging mediators to abide by the regulations.[80] They found that some mediators disregard statutory periods, leaving files unresolved, while others treat the process as a check-box exercise, hastily concluding mediations via teleconference, often resulting in the failure of the mediation process. The Department of Mediation also urges the parties to 'assist the mediators'.[81]

[79] Idil Elveris, 'Mandatory Mediation is the New Game in Town' (3 March 2018) Kluwer Mediation Blog, https://mediationblog.kluwerarbitration.com/2018/03/03/turkey-mandatory-mediation-new-game-town/.

[80] Announcement made by the Department of Mediation (14 December 2020), https://adb.adalet.gov.tr/Home/SayfaDetay/arabulucularimizin-ve-kamuoyunun-dikkatine15012021093748.

[81] ibid.

However, if mediators are not adequately trained and qualified, it is unlikely that they will be able to effectively manage the mediation process and encourage the parties to engage in meaningful dialogue towards reaching a mutually acceptable solution. Therefore, it is essential to invest in the training and development of mediators to ensure that they possess the necessary skills and knowledge to conduct the mediation process successfully.

The issue of mediator quality and training initially varied greatly and posed a considerable challenge especially with respect to complex civil disputes that require special expertise.[82] In order to overcome this problem, the Ministry of Justice has established 'general' and 'specific' expertise routes for mediators. Accordingly, it has been declared that disputes related to sports law, health law, banking and finance, insurance, construction, energy and intellectual property should be referred to an expert mediator by the mediation bureaus.[83] The Department of Mediation has also published very detailed information booklets for each expertise route and has been providing trainings.[84] The booklets prepared for mediators explain the law on the relevant expertise area in detail. They also provide several fictional dispute scenarios along with an analysis on the fictional parties regarding their negotiation positions and underlying interests.[85] Overall, while mediator quality remains a concern, specialised mediator training is becoming more widespread, and the government is prioritising increased specialisation to enhance mediation's effectiveness.

CONFUSION WITH RESPECT TO THE ROLE THAT NEEDS TO BE PLAYED BY THE MEDIATOR IN SETTLEMENT NEGOTIATIONS

An interlinked issue with the mediator quality and training is that there seems to be some confusion as to whether mediators should give legal advice or provide a solution proposal to the parties. According to the regulations, mediators cannot give legal advice to the parties and they can only facilitate an interest-based settlement.[86] However, in the event that parties are unable to

---

82 ibid.

83 In effect since 10 May 2021. See the announcement by the Turkish Ministry of Justice (in Turkish), https://adb.adalet.gov.tr/Home/SayfaDetay/uzmanlik-alanlarinin-uygulamasi28042021033931.

84 See the Turkish Ministry of Justice website; https://adb.adalet.gov.tr/Home/SayfaDetay/uzman-arabuluculuk18032021014650.

85 Ministry of Justice, Mediation Department, *Becoming an Expert Mediator in Commercial Law*, p 124 https://adb.adalet.gov.tr/Resimler/SayfaDokuman/1832021210234Ticaret.pdf.

86 Regulation of Law on Mediation in Civil Disputes, Art 17 (5), (6).

reach a common solution, mediators can propose an interest-based solution.[87] So the mediation technique that was intended by the policymakers seems to be a mixture of facilitative and evaluative approaches based on their individual assessment of the specific features of a given dispute. In practice, however, mediators and the parties seem to find it difficult to abide by these principles. Anecdotal evidence suggests that parties tend to prefer to remain passive, rely on mediators to make decisions for themselves and expect them to adjudicate the dispute like a judge.[88] This lack of understanding of how mediation works can hinder the effectiveness of the process and prevent parties from fully engaging in the settlement process. This problem becomes even more challenging when there is a perceived imbalance of power between the parties, such as in labour disputes. It has also been suggested that mediators may feel pressured to end the mediation process with settlement due to the Department of Mediation's strong encouragement.[89] The crux of this issue seems to stem from a lack of comprehension regarding the differences between rights-based and interest-based approaches to dispute resolution. The prevailing mentality equates dispute resolution with a court hearing, where a judge determines who is 'right' or 'wrong'. Therefore, the onus of shifting this perspective and educating parties falls primarily on the mediators.

LACK OF SAFEGUARDS THAT ADDRESS THE VULNERABLE POSITION OF EMPLOYEES AND CONSUMERS

The extent to which the pre-action mediation provisions adequately protect the parties in a weaker bargaining position, such as employees and consumers, deserves closer scrutiny. It has long been argued that non-adjudicative ADR processes can exacerbate the disparity of power, especially when the parties are 'uncertain about what even negotiation means'.[90] Therefore, the absence of procedural safeguards in ADR processes can pose significant challenges, especially when employees or consumers lack the ability to comprehend necessary information to negotiate effectively or to assess settlement options relative to

---

87 Law on Mediation in Civil Disputes, Art 15 (7).

88 Selcan Peksan, Meltem Delen, Sayim Yorgun, 'Is hukukunda dava sarti olarak arabuluculuk uygulamasi ve arabulucularin goruslerine iliskin bir arastirma', (2020) 1 Calisma ve Toplum 344, https://www.calismatoplum.org/Content/pdf/calisma-toplum-1853-0b369327.pdf.

89 ibid.

90 Ellen E. Deason, Michael Z. Green, Donna Shestowsky, Rory Van Loo and Ellen Waldman, 'ADR and Access to Justice: Current Perspectives' (2018) 33 Ohio St J on Disp Resol, 318.

potential litigation outcomes, often owing to a lack of legal representation. The current mandatory mediation system in Turkey seems to lack sufficient safeguards to mitigate this concern. As mentioned above, according to the regulations, mediators are required to adopt a facilitative approach and only provide a settlement proposal if the parties are unable to reach an agreement. Therefore, especially employees and consumers without legal representation are particularly vulnerable in a mandatory mediation process that is conducted in a purely facilitative manner by independent mediators with varying levels of quality and experience.

The mediator training booklet for the labour law route recognises the vulnerable position of employees; however, it does not provide sufficient guidance as to how to manage these issues during mediation.[91] It merely suggests that if there is an imbalance in the bargaining power of the parties, the mediator needs to take 'the necessary measures'[92] including directing parties to seek legal advice. Mandatory mediation regulations stipulate that mediators can terminate the process if they deem it unsuitable for mediation,[93] but the exact circumstances that would justify such a decision remain undefined. Some scholars contend that this provision should obligate mediators to carefully assess the power dynamics between employers and employees, ensuring that the latter can actively participate in settlement negotiations with an adequate level of knowledge and comprehension of the potential outcomes. However, it may be unrealistic to expect mediators to make such judgments and consequently terminate the mediation process. As such, it is essential to implement further structural safeguards. A potential solution to this problem could be mandating the presence of legal counsel for employees during these meetings. Current regulations make it possible for the mediator's fees to be covered through legal aid,[94] and the availability of such aid for lawyers participating in mandatory mediation procedures is also left open.[95] However, in practice, employees still often refrain from seeking legal advice during mediation, primarily owing to financial constraints.[96] Legal representation can not only help employees participate more effectively in mediation procedures, but also aid in

---

[91] Is Hukukunda Uzman Arabuluculuk (April 2023), https://adb.adalet.gov.tr/Resimler/SayfaDokuman/10052023082837iş.pdf.

[92] ibid, p 18.

[93] Law on Mediation in Civil Disputes, Art 17(1), d.

[94] Law on Mediation in Civil Disputes, Art 13.

[95] Regulation of Law on Mediation in Civil Disputes, Art 15(5).

[96] Elif Nur Aydin, 'İşçi-İşveren Uyuşmazlıklarında Avukatlık Ücreti Ne Kadar?' (14 October 2022), https://www.unalaydin.av.tr/post/i-şçi-i-şveren-uyuşmazlıklarında-avukatlık-ücreti-ne-kadar.

adjusting their expectations. Consequently, this can increase the likelihood of reaching a settlement, benefiting both the employee and the employer.

The lack of structural safeguards is especially problematic given the fact that there have been persistent ethical issues in practice. This problem was highlighted in a judgment delivered by the Antalya Regional Court of Justice in March 2023. Accordingly, the court deemed a settlement agreement, signed as part of the mandatory mediation process, invalid owing to concerns about the mediator's impartiality.[97] It was revealed that the defendant's attorney and the mediator shared the same address, and the settlement agreement was signed on the same day as the employee's termination without their knowledge of being involved in a mandatory mediation procedure. Consequently, the employee's lack of awareness led them to settle for a very unfavourable agreement.

This judgment is particularly significant as it offers a thorough legal analysis of the employee's weaker position in a mediation setting, in relation to the doctrine of 'gross disparity' under the Turkish Code of Obligations.[98] The doctrine aims to protect a party from being unfairly disadvantaged owing to an imbalance in the obligations or benefits between the parties in a contract. In their reasoning, the court emphasised that the inequality between employers and employees is a fundamental consideration of labour law, aligning with the purpose behind the legal principles of the doctrine of gross disparity. The court also made notable remarks on the need to protect the weak while also signalling an implied disapproval of using mediation to resolve such disputes:

> In our era, where all regulatory rules have been abolished and everything is left to the free, yet ruthless competition of the free market, the threat of such exploitation is at its highest level. In the face of this development, jurists and judicial bodies, who do not want to merely observe the situation, should interpret the existing protective provisions in our legal order in accordance with the demands of the times.[99]

Anecdotal evidence suggests similar ethical issues have arisen since the introduction of mandatory mediation. For example, reports from 2018 indicate that some employers select certain mediators as their 'favourites' and request their appointment from mediation bureaus.[100]

In the same line, existing provisions do not incorporate any structural measures specifically tailored to the unique dynamics of consumer disputes, where the consumer's weaker bargaining position can be further exacerbated in a facilitative mediation setting. The mediator training booklet for consumer

---

97 9th Circuit of Antalya Regional Court of Justice, 2023/6 E., 2023/935 K.

98 Turkish Code of Obligations, No 6098, Art 28.

99 9th Circuit of Antalya Regional Court of Justice, 2023/6 E., 2023/935 K, p 8.

100 Elveris.

disputes acknowledges that, 'the most effective, easiest, quickest and cheapest method' is essential for resolving consumer disputes, and it underscores that 'mediation [shall be] carried out without forgetting the fact that the consumer is the weaker party of the transaction as a rule'.[101] Further, the handbook asserts that mediators bear a responsibility to 'enlighten the consumer about their rights and warn them when necessary',[102] which indicates an implicit encouragement towards an evaluative style of mediation for consumer disputes. However, this can only be fulfilled if the mediator possesses substantial expertise in consumer law. Overall, this problem needs to be addressed through structural safeguards, as reliance on the mediator's quality on its own is clearly not sufficient.

THE CHALLENGE OF INCENTIVISING MEANINGFUL ENGAGEMENT WITH SETTLEMENT NEGOTIATIONS

Another persistent problem is the fact that mandatory mediation can often be practised as a rubber-stamping exercise.[103] Consequently, once mandatory mediation is attempted, failed and out of the way, the parties often lose sight of the possibility of settlement. Although the Law on Mediation in Civil Disputes allows the parties to resort to mediation during the course of proceedings,[104] this only happens on very rare occasions in practice.[105]

As mentioned above, the cost sanction provision was annulled by the Constitutional Court. However, this was already an overlooked feature with little practical value[106] and parties were able to easily avoid these sanctions by

---

[101] Department of Mediation, 'Expert Mediation in Consumer Law' (January 2021), Introduction, XVI, XVI, https://adb.adalet.gov.tr/Resimler/SayfaDokuman/1832021210432Tüketici.pdf.

[102] ibid.

[103] Idil Elveris, Seda Kalem, 'National Report: Turkey', Global Access to Justice Project, https://globalaccesstojustice.com/global-overview-turkey/.

[104] If parties would like to proceed with mediation during course of litigation, the proceedings shall be suspended by the court for three months, which can be further prolonged for another three months upon the parties' request. Law on Mediation in Civil Disputes, Art 13(1), 15(5).

[105] Kinikoglu, Parmaksiz, (n 338).

[106] This issue was brought to light by a 2022 Court of Cassation decision that reversed a labour court of first instance's ruling based on the legal costs. The appellate court concluded that the lower court should have ordered the party who terminated the mediation process by failing to attend the first meeting without a valid excuse to pay the full cost of the proceedings, including attorney fees. 9th Civil Circuit of the Turkish Court of Cassation, 2022/4 E., 2022/1034 K, available at https://www.cankayaarabuluculuk.com/bilgi-bankasi/kararlar/dava-sarti

simply attending the initial mediation information meeting without necessarily needing to meaningfully engage with settlement negotiations. Additionally, attendance at mediation sessions does not have to be in person; parties may also participate through their legal representatives or lawyers. A lack of direct involvement might diminish the effectiveness of the settlement negotiations. Following similar concerns, Italy has made amendments to their mandatory mediation provisions requiring in-person attendance at the first mediation meeting.[107]

Alternatively, in order to promote meaningful engagement with pre-action mediation, the mechanism of cost sanctions could be utilised more effectively, extending the requirement beyond simply attending the first mediation meeting. In particular, in a typical commercial dispute, where both parties have access to legal counsel, the cost sanctions mechanism could be extended to include the rejection of a reasonable settlement proposal made by one party during mandatory mediation or later in the litigation process. As mentioned above, similar provisions exist in jurisdictions across Europe and can act as a strong incentive for settlement.

THE CHALLENGE OF DEVELOPING A CULTURE OF SETTLEMENT BEYOND MANDATORY MEDIATION

This final point addresses a fundamental issue: a widespread culture which perceives settlement as the best possible outcome of a dispute is crucial for the effective operation of the mandatory mediation system and its desired impact on court congestion and delay. While mandatory mediation has become a part and parcel of the Turkish system for a large number of civil disputes, it is perceived to sit in sharp dichotomy with the court system and the judicial role. In other words, the stakeholders often perceive it as a hurdle to reaching the court, rather than an opportunity for optimal dispute resolution. This perception is exacerbated by policymakers treating mandatory mediation merely as an efficiency band-aid. Consequently, the legal profession and judiciary remain largely sceptical, perhaps, as a way to express disapproval of the top-down and hasty approach to ADR reforms. The judgment by the Constitutional Court as Turkey's highest court, examined above, highlights this scepticism.

To this end, it is necessary to closely examine the Turkish regulations on the courts' role in encouraging settlement during the litigation process. Turkish judges have long been required to encourage parties to settle at the preliminary

-arabuluculukta-oturuma-mazeretsiz-katilmayan-davali-yargilama-giderlerinden-sorumlu-olur.

107 Art 8, Legislative Degree 28/2010 (amended by Legislative Degree 149/2022).

hearing under the Turkish Law on Civil Procedure.[108] In 2012, the relevant section of the law was amended to also include the word 'mediation' in addition to 'settlement'. In 2020, the same section was amended once more, this time creating an obligation on the part of the judge to encourage parties to settle or mediate the dispute 'by informing about the principles, process and legal consequences of conciliation and mediation'.[109] Furthermore, as highlighted in the preamble of the Turkish Law on Civil Procedure,[110] even if parties disregard the judge's settlement invitation and do not request additional time for 'psychological reasons', the judge may still schedule a new hearing if they 'have serious conviction that the parties can reconcile'.[111] Despite the effort shown by the policymakers in drafting this judicial obligation in order to make settlement more attractive for the litigants, in practice, this requirement is usually performed in a very legalistic manner and has little effect on the attitudes of the parties[112] as judges often do not meaningfully engage with this duty, primarily owing to their heavy workload.[113] This issue has also been acknowledged by the Turkish Court of Cassation in a 2020 judgment, where the 17th chamber has highlighted that: '(the judicial obligation to encourage settlement or mediation) should be conducted in a way that would encourage the parties to focus on the outcome and end their dispute rather than merely as a rubber-stamping exercise'.[114]

Given the importance of the judge as an authority figure, if this obligation is to be taken seriously by the judges, it can potentially play a significant role in changing the culture. Such procedures could also substantially alleviate concerns regarding disparity of bargaining power between the parties in labour and consumer disputes. Excessive workload in labour courts undoubtedly affects the feasibility and effectiveness of such judicial alternative dispute resolution methods, as they would necessitate additional resources and time. Concurrently, judicial culture may be resistant to adopting a more flexible approach to duties encompassing not only adjudication but also conciliation. Nevertheless, such change is possible, even in systems where the judiciary

108 Law on Civil Procedure, Law No 6100 (12 January 2001), Art 140(2).
109 ibid.
110 Draft Law on Civil Procedure and Justice Committee Report, (16.04.2008), Art 145, https://www5.tbmm.gov.tr/sirasayi/donem23/yil01/ss393.pdf.
111 ibid.
112 Efe Kinikoglu, Yigit Parmaksiz, 'Practical Law Q&A: Mediation in Turkey' (British Chamber of Commerce Turkey, 2019) https://www.bcct.org.tr/news/practical-law-qa-mediation-in-turkey/68731.
113 Adem Albayrak, 'Hukuk Yargilamasinda On Inceleme' (January 2020) 11 (41) TAAD 511, 521 https://dergipark.org.tr/tr/download/article-file/1500728.
114 17th Civil Circuit of the Turkish Court of Cassation, 2020/70E., 2021/342K.

is initially resistant and overburdened with backlog. Italy offers a compelling example of how gradual reform can shift judicial attitudes and practices toward greater acceptance of mediation.[115] Additionally, creating opportunities for settlement beyond the pre-action phase could ultimately enhance the effectiveness of compulsory mediation. When parties recognise that the initial mandatory mediation session is just the beginning of a broader effort to encourage settlement, even after litigation begins, they might be more likely to take it seriously. However, without further incentives to settle during the litigation process, failed mandatory mediation attempts may be easily dismissed as procedural formalities and viewed as a waste of time. Therefore, integrating settlement mechanisms more fully into court proceedings would help shift this perception.

CONCLUSION

Turkish policymakers have made remarkable strides in introducing mandatory mediation for a significant portion of civil disputes within a short period, despite the prevalent continental European legal culture that traditionally prioritises adjudication over amicable settlement. The implementation of mandatory mediation reforms has significantly raised the profile of mediation in Turkey, achieving high settlement rates, especially in labour disputes, considering that prior to these reforms, ADR was largely unheard of by society. However, the analysis above reveals that the hasty, one-size-fits-all approach to the reform of mandatory mediation has created problems in its implementation. Consequently, these reforms seemed to have had little effect on improving backlog and delay.

To this end, this chapter advocates for a more nuanced approach that pays greater attention to the specific characteristics of different categories of civil disputes. To enhance the effectiveness of mandatory mediation and avoid its reduction to a mere checkbox exercise, better safeguarding mechanisms should be in place to prevent mediation procedures from being perceived as second-class justice. If a more nuanced approach is not adopted, the significant problems encountered in practice could create a negative image of mediation.

---

115 Turkish and Italian ADR reforms present strong parallels. Italy also had a very resistant culture towards the idea of amicable settlement, but recent developments show that the culture has significantly evolved, particularly among the judiciary. For an in-depth comparative analysis between Italian and Turkish ADR reforms, see, Fatma Arslan, 'Fostering ADR without the stick of high litigation costs: the cases of Italian and Turkish ADR reforms', in Masood Ahmed, Adriani Dori, Xandra Kramer, Carlota Ucin, *Sustaining Access to Justice: New Avenues for Costs and Funding* (Hart, 2025).

This chapter also advocates for a holistic approach: developing a widespread culture of settlement and integrating it as a core philosophy of civil litigation, rather than merely using mandatory mediation as an efficiency tool. Although achieving these objectives can be a challenging, long-term endeavour, it may well be the missing piece that can most effectively increase the efficiency of the civil justice system.

Finally, a comprehensive evaluation of the system's efficacy ultimately necessitates more robust and accessible data. This data should also encompass feedback from all stakeholders and more detailed empirical evidence on mandatory mediation outcomes to identify areas for improvement and ensure the long-term success of the reforms.

4. Mediation within the Nigerian civil justice system

Chinwe Egbunike-Umegbolu

4.1 INTRODUCTION

Before implementing appropriate or alternative dispute resolution (ADR) in Nigeria, the country's justice system faced several challenges. These included issues such as high costs,[1] congested courts,[2] delays,[3] and complex processes. As a result, there was a growing need for reform in the litigation process.[4] Both the stakeholders and litigants were in desperate need of a solution to address these pervasive issues.[5] For instance, the litigants complained about their cases languishing in courts for years owing to the high cost of litigation,[6] stemming from lawyers' fees and court document-filing expenses. Additionally, the

1 Kevin Nwosu (ed.), *Legal Practice Skills & Ethics in Nigeria: In Honour of Chief Babatunde Abiodun Ibironke*, SAN, DCONconsulting, 2004, p. 9.

2 Emilia Onyema, 'The Multi-Door Court House (MDC) Scheme in Nigeria: A Case Study of the Lagos MDC' (2013) 2 Apogee Journal of Business, Property and Constitutional Law, p. 4.

3 Ibid.

4 Leo Levin and Wheeler, Russell, *The Pound Conference: Perspectives on Justice in the Future Proceedings of the National Conference on the Causes of Popular Dissatisfaction with the Administration of Justice* (West, St Paul, Minnesota, 1979), p. 51.

5 Emilia Onyema, 'The Multi-Door Court House (MDC) Scheme in Nigeria: A Case Study of the Lagos MDC' (2013) 2 Apogee Journal of Business, Property and Constitutional Law, p. 6.

6 John Chuks Azu, Court of Appeal Embraces Alternative Dispute Settlement (Daily Trust 2018) <https://dailytrust.com/court-of-appeal-embraces-alternative-dispute-settlement-260224/> accessed 24 July 2024.

prevalent issue of corruption has further eroded trust in the judiciary.[7] Judges were regarded as potential saviours by those facing persecution.[8]

For example, the Supreme Court case in 2016, the *Federal Republic of Nigeria v Justice Sylvester Ngwuta*, corroborates the above statement. Justice Ngwuta was arrested by the Department of State Services (DSS) during a midnight raid on several judges' residences. They found a significant amount of foreign and local currency allegedly linked to bribes in high-profile political and electoral cases. Similarly, in Trinidad and Tobago, although corruption in the judiciary is not as systemic as in some other jurisdictions, there is significant concern about it. For instance, Chief Justice Ivor Archie has faced a series of allegations, such as advising that security contracts be awarded to private individuals (friends and acquaintances), and several judges have expressed concerns about a lack of confidence in his judicial leadership.[9]

Against this backdrop, in developing countries like Nigeria and Trinidad and Tobago, there is an opportunity to transform the judiciary into a more impartial protector of justice. Currently, the perception is that access to justice is limited to those with financial resources, a view evidenced above and by the increasing backlog of cases. Addressing these challenges can help foster a more efficient and equitable judicial system. This is where reforms come in. Therefore, it is essential to restore public trust and reaffirm the judiciary's vital role as an independent and unbiased guardian of rights and liberties for all citizens.

It is imperative to state that many people find ADR methods, particularly mediation, to be more transparent, efficient, and less vulnerable to corruption.[10] Implementing systemic reforms is essential to further enhancing the effectiveness of mediation and rebuilding trust in the formal justice system. Initiatives focused on improving judicial accountability and ensuring institutional independence can significantly contribute to a more robust and trustworthy justice framework. Regrettably, many disputants (or litigants, as the case may be) live below the poverty line in Nigeria and consequently lack

---

[7] Gbenga Oduntan, 'Prescriptive Strategies to Combat Corruption Within the Administration of Justice Sector in Nigeria' (2017) 20(1) Journal of Money Laundering Control, p. 36.

[8] Ibid.

[9] Derek Achong, Guardian Trinidad and Tobago (2025) <https://www.guardian.co.tt/news/latt-seeks-advice-from-regional-senior-counsel-on-conduct-of-cj-6.2.2273820.268973b1b4> accessed on 23 June 2025.

[10] The interview I had with the users of the Multi-Door Courthouse in Nigeria–Lagos and Enugu State respectively in 2020 and with the stakeholders in 2020–2023.

the financial means to pursue their claim in the courts of law.[11] Therefore, mediation is an informal process that is party-directed without compromising the parties' positions;[12] it offers an escape from congestion, undue and excessive delays, prevalent corruption, high cost, lack of trust, and other issues associated with litigation.[13] The difference of the masses' experiences with the law in underdeveloped economies like Nigeria, compared with that of the more affluent middle class, can find some resonance in George Orwell's novel *Animal Farm*.[14] In this book, the author uses the animals and their activities to demonstrate the gap between most Russian people, who suffered from high inequality, and the ruling class, which had money and food.[15] The author's insight helps expose the injustice and inequality in the lack of access to justice in Nigeria, which tends to favour a particular class to the detriment of the country's larger citizenry; instances such as these are the springboard for this chapter.

4.2 THE HISTORY AND DEVELOPMENT OF THE NIGERIAN CIVIL JUSTICE SYSTEM

Litigation was commonly the most frequently used and favoured method for resolving conflicts. Many saw it as the only reasonable means of settling disputes.[16] However, ADR means have been explored and adequately developed over the years.[17] In Nigeria, ADR methods are widely used to settle a wide range of disputes, including criminal cases and simple offences like misdemeanours, breaches of the peace, assault, and battery. Some of these appropriate means are mediation, negotiation, ombudsman, conciliation, neutral

---

[11] Nokukhanya Ntuli, 'Africa: Alternative Dispute Resolution in a Comparative Perspective' (2018) 22 Conflict Studies Quarterly, p. 38.

[12] Expert Views on ADR Vid/Podcast Show, A Beginner's Guide to Early Dispute Resolution (EDR) with Co-Chair Ellie Vilendrer (2024) <https://podcasts.apple.com/gb/podcast/a-beginners-guide-to-early-dispute-resolution-edr/id1538506713?i=1000661665096> accessed 20 August 2024.

[13] Masood Ahmed, 'Bridging the Gap Between Alternative Dispute Resolution and Robust Adverse Costs Orders' (2015) 66 Northern Ireland Legal Quarterly, p. 74.

[14] George Orwell, *Animal Farm: A Fairy Story* (Penguin 2003), p. 2.

[15] Ibid, 4.

[16] Kevin Ndubuisi Nwosu (ed.), Legal Practice Skills & Ethics in Nigeria in Honour of Chief Babatunde Abiodun Ibironke, SAN (2004). Published by DCONconsulting, cited in Umegbolu, Chinwe, Behind the Legal Frustration (Mediate.com 2019).

[17] Julius Miner and William Campbell, 'Court Congestion: A New Approach' (1959) 45 American Bar Association Journal 12, p. 1.

evaluation, collaborative law and arbitration. This discourse will focus on mediation, the most widely used and accessible ADR mechanism in Nigeria.[18]

Theoretically, mediation is a process in which a neutral third party facilitates communication between two or more disputing parties to help them reach a voluntary agreement. It is confidential, impartial, empowering, and humane.[19] The essence of mediation lies in prioritising the fundamental needs and interests of the parties involved, as opposed to their specific positions or demands.[20] In response to the challenges faced in the commercial sector, there was a growing need for an option other than litigation that could efficiently resolve commercial disputes while maintaining business relationships. To address this issue, the Nigerian government made amendments to the constitution of the Federal Republic of Nigeria, with Section 36 believed to be an antidote or a remedy to the problems associated with the justice system.[21]

Conversely, Section 36 of the Constitution of the Federal Republic of Nigeria 1999[22] guarantees the right to a fair hearing within a reasonable time by a court or other tribunal established by law and constituted in a manner that ensures its independence and impartiality.[23] Furthermore, in recent years, the Supreme Court of Nigeria has recognised the right of disputants to take steps to narrow down issues between them. This was well illustrated in the case of *Ogunleye v Oni*, where the court stated 'that parties to an action could settle their matters to save the court's time by agreeing on those facts that are not in the contest and leaving the court to decide the justice of the case based on the received evidence'.[24]

This approach has led to a shift in culture where delays are seen as necessary for justice, and efficiency is sometimes questioned. However, it is essential for parties to feel heard and understood.[25] These issues highlight the challenges of

---

18 Chinwe Umegbolu, 'Dispensation of Justice: Lagos Multi-Door Courthouse (LMDC) as a Case Study in Nigeria'. A PhD thesis submitted to the Business and Law Faculty at the University of Brighton (2021), p. 78.

19 Nathy Rass-Masson and Virginie Rouas, 'Effective Access to Justice – European Parliament' (*Europa EU,* 2017) <https://www.europarl.europa.eu/RegData/etudes/STUD/.../IPOL_STU (2017) 596818_EN.pdf> accessed 21 May 2019.

20 Roger Fisher and William Ury, Getting to Yes, Negotiating Agreement Without Giving In (Penguin Books 2011), p. 8.

21 Bob Osamor, Fundamentals of Criminal Procedure in Nigeria (Dee-Sage Nigeria Limited 2004) p. xiv.

22 Ibid.

23 Ibid.

24 *Joshua Ogunleye v Babatayo Oni* (SC 193 of 1987) [1962] NGSC 1 (27 April 1962) cited in Anyim (2019) at p. 93.

25 Interview with the Director 2 of the LMDC on 3 October 2020.

litigation, which have led to increased awareness of the benefits of ADR methods among users such as business associates, stakeholders, and legal practitioners. Consequently, many contracts now include provisions for resolving disputes through ADR mechanisms such as mediation, arbitration, or a combination of both (med-arb). ADR is cost-effective, as the parties, mediators and tribunal[26] can schedule meetings and hearings based on their availability. Unlike court proceedings, ADR processes are not plagued by unnecessary adjournments and delays.[27]

It is worth noting that shorter proceedings and a flexible procedure can prevent increasing costs and save time.[28] The courts now refer parties from the magistrates' court, High Court, and Court of Appeal to the Multi-Door Courthouse (MDC), attached to the High Court, to explore settling their dispute through one of the ADR mechanisms.[29]

4.3 THE MULTI-DOOR COURTHOUSE – INSTITUTIONALISATION OF MEDIATION

> 'Having spent most of my early practice years in courtrooms, it became crystal clear to me that the justice system was in desperate need of an overhaul.'[30] (Kehinde Aina)

In 1995, Kehinde Aina founded the Negotiation and Conflict Management Group, a non-profit private organisation seeking a practical legal system to cope with the surge of disputes that overwhelmed the courts.[31] In 2002, the Negotiation and Conflict Management Group embarked on a campaign to establish collaboration with the Lagos State government. Then, it adopted appropriate dispute resolution (ADR), notably the Multi-Door Courthouse

---

26 The Association of Multi-Door Courthouse of Nigeria, A Compendium of Articles on Alternative Dispute Resolution (ADR), Vol. 1 (2013), p. 15.

27 Emilia Onyema, 'The Multi-Door Court House (MDC) Scheme in Nigeria: A Case Study of the Lagos MDC' (2013) 2 Apogee Journal of Business, Property and Constitutional Law, p. 5.

28 The Association of Multi-Door Courthouse of Nigeria, A Compendium of Articles on Alternative Dispute Resolution (ADR) (2013), Vol. 1, p. 17.

29 Ibid.

30 The Lagos Multi-Door Courthouse, The Lagos Multi-Door Courthouse Neutrals' Handbook (2016), p. 12.

31 Ibid.

(MDC), as an institutional repository of ADR mechanisms.[32] To encourage dispute resolution in an atmosphere free of acrimony and contestation.

The LMDC Act was enacted in 2007, and the Lagos Multi-Door Courthouse (LMDC) is situated within the Igbosere High Court in the mainland of Lagos State. The LMDC was created to help settle conflicts or disputes among business partners or people in business, tenant and landlord disputes, land disputes, and matrimonial cases, to bring about speedy and efficient administration of justice.[33] Several states in Nigeria have emulated the LMDC by replicating its model because of its effectiveness in delivering speedy dispensation of justice to the citizenry.[34]

Consequently, the acceptance of ADR in the Lagos landscape indicates the wind of change, which is opposed to the adversarial relationship – the win–lose.[35] The acceptance of ADR means turning an adversarial pursuit into a problem-solving partnership, which connotes a win–win[36] for all the parties involved. Evidence supporting this position can be found in Kehinde Aina's statement, where he pointed out that 'the new face of justice is also assuming a human countenance'.[37] This means that disputants, litigants, and providers will have the autonomy to co-create an expeditious and effective process for settling a dispute in a private dispute setting on the courts' premises.[38] Judges and Magistrates get to refer their cases. Even with the walk-in instances that are not referred by the judge, when the parties sign the Terms of Settlement (TOS), it is sent to the ADR Judges,[39] and they will enter it and endorse it as a consent judgement in court.[40] The above-stated submission is the reason why

---

32 Chinwe Egbunike-Umegbolu, For the Love of ADR: Mass Awareness Advocacy via Podcast, Enugu State Multi-Door Courthouse (ESMDC): its Journey So Far in O42/Coal City <https://blogs.brighton.ac.uk/chinwe/2022/12/17/enugu-state-multi-door-courthouse-esmdc-the-journey-so-far/1> accessed 20 August 2024.

33 The Lagos Multi-Door Courthouse, The Lagos Multi-Door Courthouse Neutrals' Handbook (2016), p. 13.

34 Ibid.

35 Susan Marks *Watching the Wind Conflict Resolution During South Africa's Transition to Democracy* (United States Institute of Peace 2000), p. 17.

36 Ibid.

37 The Lagos Multi-Door Courthouse, The Lagos Multi-Door Courthouse Neutrals' Handbook (2016), p. 82.

38 K. Aina, 'Alternative Dispute Resolution', The Guardian Newspaper (Nigeria 2008) at p. 18.

39 ADR Judge – A High Court Judge is appointed by the Chief Judge of a state to oversee all matters sent to the MDC.

40 Chinwe Umegbolu, Dispensation of Justice; Lagos Multi-Door Courthouse (LMDC) as a Case Study in Nigeria. Thesis submitted to the Business and Law

the LMDC is referred to as a court-connected ADR[41] or 'one-stop dispute resolution service', otherwise known as the 'one-stop shop' as Professor Mark Feldman termed it.[42]

This means the assimilation of ADR with the court system, where parties have the power to select other ADR methods appropriate to their case.[43] This method gives room for screening and referral[44] and places cases and disputants on the right track that suits their disputes.[45]

According to Moore,

> All knowledge claims are socially constructed and represent particular situated perspectives.[46]

This statement aligns or is in alignment with what Aina described as frustration;[47] he faced the Nigerian courts after five years in legal practice and was a partner in the law firm of Aina Blankson & Co. as head of litigation.[48] Aina stated:

> Those short, glorious years were, for the most part, spent in courtrooms, a place of passion and great delight but very little satisfaction. It was my view then (and still is) that access to Justice means much more than access to the courtroom; access to justice means providing an opportunity for a 'just and timely result.' Not only did I not experience that just and timely result in those five years, none of those I represented did.[49]

The above statement signifies that Aina was motivated by his 'situatedness' at that point, which was the ineffectiveness of the court system in Lagos. Hence,

School, University of Brighton (2020), p. 106.

41 Ibid.

42 'One-stop' Commercial Dispute Resolution Services: Implications for International Investment Law, Handbook of International Investment Law and Policy (J. Chaisse, L. Choukroune, S. Jusoh, eds.) (Springer 2021), p. 2.

43 E.O. Ezike, 'Developing a Statutory Framework for ADR in Nigeria' (2011–2012) 10 Nig J R, p. 248.

44 Practice Direction on Mediation Procedure (2008) at p. 3.

45 G.M. Goh, Dispute Settlement in International Space Law: A Multi-Door Courthouse for Outer Space (Leiden University 2007) at p. 8.

46 D. Moore, Methodological Assumptions and Analytical Frameworks Regarding Religion. Part Three (Harvard Divinity School 2015), p. 82.

47 K. Aina, 'Alternative Dispute Resolution', The Guardian Newspaper (Nigeria 2008) at p. 4.

48 K. Aina, 'ADR 2000 – Resolving Corporate Disputes In the 21st Century' (Institute of Directors (IOD) Members Evening 2007), p. 7.

49 Levin & Russell (1979), note 4, at p. 19.

he decided to seek a solution and was stimulated by Professor Frank Sander's speech – he founded the Multi-Door Courthouse in America.[50] Sander first introduced this concept in a speech at the National Conference on the causes of popular dissatisfaction with the administration of justice in St Paul, Minnesota. In this very place, Roscoe Pound brought to the fore the causes of popular dissatisfaction with the administration of justice.[51] The MDC has been tested in domestic jurisdiction in the United Kingdom and implemented in parts of the United States, as well as Australia, Canada, New Zealand, Singapore, and other Commonwealth countries.[52]

Professor Sander emphasised the five criteria[53] for determining how best disputes can be resolved, and this criterion contributes to the effectiveness of the MDC process, which is as follows:

- the nature of disputes;
- the relationship between disputants;
- the amount in dispute;
- cost and time; and
- speed.

It has been observed that the LMDC emulates these five criteria; however, for this work, it will be relevant to focus on the first criterion – the nature of disputes – to form some relevant issues for determination.

(1) Do the parties have a likelihood of maintaining long-term relationships, e.g. family disputes and business disputes.[54]
    (a) Is the process fair and suitable to the type of dispute or conflict in question?
    (b) Is the dispute amenable to mediation or ADR? For instance, in a matrimonial cause, only the courts have the power to make a decree nisi or absolute. A party cannot submit a divorce to mediation. However, a party can submit matters on maintenance–alimony and custody of children to mediation.[55]

---

50 Ibid.

51 Ibid.

52 Goh (2007), note 45, at p. 7.

53 Levin and Russell (1979), note 4, at p. 13.

54 Ibid.

55 The Lagos Multi-Door Courthouse, The Lagos Multi-Door Courthouse Neutrals' Handbook (2016) at p. 13.

(c) Will the LMDC will need to determine if the proper parties are listed before the court? When they are, the dispute will be readily sent to the MDC.[56]
(d) Finally, will the parties voluntarily or willingly want to settle in ADR?[57]

Without doubt, mediation was integrated into Nigeria's legal framework with the establishment of the LMDC. Since then, the MDC model has spread across the country, with states such as Enugu, Abuja, Kano, Rivers, and Ogun adopting it. Essentially, these courthouses operate as adjuncts to the judiciary, enabling court-referred and walk-in mediation services. They have proven particularly effective in civil disputes.[58]

4.4 MEDIATION AND TRADITIONAL AFRICAN METHODS OF SETTLING DISPUTES

Mediation's success in Nigeria can also be attributed to its deep roots in traditional African dispute resolution methods. For instance, in the pre-colonial era, disputes between members of the same village and between different villages were settled using the traditional African methods of justice administration, placing a premium on reconciliation and social harmony rather than punishment.[59] This involved the involvement of older persons, headmen of the neighbourhood, Ozo titled men (chiefs),[60] Olubadan (traditional head[61] or Emir, traditional leader of the Hausa land),[62] and Umuada (Daughters of the Land). In the native courts, disputants pleaded their case, although this could be done in default; however, parents, guardians, or relatives could act on their behalf owing to age, status, or disability.[63]

---

56 Section 3 (6) Lagos State Multi-Door Court Law 2015.

57 Menkel-Meadow C, 'Maintaining ADR Integrity' (2009) 27 Wiley InterScience at p. 2.

58 Expert Views On ADR (EVA) Vid/Podcast Show <https://podcasts.apple.com/us/podcast/episode-5-what-are-the-factors-that-could-influence/id1538506713?i=1000500589174> accessed 12 August 2024.

59 Ibid.

60 Ibid.

61 Olubadan (traditional head of the Yoruba who acts as an arbitrator in many disputes) cited in Jerome T. Barrett and Joseph Barrett, History of Alternative Dispute Resolution: The Story of a Political, Cultural, and Social Movement published in affiliation with the Association for Conflict Resolution (2004), p. 5.

62 K. Aina (2008), 'Alternative Dispute Resolution' The Guardian, p. 13.

63 Kevin Ndubuisi N (eds), (2004), note 16, p. 91.

The cases *Nezianya v Okagbue* [1963], *Nzekwu v Nzekwu* [1989], and *Mojekwu v Mojekwu* [1997] demonstrate how Traditional African Methods of Settling Disputes (TAMSD), often rooted in cultural and religious beliefs, continue to shape conflict resolution practices in many Nigerian communities. Rituals such as forcing a widow to drink the water used to bathe her deceased husband reflect long-standing customs tied to notions of justice, morality, and communal harmony. While these practices may raise serious human rights concerns, they also highlight the communal and non-adversarial spirit that underpins traditional dispute resolution.

This communal ethos is mirrored in mediation, which has emerged as the most widely accepted and culturally compatible form of ADR in Nigeria. Like TAMSD, mediation emphasises restoration, consensus, and reconciliation, rather than punitive outcomes. Its flexibility allows it to integrate cultural norms and customary law, making it a more acceptable and accessible method of resolving disputes – especially in settings where formal litigation is viewed as alien or adversarial. Thus, mediation serves as a bridge between traditional values and modern legal frameworks, offering a respectful, rights-based alternative to harmful customary practices. The TAMSD align with modern mediation's restorative ethos, making it more acceptable to the general population. Thus, mediation bridges formal legal systems and customary practices, preserving cultural nuances while upholding justice.

4.5 NIGERIAN LEGISLATIVE AND JUDICIARY SUPPORT

As the saying goes, 'the only constant thing in life is change'. In the words of Professor Yakubu:

> The dynamic nature of law necessitates its constant change … It must reflect the ethos and values of the people. Law does not emphasise the ethos and values of bygone days but considers the utility, relevant and acceptability of a rule of conduct at a point in time.[64]

These sentiments resonate with the writer, and this philosophy is embraced by re-emphasising the changes that have occurred from the pre-colonial era (when the traditional system was dominant and was the only door) up through the colonial era (the introduction of litigation into Nigeria) and finally in the post-colonial era (where the traditional system has been repackaged as the new ADR and litigation has been infused with ADR). This link to the eras is

---

[64] Nwosu (2004), note 1, p. 341.

crucial because Yakubu mentioned that 'law changes with time'.[65] The law as we know it is never static. Thus, if a law is no longer serving its purpose or if it does not meet the purpose for which it was created, it is either overhauled or amended to conform to the required standards to sufficiently tackle the challenges in the law.[66]

Perhaps the most dramatic evidence is that because litigation could not solve the problem of congestion of the system,[67] it became necessary that an independent, party-reliant, and speedy process that could generate effective results was sought; hence the birth of the LMDC. The focal point here is that, when the westerners left Nigeria, Nigerian law was changed, and various rules of law and enactments were put in place to reflect the needs of the 'commercial village'. In this context, present-day Nigeria[68] and Lagos State took appropriate steps to 'encourage' the stakeholders – judges (to enforce adherence to ADR clauses in commercial agreements), Senior Advocates of Nigeria (SAN), magistrates, lawyers and citizens – to embrace ADR and LMDC.[69]

Lending credence to the above is the High Court of Lagos State (Civil Procedure) Rules, Order 3 Rule 11 2019, which states thus:

> all originating processes filed in the Registry shall be screened to determine the suitability for Alternative Dispute Resolution (ADR) mechanisms and may be referred to the Lagos Multi-Door Court House or any appropriate ADR institution.[70]

Subsequently, the 2012 rules were amended in 2019, and the abovementioned provisions were inserted accordingly, apart from encouraging the screening for suitability of ADR, which is continuity from the old rules.[71] A new provision came in, the Expeditious Disposal of Civil Cases Practice Direction No. 1 of 2019.[72] Its primary focus is the timely disposal of backlog cases before litigation commences in the Lagos State Judiciary.[73]

---

65 Ibid, p. 341.

66 Ibid.

67 Ibid, p .37.

68 B. Faturoti, 'Institutionalised ADR and Access to Justice: The Changing Faces of the Nigerian Judicial System' (2014) Research Gate, p. 16.

69 The Lagos Multi-Door Courthouse, The Lagos Multi-Door Courthouse Neutrals' Handbook (2016) at p. 12.

70 High Court of Lagos State Rules Civil Procedure Rules 2019.

71 Ibid.

72 Expeditious Disposal of Civil Cases Practice Direction: Pre-Action Protocol Lagos State Judiciary 2019.

73 The Association of Multi-Door Courthouse of Nigeria, A Compendium of Articles on Alternative Dispute Resolution (ADR), Vol. 1 (2013), p. 15.

The 2019 rule amended the 2012 rules and introduced some of the above-stated provisions. However, both Acts placed responsibility on the court to decide on matters as it deems fit regarding expeditious justice delivery in the State.[74] It has restored a sense of timely justice and equal footing to the common person so that the people can put an end to long-standing disputes. The English Court can only 'encourage' and does not mandate or compel parties to engage in ADR, including mediation; however, it does not hold back when sanctioning parties that have wasted the court's time, especially when the parties refuse to settle in ADR.[75] The case of *DSN v Blackpool Football Club Ltd* lends credence to the above claim.[76]

However, Master McCloud's directions in the case highlighted that:

> At all stages, the parties must consider settling this litigation by any means of Alternative Dispute Resolution (including Mediation); any party not engaging … must serve a witness statement giving reasons.[77]

After extensive examination of the above directions by Griffiths J, he admitted that Blackpool Football Club's reasons for failing and refusing to engage in settlement discussions were inadequate.[78] Although losing the claim does not validate an award for indemnity costs, in this case, Mr Justice Griffiths believed that based on their conduct, they deserved it.[79] This judgment was inescapable as it is clear the English courts can wholly sanction parties that refuse to settle under ADR and, in some cases, award indemnity costs.[80] The reason behind this is to provide an effective justice system so future claims can follow this rule and parties will desist from wasting the court's time, which in turn affects the court's dockets. Hence, in this case, the ruling brings out a peculiar feature that other jurisdictions like Nigeria, particularly Lagos State, can use as a case precedent. Sir Anthony Clarke MR pointed out that without an:

> effective civil justice system, substantive civil laws are no more than words and the rule of law becomes an 'aspiration' rather than a reality.[81]

---

[74] Ibid 16.

[75] *DSN v Blackpool Football Club Ltd* [2020] EWHC 670 (QB).

[76] Ibid.

[77] Ibid.

[78] Ibid.

[79] Ibid.

[80] Ibid.

[81] H. Genn, Paths to Justice: What People Do and Think About Going to Law (Hart, Oxford, 2019) p. 18.

This aligns with the case of *Nweke v FRN*, where the victim still awaits justice. This case has been at the trial court for eight years now and has yet to commence.[82] However, it has gone from one court to another.[83] This rule has provided an effective justice mechanism that can tackle such cases, which is a step in the right direction; the judge, in his discretion, can unburden the courts and achieve swift justice either through litigation or through ADR in the LMDC or any other ADR Centre. However, it is argued that the issue of 'referring parties'[84] comes across as ambiguous or vague. It could also connote a different meaning: 'forcing or controlling parties' to use ADR.

However, it is pertinent to note that this was before the *Churchill v Merthyr Tydfil County Borough Council* case in 2023.[85] In November 2023, the UK Court of Appeal found that parties to a dispute can be ordered by the court to engage in ADR.[86] The judgment, handed down in the *Churchill v Merthyr Tydfil County Borough Council* case, overturned a previous ruling in the *Halsey v Milton Keynes General NHS Trust* case (*Halsey*),[87] which argued that compulsory ADR 'would be regarded as an unacceptable constraint on the right of access to the court'.[88] This case signifies that parties to a dispute can be ordered by the court to engage in ADR.

Despite its benefits, the expansion of mediation in Nigeria is not without obstacles. These challenges include awareness, as most lawyers do not encourage their clients to use ADR, which is often perceived as 'a drop in revenue'; a lack of confidence in its outcomes; a lack of funding; and the need for greater standardisation in training and credentialing across jurisdictions to ensure consistency.[89]

---

82 Bolaji-Yusuff Misitura, Rev Fr. Silas C. Nweke v The Federal Republic of Nigeria (2016) LLJR-CA. Law Global-Hub Lead Judgment Report (2024) <https://www.lawglobalhub.com/rev-fr-silas-c-nweke-v-the-federal-republic-of-nigeria-2016-lljr-ca/> accessed 15 September 2024.

83 *Nweke v FRN* (2019) LPELR-SC.

84 Order 2 (1) of the 2019 Constitution of the Federal Republic of Nigeria 1999.

85 Rachael Johnson, The New Landscape for ADR Post-Churchill (2024) <https://www.ibanet.org/the-new-landscape-for-adr-post-churchill> accessed 15 September 2024.

86 Ibid.

87 Ibid.

88 Ibid.

89 Interviews I conducted at the ESMDC and LMDC between 2021 and 2023.

4.6 MEDIATION IN NIGERIA

Mediation is a form of ADR encompassing a wide range of non-binding and voluntary dispute resolution processes.[90] Mediation has a long history in various civilisations despite its perception as a modern process, as illustrated by the African/Nigerian and Chinese perspectives.[91] In the fifth century BC, the Confucian viewpoint emphasised resolving disputes through moral persuasion and agreement rather than sovereign coercion.[92] It is essential to note that any settlement reached during mediation can become a legally binding contract.[93]

Hypothetically, the concept encourages disputants to use mediation to reach agreements through reasonable and productive discussions with a neutral third party, rather than resorting to the adversarial process.[94] The parties must appoint a mediator, but the mediator cannot make binding decisions on their behalf. Instead, he or she will facilitate their decision-making process and help them find solutions to their conflict.[95] Mediators prioritise fairness over legal rights.[96] In addition to voluntariness, mediation offers the advantage of providing a high level of privacy and shielding the parties' issues from the public eye.[97] Furthermore, the informal process, where the parties control their decision, is often quicker, less costly, and less adversarial than litigation. Given the merits of mediation mentioned above, it is no surprise that the judiciary usually encourages mediation first before resorting to litigation in many cases.[98] When compared to litigation, the advantages of this process sometimes portray mediation as beneficial and the latter as unfavourable. However, mediation is not always appropriate and does not always result in an agreement. For example, Mr E, who came for a mediation session at the LMDC with Mrs E, may decide to end the session before it reaches the final stage after realising

90 Penny Brooker, Mediation Law: Journey through Institutionalism to Juridification (Routledge (2013), p. 8.

91 Jay Folberg and Alison Taylor, 'Reviewed Work Mediation: A Comprehensive Guide to Resolving Conflicts without Litigation' (1986) 84 Michigan Law Review, p. 17.

92 Ibid.

93 Ibid.

94 K. Aina, 'Alternative Dispute Resolution', The Guardian Newspaper (Nigeria 2008), p. 11.

95 Ibid.

96 Parkinson L, *Family Mediation* (3rd edn, Family Law 2014), p. 10.

97 [2004] EWCA Civ 576.

98 Ibid.

that he might not keep his word. Both parties might opt out because they feel the decision reached was unreasonable, especially in financial arrangements.[99]

It is important to recognise that mediation has its limitations and may not be the best approach for cases involving unequal bargaining power and domestic violence.[100] Hyman emphasised the role of mediators, stating that it is not their responsibility to determine who is right or wrong; that decision falls to juries, judges, and arbitrators.[101] When mediators operate within these limitations, it's crucial for them to remain neutral and unbiased, avoiding imposing their views on the disputing parties. This is essential for maintaining the constructive nature of mediation in addressing marital breakdown and divorce.[102] Furthermore, mediation offers a valuable approach for resolving conflicts and disputes. It encompasses two distinct mediator styles, which will be outlined and discussed below.

A. Facilitative Mediation

In the 1960s and 1970s, only facilitative mediation was taught and practised.[103] This approach involves the mediator structuring a process to help the parties reach a mutually agreeable resolution.[104] The facilitative mediator refrains from making recommendations to the parties[105] but may offer advice or opinions on the case's outcome. The mediator oversees the process, while the parties are responsible for the result or outcome. The facilitative mediator asks open-ended questions, delves into the interests underlying the parties' positions, and aids the parties in identifying and analysing suitable paths to resolution.

---

[99] Chinwe Umegbolu (2021) Dispensation of Justice: Lagos Multi-Door Courthouse (LMDC) as a Case Study in Nigeria. A PhD thesis submitted to the Business and Law Faculty at the University of Brighton, p. 123.

[100] Mary Hayes and Catherine Williams, Family Law Principles, Policy and Practice (2nd edn, Butterworths 1999), p. 554.

[101] Jonathan Hyman, 'Swimming in the Deep End: Dealing with Justice in Mediation' (2005) 6 Cardozo Journal of Conflict Resolution, p. 19.

[102] Catherine Williams and Mary Hayes, Family Law Principles, Policy and Practice (Cambridge University Press, 2009), p. 554.

[103] Zena Zumeta, Styles of Mediation: Facilitative, Evaluative, and Transformative Mediation (Mediate.com, 2018), p. 1.

[104] Ibid.

[105] Mieke Brandon and Rachael Field, 'An Analysis of the Complexity of Power in Facilitative Mediation and Practical Strategies for Ensuring a Fair Process' (2020) 39 Resolution Institute | the arbitrator & mediator, p. 33.

Facilitative mediators aim to ensure that parties reach agreements based on their mutual understanding. They conduct open joint sessions with all parties in attendance, allowing everyone to share their perspectives.[106] It is important to note that at Nigeria's MDC, mediators are encouraged to use facilitative mediation.[107] However, the approach used depends on the nature of the disputes. In some cases, the mediator may choose to use both approaches or just one of them.[108]

B. The Evaluative Mediation

This type of mediation is also known as directive mediation, in which the mediator is required to provide a formal or informal recommendation to the parties regarding the potential resolution of their issues.[109] Directive in nature, this method involves the mediator structuring the process and directly influencing the mediation outcome. Therefore, evaluative mediation resembles the settlement conferences conducted by judges. An evaluative mediator helps the parties in settling disputes by pointing out the weaknesses in their cases and predicting the potential actions of a judge or jury.[110]

Evaluative mediation, simply put, is a process that may involve the mediator providing an assessment or opinion on the pros and cons of the case, along with a forecast of the likely outcome.[111] Evaluative mediators prioritise the parties' legal rights, unlike facilitative mediation, which prioritises the parties' interests. As a result, evaluative mediation emerged from the legal concept of impartiality.[112]

---

106 Susan Blake, Julie Browne and Stuart Sime, A Practical Approach to Alternative Dispute Resolution (5th edn, Oxford University Press 2018), p. 257.

107 Chinwe Umegbolu, Dispensation of Justice: Lagos Multi-Door Courthouse (LMDC) as a Case Study in Nigeria. A PhD thesis submitted to the Business and Law Faculty at the University of Brighton (2021), p. 45.

108 Chinwe Umegbolu, Episode 5: What are the Factors that could Influence the Selection of an ADR Option? <https://blogs.brighton.ac.uk/chinwe/2020/11/> accessed on 21 June 2025.

109 Zumeta, 'Styles of Mediation: Facilitative, Evaluative, and Transformative Mediation', p. 1.

110 Ibid.

111 Ibid.

112 Expert Views on ADR (EVA) Vid/Podcast Show (2024), <https://podcasters.spotify.com/pod/show/chinwe1/episodes/Series-4-Creating-Safe-Spaces-Via-ADR-How-can-Employees-in-the-US-Report-Discrimination--Harassment--Bullying-without-fear-of-losing-their-jobs-with-Ed-Watt-e2nipo7/a-abgc2lv> accessed 24 August 2024.

Evaluative mediators often conduct separate meetings with the parties and their lawyers, engaging in what is often referred to as 'shuttle diplomacy'.[113] They play a pivotal role in assisting parties and attorneys in thoroughly evaluating their legal position and carefully weighing the costs and benefits of pursuing a legal resolution versus seeking a mediated settlement.[114] This approach to evaluative mediation originated in court-referred mediation, where the attorney collaborates with the court to select the mediator.[115] It is based on the premise that the mediator possesses legal expertise in the specific area of the dispute. Given the close association between the courts and evaluative mediation and their familiarity with settlement conferences, it is typical for evaluative mediators to be legal professionals.

4.7 THE MEDIATION FRAMEWORK BEFORE THE ENACTMENT OF THE ARBITRATION AND MEDIATION ACT 2023

To reiterate, mediation has been a prevalent method for resolving disputes in the Nigerian context. The Igbo people, one of Nigeria's 370 ethnic groups, offer a compelling case study. They are dispersed across several states (36 states and the capital territory, Abuja).[116] They reside is predominantly in the southeastern region – in Abia, Anambra, Ebonyi, Enugu, and Imo states, and the eastern fringes of Delta State, parts of Akwa Ibom, Bayelsa, Benue, Cross River, Kogi, and River states.[117] In 1967, the Igbo people, feeling marginalised by other regions of Nigeria, opted to establish their nation, Biafra.[118] This decision led to a conflict to prevent secession and compelled the Igbo group to reintegrate into Nigeria.[119] Despite numerous attempts by various states to mediate between the conflicting parties, a lasting resolution remained elusive.

---

113 Diane Cohen, Evaluative Mediation (Mediate.com, 2011) <https://www.mediate.com/author/Diane-Cohen/1019> accessed 20 August 2024.

114 Expert Views on ADR (EVA) Vid/Podcast Show, <https://podcasts.apple.com/us/podcast/episode-56-exploration-into-the-concept-of/id1538506713?i=1000642886450> accessed 20 August 2024.

115 Ibid.

116 N. Okereafoezeke, Law and Justice in Post-British Nigeria: Conflicts and Interactions between Native and Foreign Systems of Social Control in Igbo (Library of Congress Cataloging-in-Publication Data 2002), p. 12.

117 Ibid.

118 Ibid.

119 Okolie Ofobuike, Nigerian Government and Politics the Changing Scene (3rd edn. John Jacob's Classic 2007), p. 38.

This highlights the need for more effective mediation strategies to address such intricate disputes.

However, introducing unofficial mediators played a significant role during the conflict between Nigeria and Biafra from 1966 to 1970.[120] These unofficial mediators, also known as go-betweens, provided a crucial communication channel, even though the Quaker mediators were unsuccessful.[121] Their involvement helped to reduce the tension caused by a lack of trust on both sides, paving the way for what is described as an 'almost miraculous mood of reconciliation'.[122] The unofficial mediators' independence from the government and non-interference allowed the parties to trust and confide in them, making mediation more appealing. Traditional mediation is still ongoing, and technology has made it possible to summon parties from wherever they reside to address their cases.

A recent incident involving Chief Emenike Mgbenena (Oboli Obosi) and Nze Okey Ogbazi (Ezeakaibe Ugeji) was reported at the Okwuolisa Traditional Supreme Council in Obosi.[123] Chief Emenike Mgbenena complained that Nze Ogbazi insulted him during a meeting of the Obosi forum held at Nze Ezeakaibe's residence in London.[124] It was alleged that Nze Ogbazi even attempted to harm Chief E. Mgbemena with an empty bottle of brandy and addressed him using his name rather than his chieftaincy title (Oboli Obosi).[125] Following an exchange of words, the other members present calmed both individuals down. The situation was resolved with the defendant offering a bottle of brandy to Chief Emenike Mgbemena, followed by a prayer, a hug, and handshake to bring amicable closure.[126] The defendant initially believed the matter was resolved but was subsequently summoned by the Traditional Supreme Council of Obosi to present his defence over the phone from his home in London. Following this, the council heads, known as the 'Isi Muo' in Igbo (Spirit head),[127] ruled in favour of the defendant, stating that the case lacked merit. In response to an appeal from Nze Okey Ogbazi to avoid

---

120 Ibid.

121 Donald Rothchild, 'Unofficial Mediation and the Nigeria-Biafra War' (1997) 3 Nationalism & Ethnic Politics, p. 37.

122 Adam Curle, 'Mediation During the Nigerian Civil War' (1967–1970) accessed 4 June 2024, <https://www.quakersintheworld.org/quakers-in-action/226/Mediation-During-the-Nigerian-Civil-War-1967-70>.

123 *Chief Emenike Mgbenena v Nze Okey Ogbazi* Traditional Supreme Council Obosi.

124 Ibid.

125 Ibid.

126 Ibid.

127 Ibid.

further conflict with Chief Mgbemena, the 'Isi Muo' of Obosi advised Nze Okey Ogbazi to select a representative to visit the complainant with a bottle of brandy, aiming for a final peaceful reconciliation. This course of action would secure the continued peaceful representation of the Obosi Kingdom.[128]

As previously discussed in this book chapter, the central theme of this case underscores the enduring presence of traditional mediation and customary arbitration in Nigeria, which closely resemble ADR.[129] The continued recognition of council heads' authority means that their decisions carry substantial weight. In this instance, the defendant complied with the rulings to prevent potential ostracism of himself and his family from the community.

As per Hon. Justice Nelson Ogbuanya, the Judge of the National Industrial Court of Nigeria, the new Arbitration and Mediation Act of 2023[130] has superseded the previous Arbitration and Conciliation Act of 1988, which formerly governed arbitration and conciliation in Nigeria.[131] This updated act marks a significant step forward by acknowledging mediation as a legitimate and effective method for resolving disputes, setting it apart from its predecessor. Unlike the Arbitration and Conciliation Act, the new Act defines 'mediation' as the procedure through which disputing parties engage an impartial third party or parties to assist them in reaching a mutually acceptable resolution for their contractual or legal relationship dispute.[132]

The UNCITRAL Model Law on International Commercial Mediation (2018) has significantly influenced the Arbitration and Mediation Act's framework.[133] It clearly defines the various types of disputes suitable for mediation under the Act, outlines the process for initiating mediation, specifies the required number of mediators,[134] details the procedures involved in mediation, and addresses important issues such as the mediator's immunity and fees. Additionally, it recognises the Singapore Convention on Mediation 2018's applicability for enforcing international settlement agreements outside of Nigeria, pending the

---

128 Ibid.

129 Ibid.

130 Expert Views on ADR (EVA) Vid/podcast Show (2024) ADR and Workplace Conflict: A Nigerian Perspective with Hon Justice Nelson Ogbuanya <https://open.spotify.com/episode/3zdfJPSETHZw6UMfgjmNrA?si=UOMpgnqBSnW4C0rzGJxIEQ>.

131 Ibid.

132 Tiwalade Aderoju, (2023), The Nigerian Arbitration and Mediation Act 2023: A comparison with the Arbitration and Conciliation Act 2004 and global practices. <https://www.ibanet.org/the-nigerian-arbitration-and-mediation-act-2023> accessed on 8 July 2024.

133 Ibid.

134 Ibid.

state's accession to the Singapore Convention.[135] However, the new Act is not applicable to labour disputes; the argument is that labour is not a commodity and, therefore, discussions involving humans cannot be commercialised because the slave trade has been abolished.[136] In other words, people can take it as a commercial dispute, as the Act talks about commercial arbitration. To that extent, it exposes humans to the commodity level, which is correct.

In the context of workplace issues, many problems are resolved through ADR.[137] For instance, Hon. Justice Nelson Ogbuanya mentioned a case involving a retired officer. The officer's proposed approach seemed likely to damage the reputation of everyone in the office.[138] Therefore, ADR appeared to be the best approach for this case. The officer did not express a desire to return to the office but instead stated, 'Pay me everything I am entitled to. If you don't, I will disclose much of what happened here.' If he disclosed the information, it could tarnish the entire organisation by highlighting unresolved issues.[139] Additionally, all the other details were already public knowledge. Even if the claims turned out to be false, it would be a challenge to convince people that the situation was not as presented in court. This is the nature of litigation.[140]

In Nigeria, ADR is an integral part of the court system. Kehinde Aina (SAN), the founder of the Multi-Door Courthouse in Nigeria, supports this assertion in a recent interview with the researcher. He noted that the Court of Appeal Mediation Center (CAMC), which is now the Court of Appeal Alternative Dispute Resolution (ADR), of which he is one of the founders, aims to expedite justice through ADR. The Center facilitates amicable resolutions for both civil and criminal appeals, helping more cost-effective solutions. The researcher also interviewed the Director of the Court of Appeal ADR center in Nigeria (covers Abuja, Port Harcourt and Lagos state) (on 19 January 2026 – the same day the researcher interviewed Mr Aina), Ms Regina T. Kuhe.

The Court of Appeal ADR center was formally the Court of Appeal Mediation centre. It is premised on two main principles of mediation: the right of self-determination and balancing the interests of the parties. The right of self-determination is saying that the Court of Appeal ADR center ensures that the parties involved, rather than a judge or arbitrator, have the power to determine the final outcome of their matter. It empowers parties to take responsibility for the decisions that lead to settlement, essentially acting as 'assisted

---

135 Ibid.

136 Expert Views on ADR (EVA) Vid/podcast Show (2024) ADR and Workplace Conflict: A Nigerian Perspective with Hon Justice Nelson Ogbuanya (unpublished).

137 Ibid.

138 Ibid.

139 Ibid.

140 Ibid.

negotiation'. On the other hand, balancing the interests of the parties aims to foster mutual understanding and ensure that solutions are not lopsided, but rather satisfy the interests of all parties involved. Thus, two principles are a responsibility on all mediators to ensure that the parties interests are paramount at any point that the interests of the parties are not balanced or on equal footing, then they stop the session.

It is imperative to state that the Industrial Court in Nigeria has the statutory authority to establish an ADR centre based on the constitution.[141] The constitution's provision is clear, and the centre utilises mediation and other hybrid processes, making ADR well-suited for addressing work disputes in Nigeria. However, the key challenge lies in effectively implementing it within the legal framework.

4.8 THE PROs AND CONs OF MEDIATION

In recent years, mediation has become increasingly prevalent as the preferred method of resolving disputes in major commercial contracts, both domestic and cross-jurisdictional. It is perceived as a more flexible, less legalistic, and more forward-thinking approach than litigation or arbitration.[142]

Corporations and individuals have recently incorporated mediation into their contractual agreements to resolve disputes.[143] This is due to mediation's recognised benefits, including speed, cost-effectiveness, efficiency, and the promotion of mutually beneficial outcomes. Consequently, there is a strong preference for hiring trained mediators who are experts in dispute resolution and possess effective communication skills.[144] It is important to note that mediation is a voluntary, party-driven, empowering, humane, non-binding, and private dispute resolution process. As a result, it typically requires the agreement of all parties involved to proceed. However, in certain jurisdictions, such as Nigeria, as discussed in this chapter, parties are encouraged to participate in mediation.

---

141 Ibid.

142 Alero Akeredolu, 'A Comparative Appraisal of the Practice and Procedure of Court-Connected Alternative Dispute Resolution in Nigeria, United States of America and United Kingdom' (University of Ibadan 2013), p. 79.

143 Chinwe Umegbolu, Dispensation of Justice: Lagos Multi-Door Courthouse (LMDC) as a Case Study in Nigeria. A PhD thesis submitted to the Business and Law Faculty at the University of Brighton (2021), p. 234.

144 Mike Whitehouse, 'Regulating Civil Mediation in England and Wales: Towards a "Win–Win" Outcome' University of Hull (2017), p. 2.

Party autonomy is fundamental in mediation and other ADR processes.[145] It is emphasised during the initial stages of the mediation process, where the parties and their legal counsel are present. Mediators consistently communicate to the parties that mediation is driven by them, and they have complete autonomy during the opening session. Additionally, mediation is often more cost-effective than other dispute resolution methods. It offers the advantage of resolving disputes promptly, which contrasts with the protracted nature of litigation.[146] Party autonomy within mediation ensures that the mediator does not unduly influence the parties to settle in a particular manner and provides them with the freedom to make concessions or compromises at their discretion.[147] Additionally, they alone can sign the TOS or appoint another person, like a lawyer, to write the TOS for him/her. The party's autonomy is revealed in the sense that the party, in the very long run, takes full responsibility for the TOS.[148] However, some critics of mediation doubt whether ADR is as rosy as proponents have depicted it to be. They claim that mediation prioritises compromise or concession over justice.[149] One of such critics is Owen Fiss, who argued as follows:

> Settlement is, for me, the civil analogue of plea-bargaining: Consent is often coerced; someone without authority may strike the bargain; the absence of a trial and judgment renders subsequent judicial involvement troublesome; and although dockets are trimmed, justice may not be done. Like plea-bargaining, settlement is a capitulation to the conditions of mass society and should be neither encouraged nor praised.[150]

The statement above has stimulated extensive debates, with arguments for and against it. This debate is echoed to some extent in the perspectives of Genn and Meadow. Initially, Professor Genn suggested that: 'Mediation is not about just settlement; it is just about settlement'[151] on the contrary, Meadow suggested that the 'demise of the adversary system of trial' is a continuing evolutionary development of our Anglo-American legal system, and that the phenomenon

---

145 Gary Born, 'Keynote Address: Arbitration and the Freedom to Associate' (2009–2010) 38 Ga J Int'l & Comp L, p. 16.

146 Centre LMDC, The Lagos Multi-Door Courthouse Neutrals' Handbook, p. 31.

147 Ibid.

148 Ibid.

149 Owen Fiss, 'Against Settlement' (1984) 93(6) The Yale Law Journal, p. 1075.

150 Ibid.

151 Joshua Rozenberg, 'Dame Hazel Genn Warns of "Downgrading" of Civil Justice' (2008) accessed 25 August 2024.

of the 'vanishing trial'[152] is not necessarily bad. If litigants and their lawyers choose other processes, we must examine why and observe.[153]

Upon reviewing the statements above, Meadow's final statement echoes Genn's perspective. In contrast to Professor Fiss, Genn suggests that parties engaging in ADR, such as mediation, often adopt a 'settlement mindset'.[154] This mindset leads them to prioritise problem-solving over legal entitlements and positional bargaining in pursuit of mutually beneficial outcomes.[155]

For instance, where a conflict arises between a husband and wife and is submitted to mediation, the potential for a constructive resolution emerges. Rather than seeking advantage from the judgement, the spouses can utilise the process to work towards restoring their marriage or relationship and achieving peaceful coexistence. This approach embodies a mindset of reconciliation and moving beyond grievances to reach a positive outcome for both parties.

Essentially, the concept of settlement emphasises the idea of waiving one's rights,[156] with most parties seeking peace or closure. It is important to note that parties are permitted to bring a lawyer if they wish. In recent years, it is evident that disputants in matters such as divorce or other disputes do not make decisions in isolation.[157] They either seek legal counsel or educate themselves about their legal position before reaching a private settlement.[158] Hence, the party's bargaining abilities are influenced by their understanding of the law to some extent. Therefore, when divorcing parents come to an agreement regarding the division of family wealth and custodial rights, they do so by negotiating within the framework of the law.

In trial courts, the primary focus is on discerning the rightful party and ensuring that they receive their due under the law, while the disadvantaged party is left to bear the consequences – a dynamic often referred to as the

---

152 Carrie Menkel-Meadow, 'Is the Adversary System Really Dead? Dilemmas of Legal Ethics as Legal Institutions and Roles Evolve, Current Legal Problems' (2005) Research Gate, p. 86.

153 Owen Fiss, 'Against Settlement' (1984) 93(6) The Yale Law Journal, p. 1076.

154 Ibid.

155 Chinwe Umegbolu, 'Bargaining in the Shadow of the Law: The Facts of Divorce As They Stand Today' (2020) 39 (1) Resolution Institute | the arbitrator & mediator, pp. 144–145.

156 Umegbolu, 'Bargaining in the Shadow of the Law: The Facts of Divorce As They Stand Today', p. 152.

157 So this can be done by mandatory or voluntary mediation.

158 Dalrock, 'Bargaining in the Shadow of the Law' (2012) <http://dalrock.wordpress.com/2012> accessed 23 September 2024 cited in Umegbolu, 'Bargaining in the Shadow of the Law: The Facts of Divorce As They Stand Today', p. 145.

win–lose approach.[159] While most cases are better suited for litigation than ADR, the researcher endorses both Genn and Meadow's perspectives on ADR.[160] There are instances, such as in divorce cases and matters requiring the establishment of legal precedent, where mediation and other ADR methods may not yield the desired outcomes. Nevertheless, the straightforward nature of ADR appears to afford inherent advantages over litigation.

4.9 RECOMMENDATIONS

The writer believes that to fully harness mediation in Nigeria's civil justice system, reforms must address legal, institutional, technological, and socio-cultural barriers. Educational campaigns are needed to build awareness and trust in mediation. Additionally, it is crucial to enhance institutional support and funding for the Multi-Door Courthouse, as well as to promote academic research and data collection to assess mediation outcomes and inform policy. Lastly, enacting national legislation to unify existing ADR frameworks is essential.

4.10 CONCLUSION

The chapter provides an overview of ADR's history, processes, advantages, and disadvantages. It also explores its impact on the speed and informality of court processes and its relevance in Nigerian jurisdictions. Furthermore, the chapter examines the significant changes in mediation. The insights provided in this chapter will help the reader understand the Nigerian civil justice system and the benefits and similarities between the TAMSD and modern-day mediation. These parallels will significantly contribute to the reader's understanding of the role and progress of mediation in the Nigerian judicial landscape, highlighting how these processes complement traditional litigation.

[159] Susan Marks, Watching the Wind Conflict Resolution During South Africa's Transition to Democracy (United States Institute of Peace 2000), p. 17.

[160] The Lagos Multi-Door Courthouse, The Lagos Multi-Door Courthouse Neutrals' Handbook (2016), p. 32.

ACKNOWLEDGEMENT

The author acknowledges Mr Kehinde Aina, SAN, Founder of the Multi-Door Courthouse (MDC) in Africa, and Ms Regina T. Kuhe, Director of the Court of Appeal ADR Centre in Nigeria, for taking time out of their busy schedules to share their insights and experiences. Their contributions were invaluable to the development of this chapter and to advancing the discourse on institutional ADR in Nigeria and Africa.

5. China's unique mediation experience: The future of judicial mediation in the information age

Peter C.H. Chan

5.1 INTRODUCTION

Judicial mediation is a unique feature of China's civil justice system. The judge acts as the mediator and employs highly directive methods to lead parties to a settlement. Judicial mediation was abused during the era when Wang Shengjun was president of the Supreme People's Court ("SPC"). Courts were encouraged to abandon adjudication altogether and settlement rates became the most important performance indicator for judges.[1] Parties complained that judges would "force" them to settle in many cases.[2] In 2013, with the change in SPC leadership, judicial mediation regained its ADR function as courts were once again encouraged to adjudicate cases. In recent years, some courts have reaffirmed the policy of the past in prioritizing mediation. Judicial mediation now plays an important role in promoting social stability, which is an absolute priority of the party-state under Xi Jinping. The problem with the "mediation first" policy is threefold. First, not all cases are suitable for judicial mediation. Some cases are so clear-cut that a swift decision by the judge should be the most desirable outcome. Second, judicial mediation has its inherent problems. For instance, the dual role of the judge–mediator exerts unwarranted pressure on parties in the mediation process, especially if the judge indicates his or her preference for a settlement. This is problematic because the mediating judge will go on to become the trial judge if the dispute does not settle. Third, using mediation as a tool for social control not only weakens the ADR function of

---

1 Yedan Li, Joris Kocken, and Benjamin Van Rooij, "Understanding China's Court Mediation Surge: Insights from a Local Court" (2018) 43 Law & Soc Inquiry 58.

2 Randall Peerenboom and Xin He, "Dispute Resolution in China: Patterns, Causes and Prognosis" (2009) 4 E Asia L Rev 27.

mediation but could also lead to a miscarriage of justice in cases where it is obvious that one party has an overwhelmingly meritorious claim.

This chapter traces the history of the development of judicial mediation in China, explains its current problems and offers potential solutions. The procedural issues relating to judicial mediation are structural, even ideological. Hence, a full picture needs to be constructed to understand the contextual implications of the promotion of judicial mediation and to introduce any form of reform in this area. With the advent of technology in the administration of justice, the role of judicial mediation may also change drastically in the future. To date, China's e-courts and e-procedures are thriving. More mediations are conducted online than at any time in the history of the people's courts. This chapter also dissects the implications for parties and judges when online procedures are gradually becoming the norm in Chinese civil justice. In the future, judicial mediation should take a new form whereby the mediating judge should be a separate person from the adjudicating judge. The principle of voluntariness, which is enshrined in China's civil procedure law, should be re-emphasized and applied in practice. Judicial mediation, being a unique feature of China's civil justice system, should remain, but drastic changes are necessary.

5.2 THE HISTORICAL DEVELOPMENT OF JUDICIAL MEDIATION IN CHINA

Judicial mediation in China is defined as a "litigation activity" that occurs within first-instance, second-instance, and retrial cases accepted by courts. It is conducted by judges, who act as the neutral third party, to resolve disputes and facilitate a settlement between the parties.[3] Judicial mediation is conducted on the statutory premise that mandatory legal provisions are not violated and the voluntariness of the parties is upheld.[4] China's judicial mediation experience is known to be efficient. In recent years, the fundamental principles and operational mechanisms of China's mediation system have been applied in other jurisdictions.[5] Judicial mediation is not only an important method of

3 Shan Feng (单锋), *Zhongguo Yujing Zhong de "Sifa Tiaojie": Yi Zhong Fei Biaozhunxing Quanshi* (中国语境中的"司法调解"—种非标准性阐释) [*"Judicial Mediation" in the Chinese Context—A Non-standard Interpretation*], Nanjing Shida Xuebao (Shehui Kexue Ban) (南京师大学报(社会科学版)) [Journal of Nanjing Normal University (Social Science Edition)], no. 4, 2015, at 52–62.

4 Peter C.H. Chan, *Mediation in Contemporary Chinese Civil Justice: A Proceduralist Diachronic Perspective* (Brill Nijhoff 2017) 37.

5 Ming Song (宋明) and Jialin Chen (陈佳林), *Lun Sifa Tiaojie Heyi Yuanze de Shiyong* (论司法调解合意原则的适用) [*On the Application of the Consensus*

dispute resolution in China but also a mechanism of social control with unique historical attributes.[6] This section traces the historical development of judicial mediation in China.

5.2.1 The "Mediation-dominant" Period (1949–1981)

For a significant period after the establishment of the People's Republic of China, the judicial mediation system served as the primary means for resolving civil and social disputes.[7] On 26 July 1950, the Supreme People's Court (SPC) explicitly stated at a national conference on judicial work that "the People's Courts must always prioritize mediation efforts, as mediation during litigation is a necessary component of our country's judicial system".[8] On 2 February 1979, the SPC issued the "Provisions on the Procedure for the People's Courts to Handle Civil Cases (Trial Implementation)", which emphasized the policy of "relying on the masses, conducting investigations and studies, resolving issues locally, and prioritizing mediation" in civil trial work.[9] During this period, when the legal system was still under construction, judicial mediation became a tool for the party-state to reorganize social order and mobilize public support for its policies.[10]

5.2.2 The "Emphasis on Mediation" Period (1982–1990)

As the standard of living improved as a result of China's economic reforms, the judiciary began to recognize the limitations of exclusively emphasizing

---

Principle in Judicial Mediation], SHANDONG SHEHUI KEXUE (山东社会科学) [SHANDONG SOCIAL SCIENCES], no. 7, 2013, at 134.

6 Yongkun Zhou (周永坤), *Zhongguo Sifa Gainian Shi Yanjiu* (中国司法概念史研究) [*Research on the History of Judicial Concepts in China*], FAZHI YANJIU (法治研究) [LEGAL STUDIES], no. 4, 2011, at 67, 72.

7 Rongdi Li (李荣棣), Dehua Tang (唐德华), *Shilun Wo Guo Minshi Susong Zhong de Tiaojie* (试论我国民事诉讼中的调解) [*Preliminary Discussion on Mediation in Our Country's Civil Litigation*], FAXUE YANJIU (法学研究) [LEGAL STUDIES], no. 5, 1981, at 40.

8 Waye Vicki and Ping Xiong, "The Relationship Between Mediation and Judicial Proceedings in China" (2011) 6 Asian Journal of Comparative Law 1–34.

9 Ibid.

10 Bowen Niu (牛博文), *Zhongguo Sifa Tiaojie de Lishi Xushi ji Chengyin Fenxi* (中国司法调解的历史叙事及成因分析) [*Historical Narration and Cause Analysis of Judicial Mediation in China*], GANSU XINGZHENG XUEYUAN XUEBAO (甘肃行政学院学报) [JOURNAL OF GANSU ADMINISTRATIVE COLLEGE], no. 2, 2014, at 110–124, 128.

judicial mediation.[11] To enhance the status of adjudication in civil disputes, statutory changes were made to formalize the operation of judicial mediation.[12] On 8 March 1982, the "Civil Procedure Law of the People's Republic of China (Trial Implementation)" was promulgated, abolishing the principle of "prioritizing mediation" in favor of "emphasizing mediation".[13] Consequently, China's civil litigation entered a new phase of strictly following statutory procedures in handling cases.

5.2.3 The "Voluntary and Lawful Mediation" Period (1991–2002)

The "Civil Procedure Law of the People's Republic of China," passed on 9 April 1991, fundamentally changed the principle of "emphasizing mediation" and established the principle of "voluntary and lawful mediation".[14] Despite statutory changes to formalize judicial mediation and protect party autonomy, some scholars still view judicial mediation to be an arbitrary process in practice.[15] During this period, however, the rate of cases concluded

---

[11] Jianhua Ma (马建华), *Lun Wo Guo Sifa Tiaojie Zhidu de Wanshan* (论我国司法调解制度的完善) [*On the Improvement of the Judicial Mediation System in Our Country*], DANGDAI FAXUE (当代法学) [CONTEMPORARY LEGAL STUDIES], no. 5, 2010, at 147.

[12] Wusheng Zhang (章武生) et al., *Sifa Xiandaihua yu Minsi Susong Zhidu de Jianzhu* (司法现代化与民事诉讼制度的建构) [*Judicial Modernization and the Construction of Civil Litigation System*] 30 (Law Press (法律出版社) 2000).

[13] In adjudicating civil cases, the people's courts shall prioritize mediation, with timely judgment rendered in cases where mediation proves ineffective. Zhonghua Renmin Gongheguo Minshi Susongfa (Shixing) (中华人民共和国民事诉讼法(试行)) [The Civil Procedure Law of the People's Republic of China (Trial Implementation)] (promulgated by Standing Comm. Nat'l People's Cong., 8 March 1982, effective 1 October 1982), art. 6, http://www.law-lib.com/law/law_view.asp?id=44928.

[14] In adjudicating civil cases, the people's courts shall mediate based on the principles of voluntariness and legality. If mediation fails, timely judgment shall be rendered. Zhonghua Renmin Gongheguo Minshi Susongfa (中华人民共和国民事诉讼法) [Civil Procedure Law of the People's Republic of China] (promulgated by Nat'l People's Cong., 9 April 1991, effective 9 April 1991), art. 9, http://www.npc.gov.cn/zgrdw/npc/xinwen/2017-06/29/content_2024892.htm?eqid=c78959be0006216e00000006642c1965&wd=&eqid=f54deeb3000131fd000000036466ddea.

[15] Weidong Ji (季卫东), *Fazhi yu Tiaojie de Beilun* (法制与调解的悖论) [*The Paradox of Legal System and Mediation*], FAXUE YANJIU (法学研究) [LEGAL STUDIES], no. 5, 1991, at 21, 24.

through judicial mediation saw a significant decline, from 59.08% in 1991 to 30.32% in 2002.[16]

5.2.4 The "Revival of Judicial Mediation" Period (2003–2012)

Entering the twenty-first century, as social disputes intensified and judicial reforms encountered resistance, coupled with the party-state's promotion of the concept of a "harmonious society", judicial mediation found its way back to the center of judicial activities from 2003. On 4 July 2003, the Adjudication Committee of the SPC passed the "Several Provisions on the Application of Summary Procedures in the Trial of Civil Cases", where Article 14 explicitly mandates that courts should first attempt mediation (before hearing cases) in handling six types of disputes, including matrimonial disputes and labor contracts disputes.[17] On 18 August 2004, the SPC passed the "Provisions on Several Issues Concerning the Civil Mediation Work of the People's Courts", proposing the work guideline of "mediating when possible, adjudicating when necessary, combining mediation with adjudication, and resolving cases thoroughly". This guideline effectively made judicial mediation the predominant method of civil dispute resolution in China. On 17 March 2009, the SPC issued the "Third Five-Year Reform Outline for the People's Courts (2009–2013)", advocating the policy of "strengthening litigation ([judicial]) mediation" in civil lawsuits attached to criminal cases.[18] The national first-instance civil case mediation settlement rate rebounded from 30.0% in 2003 to 67.3% in 2011.[19] Court leaders pride themselves on resolving cases solely by judicial mediation. Some courts even attained "zero adjudication rates", with all civil cases settled by judicial mediation. Wang Shengjun, the president of the SPC during that period, was the key advocate for promoting judicial mediation as the predominant dispute resolution method. Under this overarching policy, some judges would forcibly conclude a settlement between the parties just to boost

---

16 Zhongguo Falv Nianjian (中国法律年鉴) [Law Yearbook of China] (Press of Law Yearbook of China (中国法律年鉴出版社) 2011).

17 Guanyu Shiyou Jianyi Chengxu Shenli Minshi Anjian de Ruogan Guiding (关于适用简易程序审理民事案件的若干规定) [Several Regulations on the Application of Summary Procedure for Adjudicating Civil Cases] (promulgated by Adjud. Comm. Supr. People's Ct., 4 July 2003, effective 1 October 2003), art. 14, https://www.chinacourt.org/law/detail/2003/09/id/88124.shtml.

18 Renmin Fayuan Disange Wunian Gaige Gangyao (2009–2013) (人民法院第三个五年改革纲要 (2009–2013)) [Outline of the Third Five-Year Reform Plan of the People's Court (2009–2013)] (promulgated by Supr. People's Ct., 25 March 2009, effective 25 March 2009), art. 26.

19 *Supra* note 14.

the mediation settlement rates. Procedural abuses were rampant during this period. While voluntariness was still a statutory requirement, it was essentially ignored by most courts in China.

5.2.5 The "Reconstruction of Judicial Mediation" Period (2013–2023)

When Wang's tenure ended in 2013, so did his radical policies on judicial mediation. During this period, the principles of legality and voluntariness in judicial mediation were re-emphasized. Courts, again, were told to hear cases. The SPC president during this period, Zhou Qiang, was an advocate for procedural formalism.[20] As a result, mediation settlement rates declined drastically.[21] The Decision on Amending the Civil Procedure Law of the People's Republic of China, which was adopted on 31 August 2012, introduced a new provision as Article 133(2) of the Civil Procedure Law, stating: "For cases accepted by the People's Courts, if mediation is feasible before the trial, mediation shall be employed to resolve the disputes in a timely manner".[22] Judicial mediation became an optional pre-trial procedure if it is suitable for the specific case,[23] with adequate procedural protection for parties.[24]

---

[20] Albert HY Chen, "China's Long March towards Rule of Law or China's Turn Against Law?" (2016) 4 The Chinese Journal of Comparative Law 1–35.

[21] Ibid 11.

[22] Quanguo Renmin Daibiao Dahui Changwu Weiyuanhui Guanyu Xiugai Zhonghua Renmin Gongheguo Minshi Susongfa de Jueding (全国人民代表大会常务委员会关于修改《中华人民共和国民事诉讼法》的决定) [Decision of the Standing Committee of the National People's Congress of the People's Republic of China on Amending the Civil Procedure Law of the People's Republic of China], Zhonghua Renmin Gongheguo Zhongyang Renmin Zhengfu (中华人民共和国中央人民政府) [Cent. People's Gov't China] (31 August 2012), https://www.gov.cn/flfg/2012-09/01/content_2214662.htm.

[23] Jiansheng Zhang (章剑生), *Xingzheng Zhengyi Suqian Tiaojie Lun: Falü, Gouzao yu Pingpan* (行政争议诉前调解论：法理、构造与评判) [*On Pre-litigation Mediation of Administrative Disputes: Jurisprudence, Structure, and Evaluation*], QIUSHI XUEKAN (求是学刊) [SEEKING TRUTH], vol. 50, no. 4, 2023, at 89–101.

[24] Liping Zhang (张立平) and Milong Xie (谢米隆), *Woguo Minshi Susong Tiaojie Zhengce de Lishi Bianqian yu Yanjin Luoji: Jiyu Lishi Zhidu Zhuyi Fenxi* (我国民事诉讼调解政策的历史变迁与演进逻辑—基于历史制度主义分析) [*The Historical Changes and Evolution Logic of Civil Litigation Mediation Policy in China: Based on Historical Institutionalism Analysis*], CHONGQING SHEHUI KEXUE (重庆社会科学) [CHONGQING SOCIAL SCIENCES], no. 8, 2022, at 89–100.

5.2.6 Latest Developments (Post 2023)

In recent years, some courts have reaffirmed the policy of the past in prioritizing mediation. Judicial mediation now plays an important role in promoting social stability, which is an absolute priority of the party-state under Xi Jinping. The current president of the SPC, Zhang Jun, is an advent supporter of the quantification of judicial performance evaluation.[25] The resolution of cases in a fashion that avoids any ensuing social discontent is one of the key positive indicators of performance.[26] As such, judicial mediation, given its propensity to settle disputes and create a win–win situation for both parties, has become a naturally preferred choice of many Chinese adjudicators. While national mediation settlement rates are nowhere near their heights during the Wang Shengjun period, data show that settlement rates in some courts are rising.[27]

5.3 CURRENT CHALLENGES IN CHINA'S CIVIL JUDICIAL MEDIATION SYSTEM

The contemporary judicial mediation system in China is rooted in its traditional legal culture that promoted harmony and consensus.[28] The system inherited the value orientation of "mediating disputes and quelling lawsuits" that dated back to the early days of imperial China.[29] Thus, the institutional design of civil litigation in contemporary China exhibits a strong preference

---

25 Zheng Zhuo (郑卓), Jixiao Kaohe Zhidu Sifa Shencha de Biyaoxing ji Juti Lujing (绩效考核制度司法审查的必要性及具体路径) [The Necessity and Specific Approaches of Judicial Review on Performance Appraisal Systems], ZHONGGUO SHEHUI BAOZHANG (中国社会保障) [CHINA SOCIAL SECURITY], no. 07, 2023, at 70–71.

26 Peter C.H. Chan, "An Uphill Battle: How China's Obsession with Social Stability is Blocking Judicial Reform" (2016) 100 Judicature 14.

27 Gu Jiajie (谷佳杰), Zhongguo Tese Susong Tiaojie Zhidu Zhi 70 Nian Bianqian yu Gaige Zhanwang: Jiyu Sifa Zhengce dui Susong Tiaojie Yingxiang de Fenxi (中国特色诉讼调解制度之70年变迁与改革展望—基于司法政策对诉讼调解影响的分析) [70 Years of Changes and Reform Prospects of the Litigation Mediation System with Chinese Characteristics: Based on the Analysis of the Impact of Judicial Policies on Litigation Mediation], SHANDONG DAXUE XUEBAO (ZHEXUE SHEHUI KEXUE BAN) (山东大学学报(哲学社会科学版)) [JOURNAL OF SHANDONG UNIVERSITY (PHILOSOPHY AND SOCIAL SCIENCES)], no. 06, 2019, at 36–46.

28 Vicki Waye and Ping Xiong, "The Relationship between Mediation and Judicial Proceedings in China" (2011) 6 Asian Journal of Comparative Law 1–34.

29 Ibid 3.

for mediation.[30] However, an excessive emphasis on the mediation activities of courts has made judicial mediation a goal of civil justice, rather than a means to resolve disputes.[31] Moreover, the coexistence of judicial mediation and adjudication within the litigation process leads to inevitable inherent conflicts and the weakening of the ADR function of judicial mediation.[32]

5.3.1 Interference with the Voluntariness of Parties

Mediation is fundamentally a system where parties consensually resolve disputes. The voluntary nature of mediation distinguishes it from adjudication procedures where a decision is binding on parties whether or not the parties agree with the decision.[33] The Chinese Civil Procedure Law explicitly stipulates the principle of voluntariness in judicial mediation.[34] However, incorporating the mediation process into the litigation process could give rise to conflicts between the two procedures. With the inherent powers granted to the judge, the judge can forcibly push for a settlement or, at least, steer parties away from adjudication.[35] This deprives parties of their opportunity to be heard. This is particularly true when mediation is promoted as the preferred form of dispute resolution. In fact, empirical studies have shown that parties frequently find themselves under pressure from the judge to mediate despite having made it quite clear that they do not want to settle.[36]

---

30 Ibid 3.

31 Yanming Tang (唐延明), *Jin Fang Susong Tiaojie Guoduhua* (谨防诉讼调解过度化) [*Beware of the Overuse of Litigation Mediation*], Xingzheng yu Fa (行政与法) [Administration and Law], no. 5, 2012, at 102–105.

32 Yun Zhao, *Mediation and Alternative Dispute Resolution in Modern China* (Springer 2022).

33 Unyime Morgan, "Voluntariness of Mediation—The Mediator's Perspective" (2023) 2(3) Journal of Alternate Dispute Resolution 55–64.

34 Hao Li (李浩), *Tiaojie Gui Tiaojie, Shenpan Gui Shenpan: Minshi Shenpan Zhong de Tiao Shen Fenli* (调解归调解，审判归审判：民事审判中的调审分离) [*Mediation to Mediation, Judgment to Judgment: The Separation of Mediation and Adjudication in Civil Trials*], Zhongguo Faxue (中国法学) [China Legal Science], no. 3, 2013, at 5–18.

35 Leonard L. Riskin and Nancy A. Welsh, "Is That All There Is: The Problem in Court-Oriented Mediation" (2007) 15 George Mason Law Review 863.

36 Xin He, "Pressures on Chinese Judges under Xi" (2021) 85 The China Journal 49–74.

5.3.2 Interference with Judicial Neutrality

In a litigation process where mediation and adjudication are fused together, a judge acts as both the mediator and the adjudicator.[37] This dual role creates an inherent conflict that makes it difficult for the judge to stay absolutely neutral in the litigation process. Information obtained during mediation could influence the adjudicator's judgment of the case and infringe upon the neutrality of the judge.[38] Judicial performance in Chinese courts is linked to an array of different metrics, among which are case withdrawal rate and appellate reversal rate.[39] If a case is settled by mediation, the judge can avoid an appeal. As such, the judge has a vested interest in promoting judicial mediation. This, too, infringes the judge's ability to handle the case in a neutral manner.[40]

5.3.3 The Weakening of the ADR Function of Judicial Mediation

When judges prefer mediation over adjudication, parties often find themselves in a mediation against their own will.[41] Mediation only works as an alternative dispute resolution mechanism when parties are genuinely committed to settling a dispute.[42] The principle of Chinese civil justice of "closing the case and having the [underlying] dispute conclusively settled" (*anjie shiliao*) drives courts to settle disputes for the sake of closing the case and avoiding appeals

---

[37] Hao Zhenjiang (郝振江), Lun Woguo Fayuan Tiaojie yu Shenpan de Chengxu Fenli (论我国法院调解与审判的程序分离) [On the Procedural Separation of Court Mediation and Adjudication in China], JINAN XUEBAO (ZHEXUE SHEHUI KEXUE BAN) (暨南学报(哲学社会科学版)) [JINAN JOURNAL (PHILOSOPHY AND SOCIAL SCIENCES)], vol. 39, no. 09, 2017, at 28–37.

[38] Ibid 34.

[39] Tongtong Yang (杨铜铜), *Faguan Jixiao Kaohe Zhidu de Fei Sifahua Kundian ji Qi Tiaoshi* (法官绩效考核制度的非司法化困境及其调试) [*The Non-judicial Dilemma of the Judge Performance Appraisal System and Its Adjustment*], FAZHI YU SHEHUI FAZHAN (法制与社会发展) [LEGAL SYSTEM AND SOCIAL DEVELOPMENT], vol. 28, no. 3, 2022, at 85–104.

[40] Peter C.H. Chan, "An Uphill Battle: How China's Obsession with Social Stability is Blocking Judicial Reform" (2016) 100 Judicature 14.

[41] Deborah R. Hensler, "Suppose it's Not True: Challenging Mediation Ideology" (2002) 1 J Disp Resol 81.

[42] D.R. Hensler, "Our Courts, Ourselves: How the Alternative Dispute Resolution Movement is Re-Shaping Our Legal System" (2003) 108 Penn St L Rev 165.

(or further trouble).[43] This weakens the ADR function of judicial mediation and opens a pandora's box of procedural abuses.[44]

5.4 TECHNOLOGICAL PROGRESS AND THE FUTURE OF THE JUDICIAL MEDIATION SYSTEM IN CHINA

With the rapid development of information technology in recent years, diversified pathways have emerged in the digitalization of judicial activities. The "smart court" reforms in China have revolutionized the landscape of judicial practice, which also impacted the conduct of judicial mediation.[45]

5.4.1 Online Judicial Models in China

(a) Smart courts

China has seen a rapid rise of "smart courts" in the last decade or so. There are two dimensions to a smart court. The first is e-court hearings. The second is pre-hearing procedures conducted with the aid of information technology. Unlike traditional hearings where physical presence is required, online hearings provide a virtual space for parties to submit their cases either in synchronized or asynchronous fashion.[46] A few cities have established fully fledged online courts.[47] On this basis, successive information platforms primarily serving the needs of online hearings have been established in the past decade or so. In October 2017, a mobile-based "Micro Court" app was launched in Ningbo; in March 2019, a pilot promotion meeting for the "Mobile Micro

---

43 Feng Junhai (冯俊海), Dui Anjie Shilei Zhuiqiu de Falixue Sikao: Yi Faguan Caipan Liyi Kao liang wei Shijiao (对案结事了追求的法理学思考—以法官裁判利益考量为视角) [Jurisprudential Reflections on the Pursuit of Case Resolution: From the Perspective of Judges' Interest in Adjudication], Shandong Shehui Kexue (山东社会科学) [Shandong Social Science], no. 05, 2014, at 120–124.

44 Ibid 121.

45 Weiwei Zheng (郑维炜), *Zhongguo "Zhihui Fayuan" Zaixian Tiaojie Jizhi Yanjiu* (中国"智慧法院"在线调解机制研究) [*Research on the Online Mediation Mechanism of China's "Smart Courts"*], Dangdai Faxue (当代法学) [Contemporary Legal Studies], vol. 34, no. 6, 2020, at 141–148.

46 Weimin Zuo (左卫民), *Zhongguo Zaixian Susong: Shizheng Yanjiu yu Fazhan Zhanwang* (中国在线诉讼: 实证研究与发展展望) [*China Online Litigation: Empirical Research and Development Prospects*], Bijiao Fa Yanjiu (比较法研究) [Comparative Law Research], no. 4, 2020, at 162.

47 Jiang Huiling (蒋惠岭), Lun Chuantong Sifa Guilu zai Shuzi Shidai de Fazhan (论传统司法规律在数字时代的发展) [On the Development of Traditional Judicial Rules in the Digital Age], Xiandai Faxue (现代法学) [Modern Law Science], vol. 45, no. 05, 2023, at 125–138.

Court" was held in Ningbo, expanding the pilot scope from Zhejiang Province to courts in 12 provinces in China, including Beijing and Hebei.[48] In May 2020, the "Supreme People's Court Work Report" proposed "to fully promote the "Mobile Micro Court of China", driving the development of electronic litigation services to mobile platforms.[49] On 1 March 2022, the "People's Court Online Operation Rules" officially came into effect. The SPC transformed and upgraded the "Mobile Micro Court of China" into the "People's Court Online Service", integrating mediation, filing, document review, service, preservation, appraisal, and other litigation service functions with smart services, achieving a "one-stop, all-in-one" online service for the People's Courts.[50] The rate of online hearing has risen substantially, from 1.1% in 2016 to 37.3% in 2022, a 36.2% increase (see Table 5.1).[51]

The use of information technology in pre-hearing procedure has also seen rapid expansion in the past few years. The rate of online filings increased from 17.4% in 2018 to 39.1% in 2022, a 21.7% increase over five years; the rate of online mediation rose from 9.1% in 2018 to 93.3% in 2022, an increase of 84.2%.[52] Online evidence exchange has developed from the functional construction stage to the actual application stage, with gradually increasing usage rates.[53] By the end of December 2023, the "People's Court Online Service"

48 Zhongwen Li (李中文), Linfeng Dai (戴林峰), and Hanyang Dou (窦瀚洋), "Round-the-clock, Full-process Litigation Services Available 'in the Palm of your Hand'". (全天候全流程 诉讼服务"掌上办") (*Beijing*, 26 January 2024) http://zj.people.com.cn/n2/2024/0126/c186327-40727418.html, last visited 13 May 2024.

49 "Yidong Weifayuan" Shidian Jiang Kuozhi Beijing Deng 12 Ge Diqu ("移动微法院"试点将扩至北京等12个地区) [The Pilot of "Mobile Micro-Courts" will Expand to 12 Areas Including Beijing], YANGGUANG WANG (央广网) [CHINA NATIONAL RADIO] (23 March 2019), https://news.cnr.cn/native/city/20190323/t20190323_524553156.shtml.

50 "Zuigao Fa Fabu Renmin Fayuan Zaixian Yunxing Guize" ("最高法发布人民法院在线运行规则") [The Supreme People's Court Issues Rules for Online Court Operations], Zhongguo Fayuan Wang (中国法院网) [China Court Network] (22 February 2022), https://www.chinacourt.org/article/detail/2022/02/id/6539836.shtml.

51 Zhongguo Shehui Kexue Yuan Faxue Yanjiusuo Fazhi Zhishu Chuangxin Gongcheng Xiangmuzu (中国社会科学院法学研究所法治指数创新工程项目组), Zhongguo Fayuan "Zhihui Shenpan" Disanfang Pinggu Baogao (2018–2022) (中国法院"智慧审判"第三方评估报告(2018–2022)) [Third-party Evaluation Report on China's Court "Smart Adjudication" (2018–2022)] (Chinese Academy of Social Sciences Press (中国社会科学出版社) 2023).

52 Ibid.

53 Ibid.

Table 5.1 Comparison of the People's Court electronic litigation: 2018–2022 (unit: %)[a]

Year	Online case filing rate	Online court session rate	Online evidence exchange rate	Online mediation rate	Mobile micro-court usage rate
2018	17.4	1.1	<20	9.1	40.5*
2019	33.2	1.5	<20	24.8	93.7
2020	34.3	13.3	<20	48.1	98.7
2021	40.8	16.2	23.4	49.9	99.1
2022	39.1	37.3	32.2	93.9	99.7

Note: *In 2018, the Mobile Micro-Court had not yet been promoted nationwide. The data for 2018 represent the support rate for mobile electronic litigation in courts across various regions.

[a] Supra note 51.

platform had received over 39.05 million online filing applications and accumulated more than 5.9 billion visits.[54]

(b) Online judicial mediation

Online judicial mediation has also seen considerable growth in the past few years. On 16 June 2021, 30 December 2021, and 26 January 2022, the SPC successively issued the "People's Court Online Litigation Rules",[55] "People's Court Online Mediation Rules",[56] and "People's Court Online Operation Rules",[57] officially establishing an online judicial mediation system.[58] An online app, "Micro Mediation" has been developed to allow parties to conduct

54 Quantianhou Quanliucheng Susong Fuwu "Zhangshangban" (全天候全流程诉讼服务"掌上办") [24/7 Full-Process Litigation Service "Palm Litigation"], Renmin Wang (人民网) [People's Daily Online] (26 January 2024), http://society.people.com.cn/n1/2024/0126/c1008-40166867.html.

55 People's Court Online Litigation Rules (《人民法院在线诉讼规则》) [2021] https://flk.npc.gov.cn/detail2.html?ZmY4MDgxODE3Yjk2OTM3NTAxN2I5YmI0NmE5YTBkNGE, accessed 10 May 2024.

56 People's Court Online Mediation Rules (《人民法院在线诉讼规则》) [2021] https://flk.npc.gov.cn/detail2.html?ZmY4MDgxODE3ZTliMWVjODAxN2U5YjcyYmZhMDAwOWE，accessed 10 May 2024.

57 People's Court Online Operation Rules (《人民法院在线诉讼规则》) [2022] https://www.court.gov.cn/zixun/xiangqing/346471.html, accessed 10 May 2024.

58 Niu, supra note 10, at 115.

mediation on their cell phones. This app operates under the umbrella of the "Micro Court" app, which aims to provide a "miniaturized" mobile dispute resolution hub for court users.[59]

Currently, many online mediation platforms in China have achieved significant developments. For instance, the Hangzhou Internet Court's litigation platform (in Zhejiang Province) allows parties to apply for online pre-litigation mediation, extrajudicial consultation, expert evaluation, and online arbitration.[60] In Kunshan City, Jiangsu Province, the Public Security Bureau has introduced a "cloud mediation" model for mediating civil disputes connected to criminal cases with the involvement of people's mediators and resident lawyers.[61] In Xiamen City, Fujian Province, the Haicang District Justice Bureau has developed the "Haicang Mediation Online" app, which features real-name authentication, case distribution, automatic creation of case files, mediator assignment, uploading of various types of evidence, real-time recording of the mediation process, automatic generation of mediation agreements, and monitoring of mediation agreement enforcement.[62]

---

59 Yang He (何阳), Zhiwei Tang (汤志伟), *"Wei Tiaojie": Xiangcun Zhenxing Zhong Zhihui Tiaojie Xitong Jianzhu de Luoji Lilu* ("微调解": 乡村振兴中智慧调解系统建构的逻辑理路) [*"Micro-Mediation": The Logical Path of Constructing a Smart Mediation System in Rural Revitalization*], DANGDAI JINGJI GUANLI (当代经济管理) [CONTEMPORARY ECONOMIC MANAGEMENT], no. 9, 2019, at 49.

60 He Cui (崔鹤), *Wo Guo Zhihui Fayuan Jianshe Zhong Susong Pingtai de Guize Qianru—Yi Hangzhou Hulianwang Fayuan Susong Pingtai de Tiaojie Qianzhi Guize Wei Li* (我国智慧法院建设中诉讼平台的规则嵌入—以杭州互联网法院诉讼平台的调解前置规则为例) [*Rule Embedding in the Litigation Platform of Smart Court Construction in China—A Case Study of the Pre-Mediation Rules of the Hangzhou Internet Court Litigation Platform*], GUIZHOUSHENG DANGXIAO XUEBAO (贵州省党校学报) [JOURNAL OF THE GUIZHOU PROVINCIAL PARTY SCHOOL], 2020, no. 4, at 88–96.

61 Wei Gao (高玮), *Dang "Fengqiao Jingyan" Tazai "Kunshan Zhi Lu"* (当"枫桥经验"踏上"昆山之路") [*When "Fengqiao Experience" Embarks on the "Kunshan Road"*], RENMIN TIAOJIE (人民调解) [PEOPLE'S MEDIATION], 2022, no. 6, at 21–23.

62 Fei Long (龙飞), *Duoyuanhua Jiufen Jiejue Jizhi Lifa de Dingwei yu Lujing Sikao—Yi Si Ge Difang Tiaoli de Bijiao Wei Shijiao* (多元化纠纷解决机制立法的定位与路径思考—以四个地方条例的比较为视角) [*Legislative Positioning and Pathways for Multifaceted Dispute Resolution Mechanisms: A Comparative Perspective of Four Local Regulations*], HUADONG ZHENGFA DAXUE XUEBAO (华东政法大学学报) [JOURNAL OF EAST CHINA UNIVERSITY OF POLITICAL SCIENCE AND LAW], 2018, no. 3, at 107–116. *See also* Xing'an Kong (孔幸安) & Mingzhe Chen (陈明哲),

5.4.2 New Developments in Judicial Mediation in the Information Age

(a) Evidence checking and procedural recommendations by AI

Prior to an online judicial mediation, some courts employ AI technology to conduct a preliminary examination of the evidence submitted by parties to determine if the materials are sufficient and in compliance with the relevant procedures. The system automatically advises the parties to supplement or replace the relevant materials as necessary. It also explains the procedures of the mediation and what other avenues are available to parties should mediation fail.[63]

(b) Facial expression recognition technology

Facial expression recognition technology, as a facet of artificial intelligence, is now also being applied in online mediation. Taking the China Legal Services website as an example, it has developed an online mediation platform that utilizes facial expression recognition technology. This platform analyzes the expressions of parties during the mediation process and synchronously provides this data to the mediators.[64] This assists mediators in assessing the emotional fluctuations of the parties during mediation. To some extent, it compensates for the reduced emotional resonance caused by the lack of in-person interaction in online settings, helping mediators to identify mediation opportunities and manage the pace of the mediation process in a timely manner.

(c) Storage of mediation materials

The online mediation system not only records the whole mediation process but also stores the notes taken by the mediator during a mediation session. Should initial mediation fail, subsequent mediations can benefit from the data collected from the initial mediation.[65] This also enhances transparency and

---

"Haicang Tiaojie Zai Xian" APP: Dazao Zhijian Shang de Yun Tiaojie Pingtai ("海沧调解在线"*APP:*打造指尖上的云调解平台) [*"Haicang Mediation Online" APP: Creating a Cloud Mediation Platform at Your Fingertips*], Renmin Tiaojie (人民调解) [People's Mediation], 2017, no. 2, at 20–21.

63 Ibid.

64 Shuhong Sheng (盛舒弘), *"Zhihui Yun Tiaojie" Jizhi Goujian Yanjiu—Ji Yu Zhongguo Falü Fuwu Wang Pingtai* ("智慧云调解"机制构建研究—基于中国法律服务网平台) [*"Smart Cloud Mediation" Mechanism Construction Study: Based on the China Legal Service Network Platform*], Zhongguo Sifa (中国司法) [China Justice], 2022, no. 11, at 66–72.

65 Ruichang Li (李瑞昌), *Lianti yu Liandong: Zuowei Shehui Zhili Zhidu de Zaixian Tiaojie Chuangxin* (联体与联动：作为社会治理制度的在线调解创新) [*Integration and Coordination: Online Mediation Innovation as a Social*

accountability of the mediator as the records can be used to assess the impartiality of the mediation should parties challenge the process.

(d) The use of big data in judicial mediation to quell social conflicts

The use of big data in judicial mediation helps to enhance the efficiency of the process.[66] To prevent issues such as data collection gaps, poor data quality, inaccurate information, outdated data, and data silos, courts have established data collection and analysis departments[67] to collect and analyze data regarding potentially dispute-triggering social events and public sentiment information from channels such as search engine platforms, social media platforms, and short video community platforms.[68] When addressing social conflicts, mediators can refer to the data collected and apply consistent approaches for handling similar types of social conflicts.[69] Mediators can use this data to identify areas that require special attention and whether there is any need to employ preventive measures.[70]

(e) Choosing mediators in court-annexed mediation

Parties can now choose from a variety of mediation organizations and mediators with different specializations on online mediation platforms as part of some court-annexed mediation programs. Selecting the right mediator and the supervising mediation organization can greatly enhance the efficiency of mediation. The platform provides detailed information on the mediators on its panel, outlining not only their professional background but also their

---

Governance System], XINGZHENG LUN TAN (行政论坛) [ADMINISTRATIVE FORUM], vol. 27, no. 4, 2020, at 83–89.

66 Haiyun Ma (马海韵), Jinghong Yang (杨晶鸿), *Da Shuju Qudong Xia de Gonggong Zhili Biange: Jiben Luoji he Xingdong Kuangjia* (大数据驱动下的公共治理变革：基本逻辑和行动框架) [*The Transformation of Public Governance Driven by Big Data: Basic Logic and Action Framework*], ZHONGGUO XINGZHENG GUANLI (中国行政管理) [CHINESE PUBLIC ADMINISTRATION], no. 12, 2018, at 42, 46.

67 Zhong Yu (喻中), *Da Shuju yu Renmin Tiaojie de Zhinenghua Zhuanxing* (大数据与人民调解的智能化转型) [*Big Data and the Intelligent Transformation of People's Mediation*], JIANGHAN XUESHU (江汉学术) [JIANGHAN ACADEMIC], 2023, vol. 42, no. 1, at 35–42.

68 Ibid.

69 Zhang, *supra* note 23.

70 Di Zhang (张迪), *Zaixian Fayuan Goujian de Lilun Luoji yu Lujing Zhanwang* (在线法院构建的理论逻辑与路径展望) [*Theoretical Logic and Path Outlook of Online Court Construction*], LILUN YUEKAN (理论月刊) [THEORETICAL MONTHLY], no. 2, 2022, at 114–122.

mediation approaches and areas of expertise.[71] The platform can also make recommendations based on the information provided by parties. This ensures that similar cases are handled by mediators with similar expertise.

5.4.3 Online Judicial Mediation Governance Advantages and Disadvantages

Compared to traditional judicial mediation, online judicial mediation possesses unique governance advantages. Firstly, the scope of judicial mediation has expanded substantially since mediation can be conducted online,[72] as it is unrestrained by geography.[73] In relatively underdeveloped locations, parties no longer need to bear the costs and time of traveling to the city center for mediation.[74] Secondly, the operational costs of judicial mediation have gone down as no physical venue is necessary. But the online model has its drawbacks and cannot completely replace traditional judicial mediation processes.[75] Firstly, the online mediator is in a less advantageous position when it comes to "reading the room". Many physical cues are lost in online transmission.[76] In disputes where physical presence is necessary to calm the emotions of parties, like matrimonial cases, online mediation has clear disadvantages.[77] A mediator may also find it more difficult to build rapport online as human trust is usually constructed on the basis of physical interactions.[78] Secondly, technology malfunction can impede the effectiveness of the mediation process. Mere line transmission or network signal errors can cause image distortion or time

---

71 Supra note 50.

72 Dengke Xie (谢登科), He Zhang (张赫), *Zaixian Tiaojie de Shijian Kundian yu Weilai Fazhan* (在线调解的实践困境与未来发展) [*The Practical Dilemmas and Future Development of Online Mediation*], XUESHU JIAOLIU (学术交流) [ACADEMIC EXCHANGE], no. 12, 2022, at 78–92.

73 Ma, supra note 11, at 148.

74 He and Tang, s*upra* note 60, at 50.

75 Yikai Feng (丰怡凯), *Jiceng Sifa Zhili Shijian Tupu: Sifa Xiaxiang, Nengdong Sifa yu Xianshang Sifa* (基层司法治理实践图景: 司法下乡、能动司法与线上司法) [*The Practical Landscape of Grassroots Judicial Governance: Judicial Outreach, Proactive Justice, and Online Justice*], ZHONGCAI FALÜ PINGLUN (中财法律评论) [CHINA FINANCE LAW REVIEW], vol. 14, 2022, at 179–197.

76 Hu Changming (胡昌明), "Sifa de Juchanghua" dao "Sifa de Wangluohua": Dianzi Susong de Chongji yu Fansi ("司法的剧场化"到"司法的网络化": 电子诉讼的冲击与反思) [From "Judicial Theatricalization" to "Judicial Digitalization": The Impact and Reflections on Electronic Litigation], Falü Shiyong (法律适用) [Application of Law], no. 05, 2021, at 74–83.

77 Ibid 80.

78 Ibid 81.

lag, which could substantially reduce the quality of the mediation.[79] Thirdly, online mediations present security risks, including the disclosure of sensitive information about the parties.[80] Fourthly, online mediation may create unwarranted barriers for less tech-savvy individuals. For instance, if the parties lack the capability to digitize paper evidence, they may find it extremely challenging to proceed with online mediation.[81]

5.5 SPECIFIC PATHWAYS FOR IMPROVING CIVIL JUDICIAL MEDIATION IN CHINA

5.5.1 Separating Mediation and Adjudication and Developing Pre-litigation Mediation

The drawbacks of a mediation–adjudication integrated model were discussed in the previous sections.[82] China should develop a "separation of mediation and adjudication" model under which a specialized mediation institution is established within the court presided over by individuals who are not trial judges. Currently, there is no detailed statutory framework for pre-trial judicial mediation.[83] In practice, however, many grassroots courts in China have already made successful explorations in this type of mediation. For example, the Changchun Intermediate Court conducts pre-trial mediation for cases that are clear on the facts and have a small claim amount, presided over by the filing court judges after case acceptance. There is a mediation deadline of

---

79 Yongan Liao (廖永安), Zongcheng Lv (吕宗澄), *Wo Guo "Hulianwang + Tiaojie" Fazhan Kundian ji Qi Lujing Xuanze* (我国"互联网+调解"发展困境及其路径选择) [*The Development Dilemma and Path Choices of "Internet + Mediation" in Our Country*], ANHUI DAXUE XUEBAO (ZHEXUE SHEHUI KEXUE BAN) (安徽大学学报（哲学社会科学版）) [JOURNAL OF ANHUI UNIVERSITY (PHILOSOPHY & SOCIAL SCIENCES)], no. 3, 2017, at 88, 94.

80 Dengke Xie (谢登科), *Lun Zaixian Susong Zhong de Geren Xinxi Baohu* (论在线诉讼中的个人信息保护) [*On the Protection of Personal Information in Online Litigation*], ZHONGGUO ZHENGFA DAXUE XUEBAO (中国政法大学学报) [JOURNAL OF CHINA UNIVERSITY OF POLITICAL SCIENCE AND LAW], 2022, no. 1, at 127–137.

81 Ibid.

82 Chan, *supra* note 26.

83 Guanyu Shiyong Jianyi Chengxu Shenli Minshi Anjian de Ruogan Guiding (关于适用简易程序审理民事案件的若干规定) [Several Regulations on the Application of Summary Procedure for Adjudicating Civil Cases] (promulgated by the Judicial Comm. Sup. People's Ct., 10 September 2003, effective 1 December 2003), art. 14, https://www.chinacourt.org/law/detail/2003/09/id/88124.shtml.

20 days.[84] When parties settle, their settlement agreement can be confirmed by the court, something akin to a consent judgment, which is directly enforceable.[85] If the parties fail to reach an agreement, the case proceeds directly to litigation. The establishment of a specialized mediation institution serves two purposes for the court: (a) it helps divert non-complex cases to pre-trial judicial mediation and alleviate the workload of trial judges; and (b) it reduces the number of cases that fall under the traditional form of judicial mediation (i.e. mediation conducted by trial judges) and minimizes the drawbacks associated with that type of mediation. Going forward, the Chinese legislature should provide detailed procedural guidelines as to how to operate pre-trial judicial mediation to ensure uniformity and transparency for this type of mediation.

5.5.2 Adhering to the Principle of Voluntariness in Judicial Mediation

Autonomy is a fundamental principle in civil and commercial relationships.[86] In dispute resolution, party autonomy is paramount as a matter of fairness and procedural propriety. Judicial mediation in China suffers from policy interference in that judges are encouraged to direct parties to settle sometimes even in situations where parties are unwilling to do so.[87] On this front, urgent reform is necessary to uphold the principle of voluntariness in judicial mediation.[88] As long as parties are not engaged in malicious or vexatious mediation, judges should avoid excessive interference and ensure that parties maintain an active role in the mediation process.[89] This reform will go hand in hand with ongoing reforms that aim to promote procedural formalism and strengthen parties' rights in Chinese civil procedure.[90] To entrench the principle of voluntariness in judicial mediation, it is crucial to properly manage the relationship

---

84 Changchun: Weimin Youwendu Fuwu Wuzhijing (长春：为民有温度服务无止境) [Changchun: Warmth for the People, Endless Service], Zhongguo Fayuan Wang (中国法院网) [China Court] (19 December 2022), https://www.chinacourt.org/article/detail/2022/12/id/7069448.shtml.

85 Peter C.H. Chan, *Mediation in Contemporary Chinese Civil Justice* (Brill Nijhoff 2017) 235–246.

86 Heintze Hans-Joachim, "On the Legal Understanding of Autonomy" in *Autonomy: Applications and Implications* (Brill Nijhoff 1998) 7–32.

87 Supra note 39.

88 Morgan, *supra* note 33, at 57.

89 Zhang Yanhong (张艳红), Tiaojie Dui Shenpan de Fuzuo Yong (调解对审判的副作用) [The Side Effects of Mediation on Judgments], Keji Shijie (科技视界) [Technology Vision], no. 33, 2015, at 87.

90 Xie and Zhang, supra note 72.

between judicial mediation and adjudication.[91] Ultimately, the complete separation of judicial mediation and adjudication is necessary.[92] In other words, judicial mediation should be limited to pre-trial stages and must be conducted by someone other than the trial judge.[93] Courts should refrain from "chasing" mediation settlement target rates[94] and internal performance evaluation metrics should steer away from emphasizing the minimization of appellate reversals or retrials.[95] As for online mediation, parties should be given a choice to opt out of online mediation. This is important for parties who are not tech-savvy and prefer a more traditional form of mediation.[96] Parties should also be able to choose mediation to be conducted in a hybrid mode, i.e. a combination of online and offline mediation.[97]

5.5.3 Integration of Mediation Rules and Information Technology

The mediation rules are currently based on the traditional form of judicial mediation.[98] It is, therefore, important to devise a detailed set of mediation rules that take into account online mediation and the use of information

---

91 Peter C.H. Chan, "An Uphill Battle: How China's Obsession with Social Stability Is Blocking Judicial Reform" (2016) 100 Judicature 14.

92 Supra note 37.

93 Feng Yikai (丰怡凯), Jiceng Sifa Zhili Shijian Tujing: Sifa Xiaxiang, Nengdong Sifa yu Xianshang Sifa (基层司法治理实践图景: 司法下乡、能动司法与线上司法) [The Landscape of Grassroots Judicial Governance Practices: Judicial Outreach, Proactive Justice, and Online Justice], Zhongcai Falü Pinglun (中财法律评论) [China Finance Law Review], vol. 14, 2022, at 179–197.

94 Supra note 39.

95 Bin Xiao (肖滨), Shaobin Dai (戴少斌), *Panjue Yihuo Tiaojie: Jiceng Faguan Xingwei Xuanze de Zhengzhixue Fenxi* (判决抑或调解—基层法官行为选择的政治学分析) [*Judgment or Mediation: A Political Analysis of the Behavior Choices of Grassroots Judges*], Jilin Daxue Shehui Kexue Xuebao (吉林大学社会科学学报) [Journal of Jilin University (Social Sciences Edition)], vol. 62, no. 5, 2022, at 45–58.

96 Supra note 91.

97 Supra note 91.

98 Yong'an Liao (廖永安) & Pei Zhang (张培), *Lun Wo Guo Zaixian Tiaojie de Lujing Youhua—Yi Jishu—Zuzhi Hugou Lilun Wei Fenxi Shijiao* (论我国在线调解的路径优化—以技术—组织互构理论为分析视角) [*On the Path Optimization of Online Mediation in China: An Analysis Based on the Techno-Organizational Co-construction Theory*], Yantai Daxue Xuebao (Zhexue Shehui Kexue Ban) (烟台大学学报(哲学社会科学版)) [Journal of Yantai University (Philosophy and Social Sciences Edition)], 2021, vol. 34, no. 3, at 10–19.

technology in court-connected ADR procedures.[99] Currently, there are still numerous flaws in the information technology infrastructure in courts. For instance, interruptions of transmission can severely hamper the effectiveness of online mediation. Courts should take into account the technical risks when devising online mediation platforms and provide technical as well as regulatory solutions to tackle such problems should they arise.[100] With the advent of instant messaging technology, the mediator can better connect with parties and allow a free flow of information prior to and during the mediation.[101] Many courts in China nowadays have developed their own apps that allow instant messaging and scheduling for online mediation and other procedures.[102] For instance, the author is a people's assessor (a lay adjudicator) in a Shenzhen district court. The court operates an app where adjudication duties are assigned online. The court and lay adjudicators communicate via instant messaging. The app also allows adjudicators to review the case files online.

5.6 CONCLUSION

Judicial mediation in China has many virtues: efficient, user-friendly, and cost-effective. Apart from its usual ADR function, it also plays an important policy function of maintaining social stability. However, policymakers should refrain from overemphasizing the social function of judicial mediation. Judges should not work under the assumption that their leaders prefer mediation over adjudication. It is true that some cases are more suitable for mediation than

---

99 Yingchao Jiang (姜英超), *Wo Guo Zaixian Tiaojie Jizhi Shi Xiao Hua Kunnan Ji Duice* (我国在线调解机制实效化困境及对策) [*The Practical Dilemmas and Strategies for the Online Mediation Mechanism in China*], Shenyang Nongye Daxue Xuebao (Shehui Kexue Ban) (沈阳农业大学学报(社会科学版)) [Journal of Shenyang Agricultural University (Social Science Edition)], 2018, vol. 20, no. 2, at 252–256.

100 Shitong Qiao, Zhiyu Li, and Benjamin Chen, "How Technology is Changing Justice in China" (2022) Judicature International 1.

101 "Li Shen Zhi 'Yun Shang Ban', Zhihui Fayuan Bu Dayang" ("立审执'云上办'，智慧法院不打烊") [Online Handling of Filing, Trials, and Enforcement, Smart Courts Never Rest], Zhongguo Xinwen Wang (中国新闻网) [China News Network] (13 October 2022), https://www.chinanews.com.cn/gn/2022/10-13/9871922.shtml.

102 "Sifa Bu: 26 Ge Shengfen Yingyong Zhinen Yidong Tiaojie Xitong" ("司法部：26个省份应用智能移动调解系统") [Ministry of Justice: 26 Provinces Use Smart Mobile Mediation System], Zhongguo Zhengfu Fazhi Xinxi Wang (中国政府法制信息网) [China Government Legal Information Network] (6 December 2021), https://www.moj.gov.cn/pub/sfbgw/fzgz/fzgzqt/fzgzkjxxh/202112/t20211206_443214.html.

others. But it is not for the court to make that determination. Party autonomy should be upheld. This could be difficult when courts currently adhere to a quantitative performance evaluation system under which their social functions are crucial in determining their performance.[103] On a more fundamental level, judicial mediation should be separated from adjudication altogether to avoid the inevitable conflicting roles trial judges play under the current system. This will ensure the neutrality of the mediator. As Chinese courts continue to embrace information technology, online mediation should be better regulated. Currently, the rules governing online mediation are thin. Many of the technological problems associated with online mediation have not been tackled. When these reforms are put in place, the true potential of judicial mediation in China can be unlocked.

103 Supra note 39.

6. Mediation within the modern Dutch civil justice system

Emma van Gelder and Marc Simon Thomas

INTRODUCTION

The right to access to justice lies at the heart of every democracy based on the rule of law. If individuals encounter difficulties in enforcing their rights in practice, the law remains nothing more than a dead letter.[1] While the traditional arena for resolving disputes is the court, this pathway is often difficult to access owing to barriers of time, complex procedures, and high costs. Since this issue is not unfamiliar to the Dutch judicial system, the Dutch judiciary has made much effort in enhancing access to justice throughout the past decades. Since the end of the 1990s, the promotion of out-of-court dispute resolution (alternative dispute resolution, 'ADR') and especially of mediation has fulfilled an important role within the Dutch judicial policy.[2] Indeed, ADR pathways typically offer a less complex, low-cost, and timely alternative to litigation in the court.[3] ADR settlements, either within or without the court arena, have therefore become an established part of the Dutch legal culture.[4] In line

[1] Gerhard Wagner, 'Private Law Enforcement Through ADR: Wonder Drug or Snake Oil?' [2014] 51 CMLR 165, 167; Francesco Francioni, 'The Rights of Access to Justice under Customary International Law', in Francesco Francioni (ed.), *Access to Justice as a Human Right* (Oxford University Press 2007).

[2] This development was also supported by some Dutch politicians, such as former minister of Security and Justice Ard van der Steur and former minister of Legal Protection Sander Dekker.

[3] Bert Niemeijer, Machteld Pel, Court-Based Mediation in the Netherlands: Research, Evaluation and Future Expectations, [2005] 110 DLR, 345, 365.

[4] For instance, the *Geschillencommissies* resolve numerous consumer disputes annually; Liane Schmiedel, 'Mediation in the Netherlands: Between State Promotion and Private Regulation', in: Klaus Hopt, Felix Steffek (eds), *Mediation: Principles and Regulation in Comparative Perspective* (Oxford University Press 2013), pp. 697–774, p. 699.

with this long-standing tradition of promoting settlements, it does not come as a surprise that the Netherlands is also a strong proponent of mediation.[5]

The support for mediation also fits within the Dutch culture known for its 'polder' behavior. This behavior entails that Dutch citizens are often inclined to solve disputes bilaterally through negotiation.[6] Mediation finds its roots in the 1970s and has gained a more official face since the 1990s when mediation organizations began to appear. The benefits of mediation quickly became acknowledged as having the potential to resolve conflicts in an amicable manner, to offer a simpler, faster, and less costly pathway to redress than the court procedure, and thereby to contribute to enhancing access to justice. Parties can resort to mediation at their own initiative or can be referred to mediation by the court or a legal aid desk.[7]

Next to the promotion of mediation, the digitization of justice has been a key priority in justice reforms in the Netherlands as it holds the promise to further enhance the efficiency of procedures and reduce the costs of litigation both for parties and for the courts.[8] In line with this development, mediation bodies also increasingly move (parts of) their procedure online, further fueled by the influence of the EU legislator as well as the Covid-19 pandemic.

This chapter aims to offer an overview of the mediation landscape in the Dutch modern civil justice system. It critically examines key issues such as the development of mediation as part of the civil justice system; the regulation of mediation as well as the interaction and interconnection between mediation and the civil court. It first discusses the rise of mediation in the Netherlands. The chapter then elaborates on the development of mediation as part of the Dutch civil justice system. Subsequently, this chapter discusses the regulation

---

[5] Liane Schmiedel, 'Mediation in the Netherlands: Between State Promotion and Private Regulation', in: Klaus Hopt, Felix Steffek (eds), *Mediation: Principles and Regulation in Comparative Perspective* (Oxford University Press 2013), pp. 697–774, p. 699; Marc Simon Thomas, 'Mediation in Nederland', in: Dick Bonenkamp et al. (eds), *Handboek Mediation* (Sdu 2024), pp. 59–77.

[6] Machteld Pel, 'Regulation of Dispute Resolution in the Netherlands: Does Regulation Support or Hinder the Use of ADR?', in: Felix Steffek and Hannes Unberath (eds), *Regulating Dispute Resolution, ADR and Access to Justice at the Crossroads* (Hart Publishing 2013), pp. 297–329, p. 298; Alex Brenninkmeijer, 'Mediation', in: Alex Brenninkmeijer et al. (eds), *Handbook Mediation* (Sdu 2017), pp. 25–47.

[7] Pel (n 6) 300.

[8] Xandra Kramer, Emma van Gelder, Erlis Themeli, 'e-Justice in the Netherlands: the Rocky Road to Digitised Justice', in: Wendland and Weller (eds), *Digital Single Market* (Tubingen 2018), pp. 209–235.

of mediation. Then it goes into a more recent development of online mediation, after which the chapter concludes with the authors' reflections.

THE RISE OF MEDIATION IN THE NETHERLANDS

The Netherlands has a long tradition of out-of-court dispute resolution. Since the 1970s an increasing number of disputes are being resolved out of court through myriad different redress pathways including arbitration, binding advice, and mediation. This development fits within the broader Florence access to justice movement that emerged in Europe in the 1970s and aimed to study how law procedures could be made more effective.[9] This movement aimed at finding solutions for the increasing pressure on courts to safeguard the fundamental right to access to justice. While access to justice was traditionally associated with access to *courts*, one of the outputs from the Florence movement is that 'justice' became broadened to include those remedies that are offered by out-of-court dispute resolution bodies.

This movement also reached the Netherlands and resulted in the rise of various ADR procedures, of which the three main types are arbitration, binding advice[10] and mediation, in which mediation serves party autonomy the best.[11] Mediation procedures are subject to less public regulation when opposed to binding advice and arbitration procedures owing to their voluntary participation nature and the fact that they typically result in non-binding outcomes. Therefore, mediation procedures do not in principle challenge parties' right of access to court as safeguarded by Article 6 of the European Convention

[9] Andrea Fejös, Chris Willett, 'Consumer Access to Justice: The Role of the ADR Directive and the Member States', [2016] 24 *ERP*, 33, 37; Iris Benöhr, 'Alternative Dispute Resolution for Consumers in the European Union', in: Christopher Hodges, Iris Benöhr, Naomi Creutzfeldt-Banda (eds), *Consumer ADR in Europe* (Hart Publishing 2012), pp. 1–23, p. 2; Estelle Hurter, 'Access to Justice: To Dream the Impossible Dream?', [2011] 44 *CILSA* 408, 409.

[10] Binding advice is a form of alternative dispute resolution based on Article 7:900 of the Dutch Civil Code. This entails that Dutch law needs to be the law applicable to the contract. The decision is considered binding between parties. Binding advice comes in two different forms: declaratory (*zuiver*) and adjudicatory (*onzuiver*) binding advice or rather binding advice without a legal dispute and binding advice in a legal dispute. In the first form, the parties agree to leave the determination of their undetermined or partially determined legal relationship to a third party to whose judgment they commit themselves in advance. In the second form, a third party gives a binding decision on behalf of the parties in a legal dispute between them.

[11] Rob Jagtenberg, 'Mediation & Rechtswetenschap. Tien jaar verder', [2007] 1 TMD 13; Marc Simon Thomas (n 5) 59–77.

on Human Rights (ECHR).[12] While the voluntary nature of mediation allows parties to refrain from participating in the procedure at any time, arbitration and binding advice are based upon an agreement. In contrast to mediation, the neutral third party in an arbitration or binding advice procedure imposes a binding solution upon parties.[13] In contrast to arbitration, the decision of a binding advice procedure in principle has the force of an agreement, not of an 'exequatur'.[14] Consequently, a binding advice cannot be directly enforced against an unwilling debtor, while an arbitral award can be directly enforced.[15]

One of the first uses of mediation in the Netherlands can be traced back to the procedure offered by the umbrella organization for the resolution of consumer disputes that was established in the 1970s: The Complaint Board (*Stichting Geschillencommissie*, SGC). This organization hosts numerous sectoral consumer complaint boards resolving consumer disputes in a wide range of sectors including the clockwork, natural stone, and bicycle sectors.[16] These boards started pioneering forms of ADR and one of these forms was mediation. Mediation still forms a core part of the procedure offered by the complaint boards.[17] The members of the board first aim to resolve the dispute through mediation and only if this does not result in a satisfactory solution can the board escalate the complaint into a binding advice procedure.[18]

Furthermore, the roots of mediation can also be traced back to the field of divorce law. Hence, lawyers became increasingly aware of the importance of the psychological side of divorce. Therefore, divorce lawyers became eager to explore the option of mediation as they were keener to use a process that was focused on the interests of the parties and on reaching a mutual agreement between them than to focus on who was (legally) right and on filing a binding

---

12 Emma van Gelder, *Consumer Online Dispute Resolution Pathways in Europe* (Eleven 2022), p. 35.

13 Anna Plevri, 'Alternative Dispute Resolution (ADR) & Online Dispute Resolution (ODR) for EU Consumers: the European and Cypriot Framework', in: Tatiana Synodinou et al. (eds), *EU Internet Law in the Digital Era* (Springer 2020), pp. 367–392, p. 369; Marc Simon Thomas (n 5) 64.

14 Pauline Ernste, 'De rol van bindend advies naast arbitrage', *TvA* 2012, pp. 1–6, p. 1.

15 Pauline Ernste, 'Niet-bindend advies bij de Geschillencommissie van Kifid', *TvC,* I.1, 2015, p. 9.

16 In 2020, there were around 50 sectoral consumer complaint boards, promulgating thousands of decisions annually; see: De Geschillencommissie, 'Jaarverslag 2020', 2021.

17 Schmiedel (n 5) 699.

18 The complaint board *Garantiewoningen* forms an exception as it offers an arbitration procedure 'Hoe werkt de Geschillencommissie garantiewoningen?', p. 2. https://www.degeschillencommissie.nl/wp-content/uploads/gwo-brochure.pdf.

decision.[19] In 1989, family lawyers began to establish mediation courses and established an association for divorce mediators: the Association of Lawyers (VAS), which association changed its name in 2003 to the Association for Family Law Lawyers Divorce Mediators (*Vereniging Familierecht Advocaten Scheidingsmediators*, vFAS). The vFAS consists of lawyers who are specialized in (international) family law, inheritance law, and mediation.[20]

In 1993 the mediation field in the Netherlands got an even more official face with the establishment of the Dutch Mediation Institute (*Nederlands Mediation Instituut*, NMI).[21] In 2014 the institute changed its name to the Dutch Mediation Federation (*Mediatorsfederatie Nederland*, MfN). This private organization was set up by a group of professionals with the aim of enhancing the quality and professionalism of mediation in the Netherlands and facilitating the further development of mediation.[22] The MfN had developed into an umbrella organization that offers mediation in a wide range of sectors such as family law, neighborhood disputes, workplace disputes, and business conflicts.[23] Next to the vFAS and the MfN, there are multiple other private organizations active in the Dutch field of mediation; for instance, for business mediation there is the Platform for Business Mediation (PBM).[24] Also, there are mediators active within neighborhoods.[25] For instance, data from October 2023 show that 90% of the Dutch municipalities offer neighborhood mediation.[26] The Dutch Mediation Association (*De Nederlandse Mediatorsvereniging*, NMv) is the umbrella organization that connects all professional mediators.[27] The Dutch mediation branch has developed as a private sector over the past decades; however, this has taken place in connection with political and juridical interest in it, as will be shown in the next section.

---

19 Lieke Coenraad, Marijke ter Voert, 'Mediation and rechtspraak in familiezaken', p. 129.

20 https://www.verenigingfas.nl/.

21 Marc Simon Thomas, 'Mediation – Ruim 25 jaar mediation in Nederland', in: Catrien Bijleveld, Arno Akkermans, Marijke Malsch, Bert Marseille, Monika Smit (eds), *Nederlandse Encyclopedie Empirical Legal Studies* (Boom Juridisch 2020), pp. 443–468, p. 443.

22 ibid 699.

23 MfN, 'Mediation en het MfN register', https://mfnregister.nl/.

24 Jacques de Waart, 'Noblesse oblige: mediators verenigt u!', [2022] *Tijdschrift Conflicthantering* 2, pp. 12–16.

25 Geschilbeslechtingsdelta 2019, p. 44.

26 CCV, 'Buurtbemiddeling in Nederland', https://hetccv.nl/themas/veilige-woon-leefomgeving/buurtbemiddeling/buurtbemiddeling-in-nederland/.

27 De Nederlandse Mediatorsvereniging, https://www.mediatorsvereniging.nl/.

THE DEVELOPMENT OF MEDIATION AS PART OF THE DUTCH CIVIL JUSTICE SYSTEM

From its very start, the MfN institute actively engaged in seeking contact with the Dutch government to further promote the use of mediation in the Netherlands. Mediation began to receive the ongoing attention of both the Dutch government and the Dutch Judiciary from the 1990s.[28] Indeed, the Dutch government also soon acknowledged the benefits of mediation. As mediation procedures are often characterized by a certain degree of flexibility, they allow for dealing with (non-legal) disputes in a more tailored and specialized manner compared with litigation in court. Therefore, mediation can offer a suitable solution for many disputes since disputes often involve more aspects than merely a legal conflict. Another reason for the Dutch government to encourage the use of mediation was that citizens were increasingly being viewed as capable of, and responsible for, managing their own conflicts. This paragraph goes into several projects initiated by the Dutch government to stimulate the use of mediation.

Governmental Projects to Stimulate the Use of Mediation

In 1996, the Dutch Minister of Justice launched the governmental project 'Platform Alternative Dispute Resolution'. The government appointed the platform with three main tasks: advising on strategic policy choices regarding new forms of dispute resolution; making proposals on experiments as well as contributing to the guidance and evaluation of experiments; and exploring and advising on possibilities to promote new forms of dispute resolution.[29] The policy aim of this project was – essentially – to diminish the work pressure of the courts and to reduce their growing workload by encouraging the use of mediation. Thereby, mediation could contribute to the broader aim of enhancing access to justice.[30]

In 1999, the 'Platform ADR' initiative was followed by the policy letter 'ADR 2000–2002', which letter formulated four goals to further promote ADR: the dejuridization of dispute resolution; resolving disputes in the most effective way and at the best quality; meeting the societal need for a more

---

[28] Lieke Coenraad and Peter Ingelse, Afscheid van de klassieke procedure?, Preadvies voor de Nederlandse Juristen Vereniging 2017.

[29] Staatscourant. 1996. 'Instelling Platform Alternative Dispute Resolution (ADR)', Ministerieel besluit, 12 April 1996, Stcrt. 1996, 549856/896/DRJB.

[30] Carrie Menkel-Meadow, 'Introduction', in: Carrie Menkel-Meadow (ed.), *Mediation: Theory, Policy and Practice* (Routledge 2001), pp. xiii–xxxviii; Marc Simon Thomas (n 21).

pluralistic access to justice in which parties in the first place are themselves responsible for resolving their disputes; lifting the pressure on the Judiciary.[31] To achieve these four goals, the Legal Aid Desk and the Judiciary started to offer information for and referral points to mediation.[32] These referrals can alleviate the burden on the Judiciary by reducing the number of disputes that require a court procedure as well as lowering litigation expenses for courts and parties. The following paragraph will go further into court-annexed mediation.

The Introduction of Court-annexed Mediation

Between 2000 and 2005, pilot projects on court-referred mediation started in several Dutch courts.[33] An important rationale for the introduction of this referral facility was that imposing decisions by a judge does not always lead to a sustainable solution for a problem. Especially when litigants need to continue their relationship in the future – such as in the case of a divorce between spouses with children or in the case of neighborhood disputes – mediation typically forms a more suitable option to resolve the dispute than litigation.[34] Certainly, in mediation the parties are in control in finding a solution, which allows the process to result in a win–win solution that can preserve the relationship between parties. The aim of these projects was thus to encourage the judges to evaluate the suitability of a case for mediation. If the judge had the impression that litigation was not the most suitable option for parties to end their conflict, they thus acquired the option to refer parties to mediation if both parties agreed to that. The research report 'Room for Mediation' (*Ruimte voor Mediation*),[35] and the comprehensive evaluation Mediation Monitor 2005–2008 (Mediation Monitor) evaluated these referral projects and showed a growth in the use of mediation.[36] Following these pilot projects, court-annexed mediation (*Mediation naast Rechtspraak*) facilities began to be introduced

---

[31] The policy letter was entitled 'meer wegen naar het recht'.

[32] Paula Boshouwers, Hesther Uhlenbroek, Nelleke van Thiel-Wortmann, 'Kroniek Mediation', [2020] *TvC* 1, pp. 15–23, p. 21.

[33] Pel (n 6) 316.

[34] M. Gerritsen et al., 'Mediation naast rechtspraak: kosten en doorlooptijden' (SDU 2009), p. 7.

[35] Lia Combrink-Kuiters, Edwin Niemeijer and Marijke ter Voert. *Ruimte voor Mediation. Evaluatie van projecten bij de rechterlijke macht en gefinancierde rechtsbijstand* (Boom Juridische uitgevers 2003).

[36] Maurice Guiaux, Frederike Zwenk and Maureen Tumewu, *Mediation Monitor 2005–2008. Eindrapport* (Den Haag WODC 2009).

within more and more of the Dutch courts, and eventually in 2007 mediation became available in every court.[37]

If the judge proposes mediation to the parties and the parties agree to this, a designated mediation office within the court contacts the parties. This office subsequently supports the parties in choosing a mediator who is registered with the Council for Legal Aid. The office proposes a mediator to the parties who is suitable for their case taking into account factors such as the mediator's background, their experience, place of residence, and hourly rate.[38] The first meeting with the mediator usually takes place within two weeks and takes approximately two hours. If the parties' court case was already pending, the judge temporarily suspends the court procedure for the duration of the mediation procedure.[39] The mediator may not have any knowledge of these court documents in order for them to guide the parties in an impartial and independent way. If the parties find a solution for their problem through mediation, the agreements are typically laid down in an agreement and the court case ends. If the parties only find a solution for certain issues, the mediator can lay down part of the agreement and the court case can proceed for the other parts.

The referrals from the courts to mediation increased from around 3,000 in 2014 to 3,700 in 2018.[40] There has been a consistent rise in referrals from 2014 to 2018. This indicates a clear trend toward strong judicial support for mediation as well as a clear trend among parties towards favoring mediation over court litigation. If this trend continues in the coming years, further increases in court-referred mediation can be expected, resulting in positive developments such as the reduced backlog of courts, reduction of costs, and flexibility. Next to these efficiency advantages, there are also concerns about an increase in court-referred mediation, such as the fact that not all cases are suitable for being resolved through mediation, as well as the potential under-enforcement of substantive rights. Regarding the latter, it indeed seems difficult to reconcile the objective of enforcing substantive rights with the aim of mediation procedures to achieve a mutually satisfactory solution based on

---

[37] Schmiedel (n 5) 706.

[38] Mediation in een rechtszaak over een conflict, https://www.rechtspraak.nl/Onderwerpen/mediation/mediation-in-een-conflict/mediation-naast-rechtspraak#9cfc91f2-2b1f-46a2-93cf-69b77a46405a0cb75fa2-c6e2-4e29-afce-48b078857f3c1.

[39] Eddy Bauw, et al., Rechtsstatelijke waarborging van Buitengerechtelijke Geschiloplossing, Den Haag, Boom Juridisch, 2018, p. 65.

[40] Marijke ter Voert, Myrte Hoekstra, *Geschilbeslechtingsdelta 2019. Over verloop en afloop van (potentieel) juridische problemen van burgers* (WODC Cahier 2020) 44.

parties' interests.[41] While court procedures offer public hearings and usually publish their decision – as opposed to the private and confidential nature of mediation procedures – another concern is that there is a lack of transparency, and potentially malpractice may go unnoticed. Furthermore, in contrast to mediation bodies, courts are exclusively competent to interpret the law, and thereby they can contribute to the law's further development.

Mediation Techniques Used Within the Court Procedure

Judges themselves also increasingly use mediation techniques within oral hearings.[42] Judges increasingly aim to unravel parties' underlying interests and wants. This development especially occurs in specialized court procedures, including within the so-called 'Focused on Solution' procedure (*Gericht op Oplossing, GOO-behandeling*) that is offered within the Court of Amsterdam. Furthermore, mediation techniques are used by the Mediation Judge (*Bemiddelingsraadsheer*) from the Appeal Court in the Hague. Voluntariness is one of the core features for these procedures, meaning that such mediation techniques can only be used by the judge when both parties agree to this. A strong criticism of the use of mediation techniques by judges is based on the perspective that courts are public courts appointed with the task and authority to resolve legal disputes, and such tasks should not be delegated or referred to private alternative forums.[43]

Referrals to Mediation Through the Legal Aid Desks

The other referral point to mediation has been institutionalized within the Legal Aid Desks (*Het Juridisch Loket*) that are spread throughout the country.[44] When parties approach the Legal Aid Desk with their problem, the staff of the Desks will evaluate whether their case is suitable for mediation.[45]

The number of referrals to mediation through the legal aid desk decreased from 2,900 in 2014 to 1,400 in 2018.[46]

---

41 Van Gelder (n 12) 53; see also: Per Lindblom, 'ADR – The Opiate of the Legal System?', [2008] *ERPL* 16, p. 63.

42 Peter Ingelse, Nelleke van Thiel-Wortmann, 'Kroniek Mediation', [2023] *TvC* 4.

43 Owen Fiss, Against Settlement, [1984] *Yale L.J.*

44 Ter Voert and Hoekstra (n 40) 44.

45 https://www.juridischloket.nl/hoe-we-werken/mediation.

46 Coenraad, ter Voert (n 19) 131.

Financial Incentives to Stimulate the Use of Mediation

From 2005 onwards, financial support for mediation became available for those parties with less financial means in order to lower their barrier to opt for mediation. The Legal Aid Act (*Wet op de Rechtsbijstand*, Wrb) has included mediation as a dispute resolution procedure that is eligible for legal aid. This entitlement only applies to mediation procedures that have mediators who are registered at the Council for Legal Aid.[47] According to the Annual Report of the Council for Legal Aid, there were 15,370 mediations where parties were entitled to legal aid in 2023 and 13,096 in 2022.[48] In both years almost all of these mediations (99%) were related to divorce.

In March 2023, the Dutch government introduced a pilot in mediation that makes the first two-and-a-half hours of court-referred mediation cost free.[49] This pilot entails that all parties that have already paid for the court procedure are entitled to a starting fee if they have been referred to mediation by the judge. The starting fee is 150 euro for each party and has the purpose of allowing parties to explore and experience if mediation can be an option for them to resolve their conflict.[50] This starting fee will initially apply for two years and will become structural upon its success. The fee applies only to those mediations that are conducted by mediators who are registered at the Council for Legal Aid.

THE REGULATION OF MEDIATION

The regulation of mediation in the Netherlands has been mainly characterized by a hands-off approach from the legislature, who largely left the development of mediation to legal and professional practice. Mediation is thus mostly governed by soft law, such as codes of conduct issued by private organizations. At the same time, there has been and still is an ongoing discussion within the Dutch political arena to legislate mediation. In addition, the regulation of mediation has been influenced by the EU legislature with the adoption of the Mediation Directive and the ADR Directive.

---

[47] L. Coenraad, M. ter Voert, 'Mediation and rechtspraak in familiezaken' (n 19), p. 131.

[48] Raad voor de Rechtsbijstand, Jaarverslag 2023.

[49] Raad voor Rechtsbijstand, 'Invoering startbijdrage mediation vanaf 1 maart 2023', 20 January 2023.

[50] https://www.rechtspraak.nl/Organisatie-en-contact/Organisatie/Raad-voor-de-rechtspraak/Nieuws/Paginas/Mediation-naast-rechtspraak-vanaf-1-maart-gesubsidieerd-.aspx.

Soft Law

Mediation is mostly governed by self-regulatory principles such as codes of conduct and quality standards stipulated by private organizations.[51] There are numerous private organizations active in the Dutch mediation field that issue such principles, of which the MfN is the most prominent.[52] The MfN issues regulations which, *inter alia*, require parties to comply with the principle of confidentiality and has a code of conduct that also includes procedural principles such as independence, impartiality, and competency.[53] The principle of voluntariness is also embedded in the MfN regulations; Article 5(1) stipulates that mediation occurs on the basis of the voluntariness of parties and that each party, as well as the mediator, can end the mediation at any time.[54] Mediators who follow training at a certified training institute and pass an exam at an accredited examination office can be accredited as an MfN mediator and are registered in the MfN register, which is acknowledged by the Dutch Judiciary and the Legal Aid Board.[55] Once registered, a mediator is subjected to professional MfN standards, MfN rights to complain, and the MfN's code of conduct. As the number of registered mediators continues to grow, the Dutch mediation sector is becoming more and more well-organized and professionalized. For instance, while in 1994 there were only 100 registered mediators, in 2022 the MfN registered around 2,700 mediators.[56] The vFAS also has a code of conduct which, for instance, requires mediators to be impartial, to provide parties with information about their legal position, and to ensure that parties have sufficient information to negotiate on an equal footing.[57]

Aspects of Mediation that are Regulated in the Dutch Civil Code

This section discusses the regulatory framework of mediation, which can be found in the mediation agreement, the mediation clause, and the outcome of mediation.

---

[51] Gralf-Peter Calliess, Simon Johannes Heetkamp, 'Online Dispute Resolution: Conceptual and Regulatory Framework', [2019] *TLI Think!*

[52] Schmiedel (n 5) 703.

[53] Article 7 'MfN-Mediationreglement'.

[54] Article 5(1) 'MfN-Mediationreglement'.

[55] MfN, 'MfN-Mediationreglement', https://mfnregister.nl/content/uploads/MfN_Mediationreglement.pdf.

[56] MfN, 'Jaaroverzicht 2022'.

[57] https://www.verenigingfas.nl/algemeen/gedragsregels.

The mediation agreement

Parties can start their mediation procedure through a mediation agreement or through a mediation clause. A mediation *agreement* must be distinguished from a mediation *clause*. Mediation clauses are clauses that are included in an agreement between two parties in which they agree to mediate their (future) disputes.

When parties start mediation, they typically draw up a mediation agreement that is signed by the mediator and the parties. A mediation agreement typically takes the form of a contract for services (overeenkomst van opdracht) as regulated in 7:400 of the Dutch Civil Code (DCC). According to case law of the Dutch Supreme Court, private parties are not bound to mediation agreements owing to the voluntary nature of mediation.[58] This entails that parties can disregard such agreements and proceed with litigation. This is also in line with Article 5(1) of the aforementioned guidelines of the MfN. Certainly, mandatory mediation goes against the voluntary character and can challenge parties' fundamental right to access the court as stipulated in Article 6 of the ECHR and 47 of the Charter. A more recent court decision of 2 August 2017 issued by the court of first instance *Noord-Nederland* follows the line of the Supreme Court,[59] adding that a mediation clause is not on a par with an arbitration clause or a binding advice clause.[60] Where an arbitration and binding advice clause have a legal basis and parties agree to appoint an arbitrator or binding advisor to decide their case, the starting point of mediation is that parties themselves seek an amicable solution.[61] While there have been proposals within the Dutch political arena to make mediation mandatory,[62] up until now they have been swept aside in line with the case law. The main arguments to dismiss mandatory mediation are thus that it goes against the voluntary nature of mediation and it might undermine the reputation and attraction of mediation.[63]

At the same time, in 2009, the Court of Justice of the European Union held in the case of *Alassini v Telecom Italia* that mandatory mediation is justified and in line with Article 47 of the Charter of the European Union provided

58 HR 20 January 2006 ECLI:NL:HR:2006:AU3724; Niek Peters, 'The enforcement of mediation agreements and settlement agreements resulting from mediation', [2019] *CMJ* pp. 13–19, p. 15.

59 HR 2 augustus 2017 ECLI:NL:RBNNE:2017:2956.

60 HR 2 augustus 2017 ECLI:NL:RBNNE:2017:2956, r.o. 5.2.1.

61 HR 2 augustus 2017 ECLI:NL:RBNNE:2017:2956, r.o. 5.2.1.

62 *Kamerstukken* nr. 33723, Wet bevordering mediation in het burgerlijk recht.

63 Peter Ingelse and Nelleke van Theil-Wortmann, 'Kroniek Mediation', [2023] *TCR* 4, pp. 141–152, p. 141.

that certain conditions are fulfilled.[64] The requirement to mediate must have a legitimate objective in the general interest; for instance, as was the case, it must expedite the settlement and reduce its costs, thereby lightening the burden on courts.[65] The mediation must comply with the conditions that the outcome is not binding; the procedure does not result in a substantial delay in bringing legal proceedings; the time-barring period for claims must be suspended for the duration of the mediation procedure; the procedure must be free or accessible regarding costs; and access to the procedure may not be only through electronic means.[66]

In line with this EU case law, there seems to blow a new breeze in the Netherlands when it comes to the question of whether a mediation clause is legally binding. Advocate-General De Bock issued an opinion on 26 January 2024, in which she answers the question of whether a mediation clause within a business agreement between two professional parties is binding.[67] In the case, two business parties – CSW and PPSB – agreed to a mediation clause within an arbitration clause entailing that they would first attempt to resolve disputes through mediation and only in case this was unsuccessful would escalate to arbitration.[68] When a dispute occurred, PPSB started an arbitration procedure and CSW called upon the mediation clause in this procedure and requested the arbitrator to declare himself not competent to decide the case.[69] The arbitrator rejected the request and CSW started a court case at the High Court *inter alia* based on the fact that a legally valid agreement to arbitrate was lacking since a mediation procedure had not been conducted. The High Court decided that PPSB could understand the arbitration clause in such a manner that it did not contain a mandatory duty to first attempt mediation and rejected the claims from CSW. CSW continued to the Supreme Court posing the question of whether a mediation clause within a business agreement between two professional parties is legally enforceable. A-G De Bock argued that the decision of

---

[64] Judgement of 18 March 2010 in joined cases C-317/08, C-318/08, C-319/08 and C-320/08 *Rosalba Alassini and others vs Telecom Italia Spa* [2010] at p. 64.

[65] Judgement of 18 March 2010 in joined cases C-317/08, C-318/08, C-319/08 and C-320/08 *Rosalba Alassini and others vs Telecom Italia Spa* [2010] at p 64; van Duin, 2020, p. 41.

[66] Judgement of 18 March 2010 in joined cases C-317/08, C-318/08, C-319/08 and C-320/08 *Rosalba Alassini and others vs Telecom Italia Spa* [2010] at pp. 53–57; paras 58, 60, 63–65; see also P. Craig, G. de Búrca, *EU Law. Text, Cases and Materials* (Oxford University Press, 2011), p. 236.

[67] Parket bij de Hoge Raad, 26 januari 2024, ECLI:NL:PHR:2024:103, R.O. 5.1.

[68] Parket bij de Hoge Raad, 26 januari 2024, ECLI:NL:PHR:2024:103.

[69] Parket bij de Hoge Raad, 26 januari 2024, ECLI:NL:PHR:2024:103.

the High Court cannot be maintained and that a mediation clause between two professional parties to first try mediation is legally binding and thus enforceable.[70] Thereby she argued that the binding character of mediation clauses is in line with European law.

The Supreme Court filed its decision on 12 July 2024.[71] The Supreme Court acknowledged the possibility of parties entering into an agreement that they will attempt to solve a (future) dispute through mediation prior to starting or continuing a legal procedure.[72] With regard to the mediation agreement, the Supreme Court determined that the contents of an agreement must be determined by the interpretation of this agreement.[73] In doing so, it came down to the meaning that parties could, under the given circumstances, reasonably give to the mediation clause and what they could reasonably expect from each other in this regard.[74] The Supreme Court acknowledged that a mediation agreement can have a binding character and can require parties to attempt mediation prior to litigation. If a party refrains from attempting mediation prior to litigation, the Supreme Court ruled that the judge can hold a case on request of a party, but that the judge is not required to do so for instance in cases that concern an urgent matter or when it is useless to try mediation first.[75] It remains rather surprising that the Supreme Court decided that an 'urgent matter' may form a reason for a judge to not hold a court case. Court procedures typically take more time than finding a solution through mediation. Furthermore, it remains a question when it is 'useless' to try mediation first since the Supreme Court did not offer any criteria for the judge to decide when a case is useless. Also, is a judge the right person to decide when mediation is 'useless'? A mediator typically has more experience to decide when mediation is useless or not.

The outcome of a mediation procedure

The outcomes of a mediation procedure are typically laid down in a so-called *contract of settlement,* as laid down in Article 7:900 of the DCC. Not all agreements that stem from mediation, however, are laid down in such a contract. Compliance with contracts of settlements can be enforced in the civil court. The court can annul such a settlement if it is contrary to good morals or public policy or if, in the specific circumstances, it is unacceptable by standards of reasonableness and fairness.[76] Certainly, several legal rules are regarded as

70 https://uitspraken.rechtspraak.nl/details?id=ECLI:NL:PHR:2024:103.
71 Dutch Supreme Court, 12 July 2024, ECLI:NL:HR:2024:1078.
72 Ibid, r.o. 3.2.1.
73 Ibid, r.o. 3.2.2.
74 Ibid, r.o. 3.2.2.
75 Ibid, r.o. 3.2.3.
76 Articles 7:902 and 7:904(1) DCC.

being so fundamental that they cannot be deviated from, also not within a contract of settlement.[77]

Attempts to Regulate Mediation

Apart from the agreement in the form of a contract of services and the outcome in the form of a contract of settlement, mediation is thus mostly not regulated by law in the Netherlands. There have been and still are, however, several attempts to regulate mediation.

For example, in 2014, then Second Chamber representative Ard van der Steur took the initiative to achieve a legal regulation on mediation. He submitted three bills with the intention of making mediation mandatory in certain cases.[78] This submission evoked several discussions among mediators, lawyers, and judges. While some mediators argued in favor of this initiative, other mediators questioned the function and necessity of such an administrative interference. Lawyers murmured that this would mean the stimulation of inappropriate competition, and several judges argued that no alternative such as mediation was needed in the first place, because they could mediate as well. Although these bills were withdrawn in June 2015,[79] developments continued to formalize mediation within the Dutch civil justice system.

In 2016, Van der Steur – now in the role of Minister of Justice and Security – proposed a bill with the aim of supporting mediation.[80] However, the concerns of mediation professionals remained the same, so this bill never outgrew its status as a concept.

From 2020 onwards, two successive Ministers of Legal Protection have been following the political goal to legislate mediation. In 2020, Minister Sander Dekker announced his aspiration to come up with a bill to stimulate the use of mediation.[81] In June 2021, the draft Mediation Bill was withdrawn. This effort ran aground with the absence of sufficient backup from the mediation sector itself.

---

77 See also: Eva Schutte and Jacqueline Spierdijk, 'Juridical aspects', in: Dick Bonenkamp et al. (eds), *Handboek Mediation* (Sdu Uitgevers 2024), p. 544.

78 *Kamerstukken II* 2014–2015, 33.722/33.723/33.727, nr. 22.

79 *Kamerstukken II* 2014/15, 33722, nr. 23; *Kamerstukken II* 2014/1533723, nr. 14; *Kamerstukken II* 2014/1533727, nr. 12.

80 *Kamerstukken II* 2017/18, 34 775 VI; *Kamerstukken II* 2019/20, 35 300 VI.

81 Letter Minister of Legal Protection to Second Chamber, d.d., 20 January 2020, see: www.rijksoverheid.nl.

In June 2023, the Dutch Minister for Legal Protection Weerwind announced that he intends to allocate further funds to encourage the use of mediation under the broader aim of increasing access to justice in the Netherlands.[82]

By the start of 2024, it is (now outgoing) Minister of Legal Protection Weerwind who is on the barricades for promoting mediation in the Netherlands. He is preparing a (draft) bill to set up and regulate a central mediator register against the background of a motion that was adopted on 6 July 2022. This motion aimed at establishing such a central register, making the respective specialisms/fields visible and placing this register under some scrutiny of public regulation. Hence, the mediation field can be regarded as scattered and therefore difficult to navigate for parties. With this initiative, Minister Weerwind deviates from the former policy of a hands-off approach to regulating mediation. It remains to be seen whether this new aspirational policy will lead to new legislation.

The Influence of the EU Legislator on the Dutch Mediation Field

Mediation in the Netherlands is increasingly subject to public regulation *inter alia* owing to the influence of the European legislature. This paragraph discusses two instruments that have an influence on the Dutch mediation field: the Mediation Directive 2008/52 and the ADR Directive 2013/11.

The Mediation Directive 2008/52

In 2008, the EU legislature adopted the Mediation Directive 2008/52. The Mediation Directive has been adopted within the broader ambit of the EU legislature to enhance access to justice through ADR methods. The Mediation Directive has thus as its core aim the improvement of access to justice, where 'justice' refers to redress not limited to the court. Certainly, the Directive stipulates that 'the objective of securing access to justice … should encompass access to judicial as well as extrajudicial dispute resolution methods'.[83] The Mediation Directive seeks to establish minimum compliance of mediation procedures with due process principles and seeks to guarantee the enforceability

---

[82] https://www.government.nl/latest/news/2023/06/27/minister-weerwind-increases-access-to-justice.

[83] Commission of the European Communities, 'Green paper on alternative dispute resolution in civil and commercial law', COM (2002), 196 final, p. 8; Recital 9 Directive 2008/52/EC of the European Parliament and of the Council of 21 May 2008 on certain aspects of mediation in civil and commercial matters; see Alexandre Biard, 'Monitoring Consumer ADR Quality in the EU: A Critical Perspective', [2018] *ERPL* 2, 171, 176.

of mediation agreements.[84] It furthermore renews the limitation period in case of mediation, extends the possibilities for securing an executory title for party settlements in court, and affords mediators a privilege to refuse to give evidence (i.e. securing confidentiality). The latter privilege is subject to the condition that the parties have agreed to the confidentiality of the mediation proceedings beforehand. The Directive is adopted on the legal basis of Article 81 TFEU, the scope of which is limited to cross-border disputes. The starting point for the Dutch legislature in implementing the Mediation Directive was to align the new law as much as possible with the existing mediation policy.[85] In line with the Directive's legal basis, the implementation of the Directive into Dutch national law is limited to cross-border disputes.[86] Although the Directive was adopted in 2008, it was not until 1 September 2017 that this law came into force in the Netherlands.

The ADR Directive 2013/11

In 2013, the EU legislature adopted the complementary ADR Directive 2013/11 and the ODR Regulation 524/2013 with the purpose of harmonizing ADR within the consumer sector.[87] These instruments were adopted on the internal market basis of Articles 114 and 169(1)(a) TFEU. In line with the vast diversity in ADR procedures that exists throughout the EU, the scope of the ADR Directive is broad so that it can cover all these different ADR procedures. Certified mediation bodies that resolve consumer disputes thus also fall within the scope and have to comply with the ADR Directive.

The ADR Directive lays down binding quality standards for the certified bodies to comply with, including the principles of expertise, independence, impartiality, transparency, and effectiveness.[88] The Netherlands implemented the Directive within a separate implementation act, *Implementatiewet buitengerechtelijke geschillenbeslechting consumenten*, which entered into force on 9 July 2015. The principal starting point was to align this new legislation as much as possible with the already existing Dutch consumer dispute resolution field.[89]

84 Van Gelder (n 12) 36.

85 *Kamerstukken II* 2010 2011, 32555.

86 Paula Boshouwers, Hester Uhlenbroek, Nelleke van Thiel-Wortmann, 'Kroniek Mediation', [2020] *Tijdschrift voor civiele rechtspleging*, afl. 1, pp. 15–23; *Kamerstukken II* 2011/12, 33320, nr. 3.

87 ADR Directive 2013/11 and ODR Regulation 524/2013.

88 These quality standards are laid down in Articles 5–11 ADR Directive 2013/11.

89 *Kamerstukken II*, 2013/14, 33 982, nr. 3, p. 2.

In the Netherlands there are four consumer dispute resolution bodies that are certified and thus bound by the ADR Directive: the consumer complaint boards operating under the umbrella organization of The Complaint Board; the Kifid that resolves consumer disputes between consumers and financial service providers; the Foundation for Complaints and Disputes Health Insurances (*Stichting Klachten en Geschillen Zorgverzekeringen*, SKGZ) that resolves disputes in the health insurance sector; and the Rent Tribunal (*Huurcommissie*). As the Complaint Board, the Kifid, and the SKGZ use mediation as part of their procedure, the mediation is subject to the quality standards imposed by the ADR Directive.

ONLINE MEDIATION

The mediation field also went through important developments in the past decades owing to the increased influence of technology. Novel online mediation providers entered the Dutch mediation field and traditional offline mediation bodies moved their procedures (partly) online. This development fits within the broader development of digitization of justice and has been influenced by the EU legislator, as well as having been further fueled by the Covid-19 pandemic. This paragraph describes the development of online mediation in the Netherlands and elaborates on several online mediation procedures.

The Development of Online Mediation in the Netherlands

From around 2004, online mediation projects started to arise in the Netherlands.[90] At that time, online mediation already existed on a global level in the context of e-commerce. Certainly, in the mid 1990s e-commerce started and online marketplaces entered the Internet.[91] Available *offline* redress pathways proved no longer suitable to resolve the often low-value and cross-border online disputes that arose on these marketplaces. One of the earliest forms of online mediation appeared around this time when eBay partnered with Internet start-up SquareTrade, which company created an online mediation service.[92]

---

[90] SGOA, https://sgoa.eu/; Liane Schmiedel, 'Mediation in the Netherlands: Between State Promotion and Private Regulation', in: Klaus Hopt, Felix Steffek (eds), *Mediation: Principles and Regulation in Comparative Perspective* (Oxford University Press 2013), 697, 733.

[91] Van Gelder (n 12) 85, 86.

[92] Colin Rule, 'Designing a Global Online Dispute Resolution System: Lessons Learned from eBay', [2017] *U. St. Thomas L. J.*, 354, 355.

Currently, procedures offered by online platforms typically include an online mediation phase that follows an unsuccessful automated negotiation phase.[93]

One of the first Dutch projects was the e-mediation project conducted by the Foundation for Dispute Resolution Automation (*Stichting Geschillenoplossing Automatisering*, SGOA) in 2005, consisting of a telephone call with the parties and the mediators as well as a written expert opinion.[94]

Online Mediation Projects in the Netherlands

The Netherlands has various online mediation schemes representing a wide variety of forms and using a broad range of types of technology including online complaint submission mechanisms, online communication tools such as video and audio (Zoom, Skype, Microsoft Teams) and written submissions (e-mail or chat).[95] As offline mediation bodies increasingly offer their procedures online, the boundaries between ADR and ODR become increasingly vague.[96] The distinguishing factor between ADR and ODR is that in ODR the role of technology goes further than merely supporting the procedure (e.g. planning meetings through e-mail). Technology fulfills the role of the 'fourth' party.[97]

As aforementioned, one of the early online mediation projects in the Netherlands was the one offered by SGOA. The SGOA offers a 'rapid conflict resolution,' which enables parties to e-mail SGOA with a joint request within a specific online format offered by SGOA.[98] Following the receipt of this request, a back-and-forth e-mailing occurs between the mediator and parties. If a mediation session is still needed, this session in principle takes

---

93 Emma van Gelder, Anna van Duin, 'In de Schaduw van het Recht: over PayPal's Resolution Centre en kwaliteitsstandaarden voor cODR op online platforms', in: Pieter Wolters et al. (eds), *Digitalisering en Conflictoplossing* (Wolters Kluwer 2021).

94 Schmiedel (n 5) 733.

95 Van Gelder (n 12) 69.

96 Van Gelder, Van Duin (n 93).

97 The term 'fourth party' has been coined by Katsh and Rifkin: Ethan Katsh, Janet Rifkin, *Online Dispute Resolution: Resolving Conflicts in Cyberspace* (Jossey-Bass 2001); Janet Rifkin, 'Online Dispute Resolution: Theory and Practice of the Fourth Party', [2011] 19 *Conflict Resolution Quarterly* 1, pp. 117–124, p. 121.

98 SGOA, 'Reglement van de Stichting Geschillenoplossing Automatisering voor ICT-Rapid Conflict Resolution', p. 1.

place physically. Every communication takes place through written means or through online communication means.[99]

Online mediation techniques are also employed by the aforementioned consumer complaint boards, by Kifid and the SKGZ. Certainly, these boards are increasingly moving their procedures online, not only due to their objective to enhance access to justice, but also fueled by the implementation of the ADR Directive 2013 which requires the boards to be accessible online.[100] Furthermore, the Covid-19 pandemic gave an impetus for mediators to explore online options. For instance, since June 2020, the complaint boards offer online hearings through video software. The online procedure reflects the offline procedure as the boards shift mediation and binding advice to online case files and online video hearings.

A prominent online mediation platform in the field of family law is the online divorce platform *Uitelkaar.nl*.[101] The procedure they offer first explores the specific situation of parties allowing them to choose a specific 'module', which is either a mere separation plan, or a mere parental plan, or both of these plans.[102] The partner who initiates the procedure creates their own online account on the platform and fills in an online questionnaire. Upon completion, the questionnaire is sent to the other party to do the same. Subsequently, parties can make agreements in an online portal during which phase they receive online guidance by a personal-case manager through a chat function. In addition, parties can consult a mediator, with whom they can meet either physically or through video conferencing. The final agreements are reviewed by a lawyer.

The Covid-19 pandemic resulted in a general development of mediators that increasingly shift (parts of) their procedure online, such as an online request for mediation, communication with the counterparty and mediator through online video or audio communication tools, and a digital signature of the mediation agreements. While many mediation bodies in the Netherlands thus offer parts of their procedures online; their procedures, however, in most of its aspects, still reflect their offline counter parts.[103] Furthermore, most mediators do not offer a full online mediation procedure but a hybrid online procedure keeping parts of the procedure physical. A core reason for mediators to refrain from shifting fully online is the loss of non-verbal cues in an online setting. Certainly, a core task for mediators is to achieve trust in the mediation setting

99 4.1 SGOA, 'Reglement van de Stichting Geschillenoplossing Automatisering voor ICT-mediation'.

100 Article 5 ADR Directive 2013/11.

101 Uitelkaar.nl. https://uitelkaar.nl/.

102 Uitelkaar.nl, 'Scheiden via Uitelkaar.nl met mediation', p. 4.

103 Van Gelder (n 12) 70.

in order to achieve a successful mediation, and non-verbal communication is a key factor in building trust (e.g. eye contact).[104]

The suitability of online mediation also heavily depends on the type of dispute that underlies the case and on the type of parties that participate. For instance, online mediation might form a suitable option for the resolution of default consumer disputes – e.g. the late or non-delivery of a package – since parties typically do not know each other and the nature of the disputes is less sensitive. At the same time, online mediation will likely be less suitable for resolving more sensitive disputes such as those arising in the area of family law, as mediators often wish to have physical meetings so they can closely observe parties' non-verbal communication. Furthermore, parties must be digitally literate to be able to accurately participate in online mediation.[105]

The results of a survey spread among Dutch mediators in 2023 with the topic of online mediation highlight that the majority of respondent mediators indicate they work more efficiently in an offline setting than in an online setting.[106] The main reason brought forward by the respondents is that offline settings allow for better observation of non-verbal cues of parties. A possible explanation for the more skeptical view as identified in the survey results is that most of the respondents work in the field of family law, followed by the field of workplace mediation – fields with inherently more sensitive disputes.[107]

CONCLUSION

Mediation has established a professional place within the Dutch civil justice field and has become an important pathway for parties to resort to seek a solution for their dispute. This chapter has given insight into the landscape of mediation in the Netherlands. It shows that mediation is gaining more and more ground in the Netherlands and the field is becoming more professional. While the regulation of mediation is still largely left to practice, the discussions to regulate it have been and are still pending in the Dutch political arena. Also, European policymakers gave the use of and regulation of mediation a

---

104 Noam Ebner, Jeff Thompson, '@Face Value? Nonverbal Communication & Trust Development in Online Video-based Mediation', [2014] 1 *International Journal of Online Dispute Resolution*, pp. 103–124.

105 Janet Martinez, 'Designing Online Dispute Resolution', [2020] *Journal of Dispute Resolution*, p. 135.

106 Emma van Gelder, 'The Promising Potential of Online Mediation to Reduce Financial Barriers to Access Justice. A Case Study into Online Mediation in the Netherlands', in: Kramer et al. (eds), *Sustaining Access to Justice: New Avenues for Costs and Funding* (Hart Publishing 2025).

107 Ibid.

boost with the adoption of the Mediation Directive and the ADR Directive. With the mushrooming of mediation bodies and initiatives, mediation risks undermining its own success: the field becomes more and more fragmented and difficult to navigate for individuals in search of redress. Recent proposals of the Minister of Justice and Security to subject mediation to more public regulation are thus welcomed. Certainly, a single register can enhance the quality of mediation and increase the navigability of the scattered field.

7. Mediation, the pre-action protocols and judicial ADR activism in the English civil justice system

Masood Ahmed

7.1 INTRODUCTION

Mediation is on the rise. It is increasingly promoted as a necessary procedural mechanism to alleviate growing backlogs in the civil courts,[1] facilitate the efficient use of court resources, and increase access to justice.[2] Reflecting this trend, Spain has, for instance, recently implemented a mandatory pre-court mediation scheme for civil and commercial disputes.[3] Similarly, the Cypriot government has placed draft legislation before parliament which, when enacted, will require litigants with claims of up to €10,000 to engage with mediation before initiating court proceedings.[4]

1 e.g. following the introduction of mandatory mediation in Italy, the number of cases pending before the civil courts decreased by approximately 45%. See the official statistics for 2003–2023 from the Italian Ministry of Justice at https://www.giustizia.it/giustizia/it/mg_1_14_1.page?contentId=SST1287132&previsiousPage=mg_2_9_13 (accessed 2 July 2025).

2 See e.g. K. J. Hopt and F. Steffek (eds), *Mediation: Principles and Regulation in Comparative Perspective* (Oxford University Press 2012), 97–99 and 103–104.

3 Organic Law 1/2025, which came into effect on 3 April 2025.

4 The Council of Ministers in Cyprus approved an amendment bill on 3 January 2025 amending The Law on Certain Mediation Issues in Civil Disputes of 2012 (Law 159(I)/2012).

In England and Wales,[5] the integration of mediation within both traditional[6] and online civil court processes[7] has become a major policy focus.[8] It has featured prominently in successive civil justice reviews[9] and extra-judicial speeches,[10] and it dominates the case law on alternative dispute resolution (ADR).[11] Mediation has also been promoted at the pre-action stage of the litigation process through the pre-action protocols ('protocols'). The protocols, which operate outside of the formal court process, are designed to encourage the early settlement of disputes by requiring parties to exchange information and engage with ADR processes before initiating court proceedings. Where a settlement cannot be achieved, engagement with the protocols helps to narrow the issues in dispute which, in turn, facilitates efficient judicial case management. In doing so, the protocols perform an important procedural function in supporting the courts' duty to further the overriding objective of dealing with cases justly and at proportionate cost.[12] Currently, there are 17 sector-specific

---

5 Hereinafter 'England' and 'English'.

6 Practice Direction 51ZE – Small claims track automatic referral to mediation pilot scheme for claims up to £10,000. See further D. Sixsmith and A. Sixsmith's contribution at chapter 2.

7 The Online Civil Money Claims integrates mediation within the online journey see https://www.gov.uk/make-court-claim-for-money (accessed 12 June 2025).

8 e.g. *Increasing the use of mediation in the civil justice system* Ministry of Justice 26 July 2022 https://www.gov.uk/government/consultations/increasing-the-use-of-mediation-in-the-civil-justice-system (accessed 12 June 2025).

9 e.g. see Lord Justice Jackson, *Review of Civil Litigation Costs: Final Report* (TSO 14 January 2010) chp. 36, 355, Lord Justice Briggs, *Civil Courts Structure Review: Interim Report* (Judiciary of England and Wales 2015); Lord Justice Briggs, *Civil Courts Structure Review: Final Report* (Judiciary of England and Wales 2016).

10 See e.g. Lord Justice Briggs 'Mediation and the Civil Courts' Keynote Speech for the CIArb, September 2016; The Right Hon Sir Geoffrey Vos 'Mediation and Dispute Resolution' Worshipful Company of Arbitrators: Annual Master's Lecture Rathbones Investment Management Wednesday 30 March 2022; The Right Hon Sir Geoffrey Vos MR 'Mediated interventions within the Court Dispute Resolution Process' GEMME Lecture, Dublin, Ireland, Friday 28 October 2021.

11 The majority of the leading authorities on ADR, such as *Dunnett v Railtrack plc* [2002] EWCA Civ 302, *Halsey v Milton Keynes General NHS Trust* [2004] EWCA Civ 576 and *PGF II SA* v *OMFS Company 1 Limited* [2013] EWCA Civ 1288, have all concerned mediation.

12 CPR 1.1(1) provides '(1) These Rules are a procedural code with the overriding objective of enabling the court to deal with cases justly and at proportionate cost.'

protocols[13] alongside a general Practice Direction on Pre-Action Conduct[14] (PDPC) applicable to other disputes.[15]

Three recent developments have significantly enhanced the role of ADR within the English civil justice system. The first is the Civil Justice Council's[16] comprehensive review of the pre-action protocols (CJC PaP Review) which culminated in the publication of two final reports:[17] Final Report (Part 1)[18] and Final Report (Phase 2).[19] The Final Report (Part 1) proposes extensive reforms, including the introduction of a new General Pre-action Protocol (GPaP)[20] to replace the existing PDPC. The GPaP, if adopted, places greater emphasis on mediation as a means of facilitating the early consensual settlement of disputes. The second development followed three months after the publication of the Final Report (Part 1): the landmark decision of *Churchill v Merthyr Tydfil Borough Council*.[21] In this case, the Court of Appeal confirmed that the courts could compel disputing parties to engage with ADR processes, including mediation, provided any order or stay in favour of ADR did not undermine their right to proceed to a judicial hearing, and was proportionate to achieving the legitimate aim of settling the dispute fairly, quickly and at reasonable cost. The third development is the amendments to the Civil Procedure Rules (CPR) to reflect the decision in *Churchill* ('the ADR rules').

Taking mediation as its focus, this chapter critically analyses the potential of the GPaP, *Churchill* and the ADR rules in promoting proportionate dispute

13 e.g. Pre-action Protocol for Media and Communications Claims, Pre-Action Protocol for Personal Injury Claims, Pre-Action Protocol for the Construction and Engineering Disputes.

14 Practice Direction – Pre-Action Conduct and Protocols.

15 In its *Review of Litigation Funding – Final Report June 2025*, the Civil Justice Council has recommended the introduction of a pre-action protocol for mass claims.

16 The Civil Justice Council is an Advisory Public Body which was established under the Civil Procedure Act 1997. The Council's statutory duty is to review the civil justice system and make recommendations to the Lord Chancellor, the judiciary and the Civil Procedure Rule Committee on the development of the civil justice system to make it more accessible, fair and efficient.

17 In addition to the Final Report, the Civil Justice Council published its *Review of the Pre-Action Protocols Interim Report November 2021.*

18 *Civil Justice Council CJC Review of Pre-Action Protocols Final Report Part I August 2023.*

19 *Civil Justice Council CJC Review of Pre-Action Protocols Final Report (Phase 2) August 2024.*

20 See chapters 3 and 4 and Annex 2 of the *Final Report (Part I).*

21 *Churchill v Merthyr Tydfil County Borough Council* [2023] EWCA Civ 1416.

resolution during the court process and, more significantly, at the pre-action stage. It is argued that, although *Churchill* and the ADR rules strictly apply to court proceedings, they have the effect of strengthening the parties' ADR duty during the pre-action stage which will, in future, be reinforced by the GPaP. In this regard, it is argued that the courts have the powers to compel parties to a second round of mediation even though they have engaged with mediation at the pre-action stage or in compliance with a relevant protocol. This in turn serves as an incentive for parties to constructively engage with the protocols and, more importantly, with mediation. It is also argued that the courts should adopt a structured and principled approach when exercising their ADR powers when considering whether to compel parties to a second round of mediation which I refer to as 'Judicial ADR Activism'. Judicial ADR activism refers to the proactive role that judges should adopt in encouraging, facilitating, and, if required, conducting ADR processes. Judicial ADR activism requires judges to actively promote settlement-oriented approaches as part of their case management responsibilities and is rooted in the principle of proportionality and the overriding objective.

A number of points should be noted from the outset. Although the chapter focuses on mediation, it is not suggested that other forms of ADR processes are in any way inferior to mediation; indeed, as will be discussed in Section 7.5, it may be that mediation is not, in fact, the most appropriate ADR process in the circumstances in which case the courts should order the parties to engage with an alternative ADR procedure. Furthermore, although I have previously discussed judicial ADR activism within the context of court proceedings,[22] this chapter considers, for the first time, judicial ADR activism within the context of the parties' ADR duty during the pre-action stage, the future impact of that duty under the GPaP and the transition of the parties' ADR duty from the pre-action stage to the court process. Finally, this chapter does not discuss issues which have previously been dealt with by others, including the merits or otherwise of compulsory mediation,[23] the theoretical debates concerning mediation

---

22 M. Ahmed 'Harnessing the ELI-Unidroit Model European Rules of Civil Procedure in promoting "Judicial ADR Activism" in the English Civil Justice System' (2025) *Uniform Law Review* 1–16.

23 See e.g. S. Voet 'ADR, Mandatory Consumer Mediation and the Impact on Civil Litigation' in X. Kramer, M. Ahmed, A. Dori and M. Ucin (eds) *Sustaining Access to Justice: New Avenues for Costs and Funding* (Hart Publishing 2025) 217; B. Clark 'Mandatory Mediation in England and Wales: Much ado about nothing?' (2022) 2 *Amicus Curiae* 92; B. Clark 'Not So Simple? Court Connected Mediation in Scotland' (2020) 39 *Civil Justice Quarterly* 23; M. Milgo 'The Case for Express Compulsory Mediation for England and Wales' (2021) 10(1) *Journal of Law and Jurisprudence* 1.

and justice[24] and the nature and structure of the various types of mediation or other forms of ADR processes.[25]

The remainder of the chapter is organised into four parts. Part 7.2 discusses the nature of the pre-action protocols, the PaP Review and the salient features of the GPaP. Part 7.3 critically analyses *Churchill* and the ADR rules and part 7.4 considers the subsequent case law. Part 7.5 focuses on the ADR provisions of the GPaP and the impact *Churchill* and the ADR rules have on the powers of the court to order a second round of mediation. Finally, part 7.6 considers judicial ADR activism and its application to the parties' ADR duty at the pre-action stage and the transition and continuation of that duty when court proceedings are commenced.

7.2 THE PROTOCOLS, CJC REVIEW AND THE GPAP

The protocols have become a significant part of the English civil justice system. As the Court of Appeal in *Jet2 v Hughes*[26] observed, the protocols 'are now an integral and highly important part of the litigation architecture'.[27] Introduced by Lord Woolf,[28] the protocols are a procedural framework which formally sit outside of the CPR and, as such, govern the parties' pre-action behaviour as a form of soft law. They promote party cooperation through the early exchange of information which can assist in the early settlement of a dispute. Where settlement cannot be achieved, the parties' engagement with the protocols helps to narrow the issues in dispute and, consequently, facilitate

---

[24] See e.g. S. Ali *Court Mediation Reform: Efficiency, Confidence and Perceptions of Justice* (Elgar 2018); P. Chan *Mediation in Contemporary Chinese Civil Justice: A Proceduralist Diachronic Perspective* (Brill 2017); D. Anderson 'The Evolving Concept of Access to Justice in Singapore's Mediation Movement' (2020) 16 *International Journal of Law in Context* 128; D. Anderson 'Revisiting "Mandatory Mediation: An Oxymoron?": Advancing Access to Justice Through Mandatory ADR' in X. Kramer, M. Ahmed, A. Dori and M. Ucin (eds) *Sustaining Access to Justice: New Avenues for Costs and Funding* (Hart Publishing 2025) 257; V. Waye 'Mandatory Mediation in Australia's Civil Justice System' (2016) 45 *Common Law World Review* 216.

[25] See T. Allen *Mediation Law and Civil Practice* (3ed edn) (Bloomsbury 2024); S. Sime, S. Blake and J. Browne *The Jackson ADR Handbook* (4th edn) (Oxford University Press 2025); N. Nylund 'Agreements Related to Alternative Dispute Resolution' in A. Nylund and A. Cabral (eds) *Shaping Civil Litigation Using Procedural Agreements* (Eleven Publishing 2024) 85.

[26] *Jet2 Holidays Ltd v Hughes* [2019] EWCA Civ 1858. See also *Shah v Barnet LBC* [2021] EWHC 2631 (QB).

[27] *Jet 2* at [36].

[28] See *Lord Woolf, Access to Justice – Final Report (1996)*, chapter 10, para. 6.

more efficient judicial case management. In doing so, the protocols further both the private and public aspects of the principle of proportionality. The early settlement of disputes furthers the private aspect of proportionality by saving the parties from incurring high, unpredictable and disproportionate litigation costs in pursuing the matter through the courts. The early settlement of disputes also furthers the public aspect of proportionality by allowing the courts to divert their finite resources to those disputes which require judicial attention.

The decision in *Jet2 Holidays* prompted the Civil Justice Council (CJC) to conduct a detailed review of the current and future role of the protocols. The CJC's Final Report (Part I)[29] proposes a number of key reforms including making engagement with the protocols mandatory, amending the overriding objective to make explicit reference to the need for parties to comply with the protocols and for the courts to enforce them, and digitising the protocols and linking them to the court process. The Final Report (Part 1) also recommends the implementation of the GPaP to replace the PDPC. At its heart, the GPaP requires the parties to complete the following three sequential procedural steps before issuing proceedings: (i) the early exchange of relevant information; (ii) engagement with an ADR process with greater prominence being given to mediation; and (iii) if the matter cannot be settled, the parties are required to jointly complete a stocktake report which narrows the issues in dispute.

It should be noted that the ADR obligation under the GPaP is solely a process-based obligation and there is no requirement that the parties must settle their dispute. This was consistent with the Civil Justice Council's 2021 report, *Compulsory ADR*,[30] which concluded that compulsory engagement with an ADR process would not, in principle, undermine the parties' right to a fair trial under art. 6 of the ECHR provided the parties are able to revert to the court process if the matter does not settle. More significantly, it is consistent with *Churchill*, which was decided three months after the publication of the PaP Review. Furthermore, given the popularity of mediation among the judiciary and policy makers, and its future expansion within the civil justice system, mediation has been given priority in the list of ADR processes within the GPaP.

The potential effectiveness of the three procedural steps of the GPaP can be neatly illustrated by considering two very recent High Court decisions: *Mengrani v Mohamed*[31] and *Brooke Homes (Bicester Limited) v Portfolio*

---

29 *Final Report Part I* (n 15).

30 *Civil Justice Council Compulsory ADR Report June 2021*. See also *ADR and Civil Justice CJC ADR Working Group Final Report November 2018*.

31 *Mengrani v Mohamed* [2025] EWHC 1131 (Ch).

Property Partners Limited & others.[32] In *Mengrani*, the parties requested that the court order a stay of proceedings to allow the parties to engage in mediation. However, the parties disagreed on the quality of information that had been disclosed both at the pre-action stage and during court proceedings. Having considered the parties' arguments, Chief Master Shuman decided to list the matter for a further hearing to determine what issues remained outstanding and what evidence would be necessary before a stay could be ordered. As the Chief Master explained,

> After that stage the parties should be in the best possible position to resolve this case without further involvement of the court and a stay should be imposed then. If they are unable to settle the claim then at the very least they should have narrowed the issues and reduced the legal costs to achieve resolution.[33]

In *Brooke Homes (Bicester Limited)*, an insolvency matter, the claimant had made two applications seeking an equitable account and 'marshalling' to be applied. Prior to the hearing, the parties had agreed on 14 issues to be determined and by the end of the hearing, the number of issues had been reduced to four. The judge, Hugh Sims KC (sitting as a Deputy Judge of the High Court), urged the parties to engage in 'greater dialogue' and to voluntarily consider and engage with mediation, failing which he would compel the parties to mediation. The judge concluded by saying:

> I raised with the parties during the course of the hearing whether or not they had engaged in any ADR or mediation on the applications before me. They confirmed they had not. I consider this is unfortunate as it appeared to me there were a number of matters which would have benefited from further dialogue between the parties, and if such dialogue had occurred this would or should have resulted in resolution of the issue or a narrowing of the issues before the hearing. Resolution or a narrowing occurred on many points during the course of the hearing. I would be inclined to order some form of mandatory mediation between the parties to assist them in resolving any remaining disputes, should a voluntary mediation not now take place, as there are still a number of points between them, and to be worked through, on the account. I consider the amount of costs which have already been incurred on the applications are likely to have the unfortunate effect of further reducing the return likely to be made … Overall, I have gained the impression that greater dialogue is required, even if no love is lost.[34]

Had the GPaP applied in *Mengrani*, the parties would have been required to disclose and exchange key documents from the outset of the dispute. This

---

[32] *Brooke Homes (Bicester Limited) v Portfolio Property Partners Limited & others* [2025] EWHC 1305 (Ch).

[33] *Mengrani* at [62] (n 31).

[34] *Brooke Homes (Bicester Limited)* at [120] (n 32).

would have assisted them in making informed decisions about whether the matter could be settled at mediation. If settlement had not been possible, the parties would have had to cooperate in narrowing the issues before issuing court proceedings, thereby avoiding the cost and time of two court hearings. Similarly, in *Brooke Homes (Bicester) Ltd*, the parties would have been required to engage in structured dialogue at an early stage of the dispute, which could have resulted in the narrowing of issues at the pre-action stage – rather than engaging the court and consuming its finite resources to achieve what the parties could have accomplished themselves. Both cases illustrate the potential virtues of the GPaP in promoting proportionate litigation and facilitating more effective and efficient judicial case management of disputes.

7.3 *CHURCHILL* AND THE AMENDED ADR RULES

This part critically considers the landmark decision of *Churchill* and analyses the ADR rules. Given the importance of *Churchill* and its impact on the wider civil and family justice system,[35] including the issues discussed in this chapter, it is necessary to analyse the decision in detail.

(i) *Churchill*

In one of the most significant developments in English civil procedure, the Court of Appeal in *Churchill* declared that the courts could lawfully compel disputing parties to engage with ADR processes. The courts could do so provided that the order or stay allowing the parties to engage with ADR did not undermine their right to proceed to a judicial hearing, and it is proportionate to achieving the legitimate aim of settling the dispute fairly, quickly and at reasonable cost. In reaching its decision, the Court of Appeal finally departed from its controversial comments in *Halsey v Milton Keynes General NHS Trust*[36] in which Dyson LJ, giving the judgment of the Court, observed that to compel parties to engage with ADR would be contrary to their right to a fair trial under art. 6 of the ECHR.[37] Those comments were, as the Court of Appeal made clear in *Churchill*, obiter dicta and did not, therefore, bind the courts on the issue of compulsory ADR.

In *Churchill*, the claimant commenced proceedings against the defendant local authority for damages to his property caused by Japanese knotweed which had spread to the claimant's property from neighbouring land owned

---

35 For examples of family cases citing and discussing the importance of *Churchill*, see *X v Y* [2024] 2 FLR 800 and *DF v YB (Costs)* [2025] EWFC 76 (B).

36 *Halsey v Milton Keynes General NHS Trust* [2004] EWCA Civ 576.

37 ibid at [9].

by the defendant local authority. In response to the claimant's pre-action letter of claim, the defendant invited the claimant to use its internal Corporate Complaints Procedure (CCP) to try to resolve the matter. The defendant also made clear that, if the claimant decided to issue proceedings without engaging with its CCP, it would apply to the court for a stay and would also seek its costs in doing so. The claimant did not, however, engage with the CCP and issued proceedings against the defendant. In response, the defendant applied for a stay of proceedings. The deputy district judge dismissed the application for a stay. Although the judge found that the claimant had acted unreasonably by failing to engage with the defendant's CCP and behaved contrary to the general pre-action protocol, he concluded that he was bound by Dyson LJ's comments in *Halsey* that compelling parties to engage with ADR would undermine their art. 6 ECHR rights. Given the important issues of principle and practice which the case raised, the judge referred the matter to the Court of Appeal.

The appeal came before a formidable Court of Appeal which consisted of the Master of the Rolls and Head of Civil Justice, Sir Geoffrey Vos, the Deputy Head of Civil Justice and Chair of the CPRC, Birss LJ, and Lady Carr LCJ. The Court identified three issues of principle: (i) was the judge right to think that *Halsey* bound him to dismiss the defendant's application; (ii) if not, can the court lawfully stay proceedings for, or order, the parties to engage in an ADR procedure; and (iii) if so, how should the court decide whether to stay the proceedings for, or order, the parties to engage in an ADR process? The leading judgment was given by Vos MR with whom Birss LJ and Lady Carr LCJ agreed.

On issue (i), Vos MR held that the judge at first instance was not bound by *Halsey* because the passage on which the judge relied 'was not a necessary part of the reasoning that led to the decision in that case (so was not part of the *ratio decidendi* and was an *obiter dictum*)'.[38] This was so because the Court of Appeal in *Halsey* was not concerned with whether or not the courts had the power to compel ADR; rather, it was concerned with whether a costs sanction should be imposed against the successful parties on the basis that they had refused to engage with mediation. It was in that context that Dyson LJ had made his comments on compulsory ADR, which was not a necessary step in reaching the court's conclusions on the costs questions decided in the appeals. This aspect of the decision is to be welcomed in finally bringing the much-needed authoritative judicial confirmation that Dyson LJ's comments were, indeed, *obiter,* a point which was subsequently endorsed by Lord Dyson

[38] *Churchill* at [20] (n 21). See also *Darren White v Michael and Sheila Alder* [2025] EWCA Civ 392 at [19]–[20].

himself.[39] The art. 6 point in *Halsey* had created tensions within the case law, most notably at the Court of Appeal level. In *Lomax v Lomax*,[40] the Court of Appeal confirmed that the courts could compel non-consenting parties to engage with judicial early neutral evaluation (ENE) under CPR r.3.1(2)(m) because the wording of CPR r.3.1(2)(m) did not contain an express requirement for party consent before an ENE could be ordered. Although Moylan LJ distinguished *Halsey* on the grounds that it was concerned with mediation and not ENE which, by virtue of CPR r.3.1(2)(m), formed part of the court process, he appeared to cast doubt on the continuing validity of the reasoning in *Halsey* when he said, 'I would only comment that the court's engagement with mediation has progressed significantly since *Halsey* was decided'.[41] Similarly, in *McParland & Partners Limited & Anor v Whitehead*,[42] Sir Geoffrey Vos C (as he then was) recommended ENE to the parties and in doing so he explained that *Lomax* 'inevitably raised the question of whether the court might also require parties to engage in mediation despite the decision in Halsey'. Thus, *Churchill* has finally lifted the 'Halsey ADR anchor' which had, for so long, prevented the courts from recognising and exercising their ADR powers, and which has stifled the development of a coherent and consistent body of ADR case law.

On issue (ii), Vos MR held that the courts possessed the power to order disputing parties to ADR. In reaching that conclusion, Vos MR considered a number of European Court of Human Rights (ECtHR) cases, including *Deweer v Belgium*,[43] which Dyson LJ relied upon in *Halsey* in support of his art. 6 ECHR comments. *Deweer* concerned a Belgian butcher who had allegedly committed an offence of selling meat at an illegal profit. The public prosecutor ordered the butcher to close his shop until either his prosecution was completed or he paid a fine of 10,000 Belgian Francs. Although he paid the fine under protest, he brought successful proceedings for breach of art. 6(1) ECHR. The ECtHR held that the pressure brought to bear on the butcher by the threat to close his shop if he did not pay the fine was an unlawful constraint that was incompatible with art. 6. In contrast, the ECtHR has found that compulsory ADR does not undermine art. 6 where it pursues a legitimate aim and is proportionate with the aims to be achieved.[44] Vos MR also referred to the decisions of *Alassini v*

---

39 Lord Dyson MR, 'Halsey 10 Years On – The Decision Revisited' Keynote Speech, Belfast Mediation Conference, Belfast, May 2014.

40 *Lomax v Lomax* [2019] EWCA Civ 1467.

41 ibid at [27].

42 *McParland & Partners Limited & Anor v Whitehead* [2020] EWHC 368 (QB).

43 *Deweer v Belgium* [1980] ECC 169.

44 *Momcilovic v Croatia* (2019) 69 EHRR 14.

Telecom Italia SpA[45] and *Menini v Banco Popolare Societa Cooperativa*[46] in which the Court of Justice of the European Union recognised the compatibility of compulsory ADR with art. 6 rights. Vos MR then turned his attention to *R (UNISON) v Lord Chancellor.*[47] In that case, the UK Supreme Court held that the right of access to the courts could only be curtailed by express primary legislation and, therefore, the statutory instrument increasing fees to bring claims in the Employment Tribunal was unlawful because it prevented access to justice. Vos MR explained that *UNISON* was not authority for the proposition that a statutory basis was required for the court to mandate ADR because (i) it was not concerned with either staying existing proceedings for other dispute resolution processes to take place or with mandating the parties to participate in them; (ii) it did not contradict the long-established right of the court to control its own process; (iii) none of the authorities referred to in *UNISON* suggested that the court cannot make orders that delay or prevent the resolution of existing proceedings in aid of making the court system accessible, fair and efficient; and (iv) while the CPR itself is not primary legislation, nothing in *UNISON* suggested that one of the fundamental premises of the overriding objective and even the CPR itself could be unlawful without primary legislation authorising it expressly. Vos MR concluded that the courts do have the power to lawfully stay proceedings for, or order the parties to engage with, ADR. Vos MR held 'the court can lawfully stay proceedings for, or order, the parties to engage in a non-court-based dispute resolution process provided that the order made: (a) does not impair the very essence of the claimant's right to a fair trial (b) is made in pursuit of a legitimate aim, and (c) is proportionate to achieving that legitimate aim'.[48]

The Court of Appeal's conclusions on issue (ii) are manifestly correct and should also be welcomed for clearly and succinctly explaining the courts' powers to compel parties to engage with ADR. The courts' powers to compel parties to ADR have always existed and have been made clearer after *Churchill.* It is a fundamental aspect of the overriding objective, the courts' general case management powers and the courts' costs powers. By exercising those powers, the courts are able to further the principle of proportionality in achieving distributive justice across the civil justice system.[49] Following the decision in

---

45 *Alassini v Telecom Italia SpA* Joined Cases C-317/08, C-301/08, C-319/08 [2010] 3 CMLR 17.

46 *Menini v Banco Popolare Societa Cooperativa* [2018] CMLR 15.

47 *R (UNISON) v Lord Chancellor* [2017] UKSC 51.

48 ibid at [54].

49 For a detailed discussion, see J. Sorabji *A Model Civil Procedure Code for England and Wales* (Oxford University Press 2024).

Churchill, the CJEU in *Investcapital Ltd v TK*[50] reaffirmed that the Mediation Directive[51] permits Member States to adopt mandatory mediation frameworks, and that obliging disputing parties to engage with a mediation information session before or after issuing proceedings does not conflict with art. 6 of the ECHR provided the parties are permitted to access the courts.

On the issue of proportionality, however, the Court of Appeal could have more clearly articulated the importance of ADR as a significant aspect of the right to access to justice and, in particular, focused on developing a wider understanding of the concept of access to justice which comprises access to a variety of dispute resolution procedures, including access to an appropriate ADR procedure as well as access to judicial determination. Access to justice should no longer be understood in a narrow, outdated concept of simply access to the courts. Vos MR has, speaking extra-judicially, embraced a wider understanding of access to justice to encompass ADR. Vos MR has described a future digitised civil justice system which integrates sophisticated ADR procedures. As Vos MR explained, 'The whole system will be focused on resolution … continuous mediated interventions will be integrated into the whole digital justice system, making use of every available kind of dispute resolution from online or telephone to in-person mediations, early neutral evaluations or the use of AI to suggest outcomes'.[52] This understanding of access to justice is consistent with the approach being taken in Singapore where Chief Justice Menon has explained that an effective justice system should recognise that court adjudication is part of a wider universe of dispute resolution methods. This means that ADR would contribute to a wider scope within the justice system that proactively resolves disputes in the *most appropriate* manner.[53]

On issue (iii), Vos MR refused to provide a list of factors which would assist the courts in determining when to exercise its powers to compel parties to engage with ADR; it would be a matter for the courts to determine in the circumstances of each case. Nevertheless, Vos MR explained that the overriding objective, the factors identified by the claimant, the Bar Council and the *Halsey* factors were all likely to be relevant. Vos MR's refusal to provide a list of factors is understandable: lists of factors can be interpreted and applied by the courts in a mechanistic way and can, eventually, evolve into a 'judicial

---

50 Case C-658/23 *Investcapital v TK* ECLI:EU 2024:716 3 September 2024.

51 Directive 2008/52/EC of the European Parliament and of the Council of 21 May 2008 on certain aspects of mediation in civil and commercial matters.

52 The Right Hon Sir Geoffrey Vos, Master of the Rolls, 'Horizon Scanning: The Future for Dispute Resolution', The Society of Computers and Law. Sir Brian Neill Lecture 2022. Online, Thursday 17 March 2022.

53 Chief Justice Sundaresh Menon, 'Response by Chief Justice, Opening of the Legal Year 2020' (6 January 2020) at [21].

straitjacket' which restricts the court's discretion. However, there are shortcomings with the Court of Appeal's approach – it should have taken the opportunity to revisit and critically review the *Halsey* factors to ascertain whether they continue to remain 'fit for purpose' in a civil justice system where ADR is on the rise. The merits factor has been a source of considerable inconsistency in the manner in which the courts have assessed unreasonable refusal of ADR for costs purposes. On the one hand, the courts have hesitated in penalising a party that has argued that it rejected ADR because it had 'a reasonable belief' in the merits of its case,[54] while on the other hand, the courts have rejected the merits factor and have penalised parties in costs for rejecting ADR.[55] One of the principal weaknesses of the merits factor is that it does not accord with the realities of litigation: that is to say, it fails to appreciate that the vast majority of litigants who commence and defend proceedings will have at least a reasonable belief that they have a watertight case – otherwise why would they incur the substantial cost and time of engaging with the court process? Thus, the threshold set by the merits factor – reasonable belief in a watertight case – is artificially low and can easily be met by most litigants, who may therefore escape cost penalties which would otherwise apply. The Court of Appeal should have reviewed and finally dismissed the relevance of the merits factor. However, by simply reaffirming the relevance of the *Halsey* factors and therefore the merits factor, the Court of Appeal reinforced a factor which has been the source of inconsistent and divergent ADR case law. Although there are, as will be discussed in the next section, early signs in the post-*Churchill* era that the courts are more willing to exercise their costs powers where parties have rejected ADR,[56] the merits factors will continue to potentially provide litigants with an excuse not to engage with ADR.

(ii) The ADR Rules

Following the decision in *Churchill*, amendments were made to the CPR to make explicit the court's powers to compel parties to ADR. The overriding objective was amended to make clear that dealing with cases justly and at proportionate cost includes 'promoting or using alternative dispute resolution'.[57] The court's duty to further the overriding objective through active case

[54] *Gore v Naheed* [2017] EWCA Civ 369.

[55] e.g. *Thakkar v Patel* [2017 EWCA Civ 117; *PGF v OMSF* [2013] EWCA Civ 1288; *DSN v Blackpool Football Club Limited* [2020] EWHC 670 (QB).

[56] *Conway v Conway and another* [2024] EW Misc 19 (CC); *Northamber Plc v Genee World Ltd and others* [2024] EWCA Civ 428.

[57] CPR 1.1(2)(f).

management[58] was also amended to refer to the court's powers in '*ordering* or encouraging the parties to use, and facilitating the use of, alternative dispute resolution'.[59] The court's general case management powers under CPR 3 were amended to refer to the court's powers to '*order* the parties to engage in alternative dispute resolution'[60] and, when it is considering making procedural directions for cases allocated to the fast track and the multi-track, the court may make an '*order* or encourage the parties to engage in alternative dispute resolution'.[61] Finally, when considering the conduct of the parties for the purposes of costs, the court may take account of 'whether a party failed to comply with *an order* for alternative dispute resolution, or unreasonably failed to engage in alternative dispute resolution'.[62] The procedural changes to the CPR make explicit what was previously implied within the overriding objective and what was subsequently confirmed by the Court of Appeal in *Churchill*: the courts do have the power to compel parties to engage in ADR. In doing so, the revised rules provide much-needed clarity to the courts, the parties and their lawyers on the legality of compulsory ADR orders.

7.4 *CHURCHILL*, THE ADR RULES AND COURT PROCEEDINGS

This part analyses the courts' approach when exercising their ADR powers following the decision in *Churchill* and ADR rules. The case law reveals that the courts are willing to make orders compelling the parties to engage with mediation or stay proceedings in favour of mediation. Furthermore, the courts will continue to exercise their discretion in penalising the parties in costs for unreasonably refusing to engage with mediation.

The decision of *DKH Retail v City Football Group Ltd*[63] is the first case in which the court made a compulsory mediation order following *Churchill*. The case concerned a trademark dispute between the owners of the well-known 'Superdry' clothing brand and the defendant, which runs Manchester City Football Club's commercial operations. The core issue in the case was whether promotional branding appearing on professional sports players' kit was likely to be seen by the public as branding denoting the 'Superdry' brand or as branding denoting the defendant's sponsor, Asahi Super 'Dry' 0.0% lager. The words appearing on the kit included 'Super' and 'Dry'.

---

58 CPR 1.4.

59 CPR 1.4(2)(e).

60 CPR 3.1(2)(o).

61 CPR 28.7(1)(d) and CPR 28.14(f).

62 CPR 44.2(5)(e).

63 *DKH Retail v City Football Group Ltd* [2024] EWHC 3231 (Ch).

The claimant made two applications. The first was for the disclosure of the sponsorship contract between Manchester City and Asahi, and the second was an order for compulsory mediation. On the disclosure issue, Miles J found that the sponsorship agreement should be disclosed, as it had been on a list attached to the witness statement served on behalf of the club. In dealing with the application for a compulsory mediation order, Miles J referred to the decision in *Churchill* and the subsequent changes made to the CPR which made clear the courts' powers to order ADR. The claimant had argued that a 'short sharp mediation' could resolve the issues which may not be possible through litigation. The defendants resisted the application and argued that it was too late in the day to hold a mediation and availability was limited.

In granting the application for a compulsory mediation order, Miles J explained that 'Experience shows that mediation is capable of cracking even the hardest nuts. The process sometimes succeeds in cases where the parties appear at first to have intractable differences.' He agreed with the claimant's argument that a 'short sharp mediation' would focus on possible ways of resolving the issues rather than focusing on historical grievances. However, he disagreed with the defendant's argument that, if there was realistically to be a settlement, one would have been reached because the parties were commercial parties with experienced solicitors. Miles J explained the purpose of mediation when he said 'But that argument does not do full justice to experience, which shows that bringing the parties together through mediation can overcome an entrenched reluctance of parties to negotiate, even where sincere. The purpose of mediation is to remove roadblocks to settlement. I am unable to accept the submissions of the defendant that a mediation here has low prospects of success and that adjudication by a court is necessarily required. There may be solutions other than yes or no.'

It was also clear on the available material in the case that there was availability for mediation to take place. Miles J held, 'Overall I am satisfied that this is a case where I should order the parties to mediate with a view to seeking, if possible, to resolve the dispute between them and that it should take place during December 2024. The parties should report its outcome to the court as soon as possible after the mediation is complete.' The postscript to the judgement noted that 'on 13 January 2025 the parties notified the court that they had settled their dispute'.

The case of *Dover Farm Development Ltd v Smith* offers a rare example of judicial mediation and illustrates some judicial willingness to take a more interventionalist approach post-*Churchill* to ADR. In a defamation claim marked by unsuccessful cross-applications to strike out and amend the pleadings, the Master stayed the proceedings to facilitate mediation conducted by the court itself. Although the interim applications were not successful, the hearing was treated as productive because it enabled judicial engagement with ADR and allowed the parties to agree to mediate their dispute without the need for a formal ADR order. More significantly, the court considered the defendant's inability to fund a private mediation and concluded that mediation was the most proportionate and effective means of resolving the dispute. The Deputy Master conducted the mediation which resulted in the successful settlement of the dispute. The decision is significant for a number of reasons. It is an example, albeit a rare one, of judicial willingness to move beyond simply making ADR orders and leaving the parties to make the necessary arrangements to engage with ADR: the courts will actively facilitate ADR, in particular mediation, where appropriate. The decision also demonstrates how proportionality and access to justice concerns underpinned the court's decision to order judicial mediation: judicial mediation was justified not merely as desirable but as necessary to overcome costs barriers that would otherwise prevent the parties from engaging with mediation. Finally, the decision reinforces the case for judicial ADR activism, under which the court should move beyond the making of ADR orders and assume an active role in conducting ADR processes itself. This latter issue will be examined in detail in part 7.6.

A proactive approach towards ADR during proceedings was also taken by Master McCloud in *Elphick v Times Media*.[64] In that case, the Master did not hesitate to make an ADR order of her own motion in respect of the assessment of the parties' costs. In doing so, the Master referred to *Churchill* and made the following important observations:

> 136. It is my judgment essential that courts do what they can in the present congested court system to bring forward that settlement process so that assessments of costs are not needlessly listed whether in our County Courts (busy as they are) or in the Senior Courts Office …
>
> 137. I shall include a provision of my own motion that *the parties must engage in alternative dispute resolution* as to the costs claimed by the Defendant. *Good reason will need to be shown if the form of that dispute resolution is at any less engaged a level than mediation* via Costs Lawyers given that the Bill here more than justifies Costs Lawyer input. The time for commencing detailed assessment is to be extended until conclusion of *any such mediation,* or the point at which either party indicates it is not prepared to proceed and wishes to go to assessment. Any party which decides not to engage in ADR, as above or to 'call it off' must be in a position to justify that non-engagement to the Costs Judge and be alert to the provisions of CPR 44.11 and indeed the developing common law since Churchill.[65]

---

64 *Elphick v Times Media* [2024] EWHC 2595 (KB). See also *Hadley v Przybylo* [2023] EWHC 1392 (KB) and V. McCloud '"Please hold. Be assured your justice is important to us." Standards, delays and tech in the civil courts: throwing a few bricks at the façade'. J.P.I. Law 2024, 4, 259–270.

65 Emphasis added.

The decision in *Elphick* serves as an example of how the courts should embrace and exercise their ADR powers. The Master did not hesitate in exercising her powers in making an ADR order of her own motion rather than reacting to an application for an order from the parties – this proactive judicial approach should be encouraged and promoted. It is also interesting to note that the Master made several references to mediation and, more importantly, used mediation to set a benchmark on the type of structured ADR procedure that should be used by the parties, that is, one which involves a neutral third party who can assist in facilitating a settlement for the parties. Furthermore, the Master reinforced her order with explicit reference to the court's powers to penalise any party in costs for failing to comply with her order. The decision is also the first in which a senior judge has mandated ADR in costs assessment proceedings which, if allowed to proceed through the court process, further exacerbate costs and drain the courts' resources.

It is also clear that the courts will continue to exercise their powers in penalising a party in costs for unreasonably refusing to engage with ADR. Take, for example, the Court of Appeal decision in *Northamber Plc v Genee World Limited and others*.[66] A district judge had made a case management order which required the parties to engage with ADR and, if any party did not do so then that party was required to serve a witness statement giving reasons which could only be shown to the trial judge on the issue of costs. The claimant wrote to the defendants indicating its willingness to engage with mediation. The third defendant's solicitors replied by saying that they would take instructions, but there was no further response, and the second defendant did not respond at all. Neither party served a witness statement as required by the case management order. Following the trial, the judge awarded the claimant 70% of its costs. However, the judge refused to penalise the defendants in costs for their failure to comply with the case management order because there was no evidence that the claimant had chased the defendants for a reply to their invitation to engage with mediation. On appeal, the claimant argued that this aspect of the judge's decision amounted to an error of principle.

Giving the judgment of the Court of Appeal, Arnold LJ agreed that the judge had fallen into error. He noted that the defendants had remained silent in the face of an offer to mediate which was, in itself, unreasonable. To compound matters, the defendants had breached the case management order requiring them to explain their failure to agree to mediation. As Arnold LJ explained, 'If breaches of such orders are ignored by courts when deciding costs, parties will have no incentive to comply with them. That would undermine the purpose of making them, which is robustly to encourage parties to mediate.' The judge's

66 *Northamber Plc v Genee World Limited and others* [2024] EWCA Civ 428.

reasoning ignored these points. The facts that the litigation had been underway for some time and the parties had incurred substantial costs were relevant to the exercise of the court's discretion as to how to respond to the defendants' conduct. Furthermore, the litigation had continued for a further eight months, including a nine-day trial, and the parties incurred substantial costs which could have been avoided by a successful mediation. Arnold LJ also observed that the judge had wrongly concluded that the onus for chasing for a reply to its letter to mediate lay with the claimant; after the letter was sent, 'the ball was in Mr Singh's and IES's court'.

The more difficult question was how the defendants' conduct should be reflected in costs. Arnold LJ explained that 'Although costs sanctions have been imposed in a number of cases for an unreasonable refusal to mediate or for silence in response to an offer of mediation, it does not automatically follow that a costs penalty should be imposed … Rather, it is a factor to be taken into account among the other circumstances of the case.' Arnold LJ rejected the claimant's contention that the defendants should be ordered to pay 100% of the claimant's costs but did increase the claimant's costs recovery by an additional 5% to 75% in total.

Although the costs penalty in *Northamber Plc* was modest, it was, nonetheless, significant in reinforcing the principle that a party's silence in the face of an invitation to ADR will be considered as unreasonable conduct for the purposes of costs. The decision also upholds and furthers the principle of proportionality which underpins the civil justice system. As Briggs LJ succinctly put it in *PGF*, 'the constraints which now affect the provision of state resources for the conduct of civil litigation (and which appear likely to do so for the foreseeable future) call for an ever-increasing focus on means of ensuring that court time, both for trial and for case management, is proportionately directed towards those disputes which really need it, with an ever-increasing responsibility thrown on the parties to civil litigation to engage in ADR'.[67]

7.5 IMPACT OF *CHURCHILL* AND THE ADR RULES ON PRE-ACTION OBLIGATIONS

This part focuses on the relationship between the parties' ADR obligation at the pre-action stage and the courts' approach in compelling the parties to a second round of mediation when proceedings are issued. It does so by analysing the second sequential step under the GPaP – the need for parties to engage with an ADR process – and the decision in *Churchill* and the ADR rules in

[67] *PGF* at [46] (n 11).

strengthening the parties' ADR obligations and promoting and reinforcing the principle of proportionality.

Although the courts do not, at this stage, have jurisdiction over the pre-action stage of disputes, there are early signs that the courts have the power to order parties to a second round of mediation even though they have engaged with mediation in compliance with the pre-action protocols. It will be recalled that step (ii) under the GPaP requires the parties to engage with ADR with preference being given to mediation. Paragraph 4.14 of the GPaP exempts parties from any future requirement to engage with ADR if they have previously attempted ADR at the pre-action stage. Paragraph 4.14 states:

> Where the parties have engaged in mediation under this protocol [or any other dispute resolution process involving the assistance of a neutral third party such as early neutral evaluation, an Ombudsman etc.], and the dispute does not settle, *then the parties will not be required to engage in another mediation if court proceedings are started.*[68]

It is important to note that this exemption only applies to low value disputes that have already been through a pre-action ADR process; clearly, it would not be proportionate to expect small claims disputes to undergo a further round of ADR. However, *Churchill* potentially alters the position in paragraph 4.14 for higher value claims because when proceedings have been issued, the courts retain the power to order the parties to engage with ADR regardless of whether they have attempted ADR at the pre-action stage. Two recent post-*Churchill* decisions support these observations. The first case is *Heyes v Holt*.[69] In this case, the parties had attempted mediation before issuing proceedings but were unable to settle. HHJ Matthews, sitting as a judge of the High Court, ordered the parties to engage in a further mediation when he said:

> This is a case which cries out for mediation by the parties. I am aware that mediation has already been attempted between the parties … and on that occasion it failed. I commend them nevertheless for trying. But that was before the claim had even been issued. Now that the parties have full pleadings and disclosure, as well as (for what it may be worth) this judgment, the parties should try again. I will order a stay for that purpose.

The second case is *Francis v Pearson*[70] in which the parties had participated in a mediation. HHJ Matthews, sitting as a judge of the High Court, 'strongly

---

68 Emphasis added.

69 *Heyes v Holt* [2024] EWHC 779 (Ch).

70 *Francis v Pearson* [2024] EWHC 605 (KB).

recommended' that the parties re-consider engaging in another round of ADR which may include mediation. As HHJ Matthews explained:

> 88. Experience shows that it is often in entrenched cases such as this that ADR can make a real difference, often requiring honest conversations with parties as to the merits of their respective cases, and the potential downsides, as well as looking at pragmatic ways forward.
>
> 89. As part of the process, mediators might also see the parties together, without their lawyers, to try and explore ways forward.
>
> 91. The parties need to reflect on the reasons why the cases did not settle at mediation, and the costs of continuing this litigation – not just in terms of money, but the personal costs to each party for example from the time and energy spent fighting, the stress and worry the proceedings might cause, particularly in respect of outcomes, and the impact that it is going to have on the wider community in which they live.
>
> 92. I would strongly recommend that the parties re-consider some form of alternative dispute resolution process – which might include further mediation, or some other way of facilitating agreement – before matters in this case move forward and further costs are incurred.

The decision in *Holt* is one in which the court did not hesitate in staying proceedings in favour of a second round of mediation which concluded in a settlement, and in Francis the court emphasised the benefits of avoiding protracted and expensive litigation. Thus, the ADR duty is a continuing one and one which remains throughout the life of the dispute. This means that the courts, with their new *Churchill* powers and the amended ADR rules, will expect parties to not only consider engaging in a second round of mediation but will increasingly expect the parties to take constructive steps in arranging and participating in a second round of mediation regardless of whether they have done so at the pre-action stage or in compliance with a relevant protocol.

There are, however, several arguments against such an approach, in particular in circumstances where the second round of mediation does not result in a settlement. There is the obvious risk that the parties will incur increased costs and delays in bringing their dispute before the courts which, in turn, undermines access to justice. Thus, the parties may abandon their claims because they are no longer able or willing to incur additional costs in financing court proceedings. A second mediation may also undermine the principle of finality because it means the parties are unsure of whether their dispute will, despite discharging their ADR obligations, be decided by a judge. The parties may also feel impliedly compelled to settle their dispute if they are ordered to engage with a second round of mediation. Clearly, the courts cannot, as Churchill makes clear, compel the parties to reach a settlement in a mediation or in any other ADR process; to do so would undermine the right to a fair trial. However, an order of the court for a second round of mediation may be perceived by the parties as an order to reach a settlement. It is for this reason that the courts should, as will be discussed in the next section when explaining the concept of judicial ADR activism, ensure that they engage in an 'ADR dialogue' with the parties to ensure that the parties' views are taken into account and are made part of the decision-making process. Furthermore, the private aspect of the principle of proportionality may potentially be undermined if the parties do not settle during the second round of mediation and have to continue to incur costs in pursuing the matter through the courts.

There are counterarguments in support of the courts' approach. A second round of mediation may either result in a settlement or, where a settlement cannot be reached, it substantially reduces the number of issues in dispute. This argument is strengthened if the GPaP is applied. Under the GPaP, the parties are required to complete a stocktake report after having engaged with ADR which should narrow the issues in dispute. The stocktake report will not only help to support more efficient judicial case management, but it will also lay strong foundations for the parties to participate in a second round of mediation which will have a higher chance of concluding in a settlement. A second attempt at mediation also increases the likelihood of resolution, especially with the parties' statements of case and further disclosure of evidence. Finally, a second round of mediation may not simply be helpful where the gap between the parties is small. In fact, the courts perform an important function when ordering the parties to engage in a second round of mediation to avoid the delays, costs and uncertainties of litigation and, in doing so, the parties are spared from appearing weak if they were to request an order for mediation.

7.6 WAY FORWARD AND CONCLUSION

Given the courts' wide-ranging ADR powers which impact not only the court process but also have a direct impact on the pre-action protocols, it is imperative that the courts adopt a considered and structured approach when determining whether to make an order for a second round of mediation which I refer to as 'judicial ADR activism'. Judicial ADR activism refers to the proactive role that judges should play in encouraging, facilitating, and, if required, conducting ADR processes themselves. It requires judges to utilise their broad case management powers in actively promoting the use of a range of ADR processes and is rooted in the principle of proportionality and the overriding objective.

Judicial ADR activism consists of four interrelated elements which require the courts to: (i) fully embrace and exercise their ADR powers; (ii) have a detailed understanding of the nature and full range of ADR procedures, which I refer to as 'judicial ADR pluralism'; (iii) actively and constructively engage in an 'ADR dialogue' with the parties to ascertain the most appropriate ADR procedure; and (iv) increasingly conduct ADR processes themselves, including judicial mediation which is routinely and successfully conducted by judges in the Employment Tribunal.[71]

The first element of judicial ADR activism requires the courts to fully embrace and exercise their ADR powers. This means that the courts should not hesitate in making compulsory mediation orders or penalising the parties in costs for failing to discharge their ADR obligations, including any failure to engage with the protocols. This aspect of judicial ADR activism is beginning to emerge after *Churchill* with cases such as *Northamber Plc*,[72] *DKH* and *Elphick*. In *Conway v Conway*,[73] HHJ Methani KC remarked that:

> The importance of mediation can never be over-emphasised: see, for example, the recent decision of the Court of Appeal in *Churchill v Merthyr Tydfil County Borough Council* [2023] EWCA Civ 1416. The defendants will have to advance compelling reasons why the offer of mediation was rejected out of hand by them.[74]

In *Conway*, the successful defendants' costs were reduced by 25% to reflect their failure to engage with mediation. Also, in *Heathcote v Asertis*,[75] the trial judge's order that the defendant pay 75% of the claimant's costs was subsequently upheld on appeal because the defendant had refused to mediate and had failed to make a formal settlement offer.[76] Although these cases concern the parties' ADR duty after proceedings have been issued, the approach taken by the courts in those cases should also apply where the parties have failed to discharge their procedural obligations under a relevant protocol and, more significantly, where they have failed to engage with an ADR procedure. This point is a particularly important one given that the courts have historically been reluctant to enforce compliance with the protocols, an issue which was noted in the CJC's Interim Report. The preliminary consultation which formed the basis of the Interim Report found a high consensus among respondents to the courts' inconsistent approach when enforcing compliance with the protocols despite the CPR providing the courts with a range of sanctions to do so.[77]

---

[71] See e.g. Presidential Guidance: Alternative Dispute Resolution 7 July 2025; *Leeks v University College London Hospitals NHS Foundation Trust* [2024] EAT 134.

[72] *Northamber Plc* (n 66).

[73] *Conway v Conway and another* [2024] EW Misc 19 (CC).

[74] ibid at [129].

[75] *Heathcote v Asertis* [2024] EWHC 779 (Ch).

[76] Part 36 offers are formal offers to settle and are governed by CPR 36.

[77] Interim Report, Appendix 2 Preliminary Survey Results and Respondents. The range of sanctions includes ordering a stay of proceedings to allow compliance

This approach must change and the courts must enforce compliance with the protocols and in doing so they should not hesitate in sanctioning the parties in appropriate cases and the rationale justifying this approach is the need for the parties and the courts to further and promote the principle of proportionality.

It is important for judges to have a detailed understanding of the nature of the full range of consensual ADR procedures and to avoid simply fixating on mediation as the only choice for the courts and the parties. Mediation has been elevated by policymakers and judges as the most preferred ADR process in resolving civil disputes, and it has been elevated on the international stage through the enactment of the Singapore Mediation Convention[78] and the Mediation Directive.[79] This strong reference for mediation, however, risks other ADR processes being neglected and forgotten. Mediation should be considered as part of the full range of consensual ADR processes and, as such, the courts should understand the nature of each process and carefully consider whether mediation or another ADR process, such as ENE, would be the most appropriate ADR process in the particular circumstances of the dispute.

In the event that the court is inclined to make an order for a second round of mediation, it should avoid making such an order mechanistically and without having first engaged in an 'ADR dialogue' with the parties. Such an approach will allow the parties to participate in a constructive discussion with the court and for their views to be considered as to the type of ADR process that will be most suited to the circumstances of the dispute. This party participation is fundamental in upholding procedural justice. In the administration of justice,[80] the courts must ensure that they are seeking to achieve both substantive and procedural justice. Substantive justice, to borrow from Jeremy Bentham,[81] is

---

with the protocols, costs sanctions for failing to engage with the protocols or, in extremely serious cases, striking out a claim or defence.

78 United Nations Convention on International Settlement Agreements Resulting from Mediation 2018. See further B. Clark and V. Hamaiunova's contribution at chapter 9.

79 Directive 2008/52/EC of the European Parliament and of the Council of 21 May 2008 on certain aspects of mediation in civil and commercial matters.

80 As Swoboda correctly notes, 'Justice is not solely concerned with procedural propriety but also with the outcome and thereby, puts a greater emphasis on the quality of decision making.' See J. Swoboda, 'Remote hearings – the new normal? (Are they fair? Are they just?)' (2020) 3 JPLI 208.

81 J. Bentham, 'Rationale of Judicial Evidence' in J. Bowring (ed.), The Works of Jeremy Bentham (William Tait, 1843), Vol. 6, pp. 212–213. For an interesting discussion of the significance of truth in the pursuit of justice, see C.H. van Rhee and A. Uzelac, 'The Pursuit of Truth in Contemporary Civil Procedure: Revival of Accuracy or a New Balance in Favour of Effectiveness' in C.H. van Rhee and A. Uzelac, Truth and Efficiency in Civil Litigation (Intersentia, 2012).

concerned with the courts correctly applying the law to true facts or, to put it another way, deciding the case on its substantive merits.[82] Procedural justice, which consists of the rules of court as well as principles such as equality before the law, impartiality, and proportionality, is the means by which the courts discharge their constitutional function of vindicating and enforcing rights and thereby upholding the rule of law. The importance of procedural justice was explained by Lord Woolf when he said:

> Procedural justice is as important as substantive justice. *It must be seen to be fair.* The rules should, therefore, be comprehensible to the parties (whether or not they are legally represented) and to others who are concerned with the outcome of litigation. The civil process should command respect, not because it generates a sense of awe or mystery, *but because it is patently fair.*[83]

Lord Woolf's conceptual and practical understanding of procedural justice is consistent with contemporary civil procedure scholarship. De Girolomo explains that procedural justice is a concept that rests on certain elements of process that, if present, result in party perceptions of fairness in the dispute resolution process experienced by them.[84] If parties perceive those processes to be fair, then they are likely to respect and accept the outcomes from those processes because, as suggested by Hollander-Blumoff and Tyler,[85] parties care about the process by which outcomes are reached.[86] Thus, procedural justice concerns the fairness of the procedures that are used to resolve disputes, and party participation in those procedures is a fundamental aspect of procedural fairness and applies to both court and ADR processes. As De Girolomo explains in the context of mediation, which applies equally to court proceedings:

> The attendant elements of procedural justice are steeped in party participation experiences. They include the need and desire for an opportunity by parties to tell

---

[82] J. Sorabji, *English Civil Justice after the Woolf and Jackson Reforms: A Critical Analysis* (CUP, 2013).

[83] H. Woolf, *Access to Justice: Interim Report to the Lord Chancellor on the Civil Justice System of England and Wales* (HMSO, 1995), 216, para. 28–29. Emphasis added.

[84] D. De Girolomo, 'The Mediation Process: Challenges to Neutrality and the Delivery of Procedural Justice' (2019) 39(4) OJLS 4–5.

[85] R. Hollander-Blumoff and T. Tyler, 'Procedural Justice in Negotiation: Procedural Fairness, Outcomes Acceptance, and Integrative Potential' (2008) 33 L & Soc Inquiry 473.

[86] ibid.

> their story and to control its telling, a consideration of their story in a fair manner, and the need to be treated with dignity and respect.[87]

An ADR dialogue will also allow the courts to explain the courts' ADR powers and the right of the parties to return to the court process if the matter cannot be settled. This latter point is crucial in ensuring the courts refer the parties to ADR processes which preserve their rights to access the courts as explained in *Churchill*. An ADR dialogue will also allow the courts to effectively deal with any arguments, such as the merits factor, which may seek to avoid engagement with mediation and undermine the ADR duty.

Finally, if a second round of mediation is to be ordered following an ADR dialogue with the parties, the courts should undertake that second round of mediation themselves. Judges should be trained to conduct judicial mediation and other forms of ADR themselves. There is, of course, provision within the CPR on the use of judicial ENE and the King's Bench Guide provides detailed guidance on the procedure to be adopted. However, aside from the rare decision in *Dover Farm Developments Ltd* on judicial mediation, the same attention is not given to judicial mediation, which is surprising given that judges in the Employment Tribunal routinely conduct mediations and judicial mediation has a long history in other jurisdictions.[88] There is, of course, the difficult issue of a lack of resources and investment in the civil justice system; however, if the government is serious about reducing the stubborn court backlog that continues to undermine access to justice, urgent consideration must be given to investing in the training of judges in mediation and other ADR processes.

The GPaP, *Churchill*, and the ADR rules collectively represent a significant evolution in promoting proportionate dispute resolution within the civil justice system. While the benefits of encouraging early settlement, narrowing the issues in dispute, and upholding proportionality are significant, it is essential that the courts adopt a principled approach when exercising their ADR powers.

---

87 De Girolomo (n 84) 5–6.

88 e.g. Australia, Canada, Singapore, and the United States.

8. The history and trajectory of mediator neutrality

Ben Wilson

8.1 INTRODUCTION

Mediation in the United States (US) is one of the primary methods for resolving civil disputes, and neutrality is often regarded as the central tenet of a mediator's responsibility.[1] Over the last century, neutrality has been defined in vastly different ways by academics, practitioners, and institutions. Neutrality is frequently lauded as a tool for achieving trust, credibility, respect, and procedural justice, gaining entry, limiting bias and partiality, and creating the impression of fairness. However, many mediators cannot clearly define what it means to be neutral, and assessment criteria for mediator neutrality are largely absent from mediation programs. Lacking a uniform definition and prescriptive advice for mediators, in practice, neutrality emerged as an ethos or aura, rather than a skill or practice.[2]

This chapter examines the historical development of mediator neutrality by exploring the following questions: How did neutrality become the dominant mediator posture in the US? How is mediator neutrality culturally defined? And is neutrality a defining principle of mediation or merely a helpful tool for mediators? The chapter concludes by posing salient questions and pointing to future scholarship on the topic.

[1] In this chapter, mediation is broadly defined as a process for addressing conflict, in which the third (or *n*+1) party convenes and facilitates dialogue and negotiation between disputants.

[2] Carol Izumi, 'Implicit Bias and the Illusion of Mediator Neutrality' (2010) 34 Wash. U. J. L. & Pol'y 71, 77–78.

8.2 FORMALIZING FEDERAL MEDIATION

In the US, mediation gained popularity during the period of industrialization. During the first three decades of the 20th century, in particular, mediation was increasingly relied upon by the federal government to settle intense and often violent labor strikes. In 1913, as his last official act in office, President Taft signed a bill creating the Department of Labor. This legislation entrusted the Labor Secretary with, 'power to act as a mediator and to appoint commissioners of conciliation in labor disputes whenever in his judgment the interests of industrial peace may require it to be done.'[3]

In 1935, the US Congress passed the National Labor Relations Act to further balance the 'inequality of bargaining power' in labor disputes by preserving the right of private employees to organize unions, engage in collective bargaining, and assemble strikes and mutual aid efforts.[4] After World War II, Congress established the Federal Mediation and Conciliation Service (FMCS) through passage of the Labor–Management Relations Act of 1947 to prevent or minimize labor stoppages by providing mediation and other services.[5] FMCS mediators were tasked with maintaining absolute neutrality in their efforts.[6]

Widespread racial conflict, partially characterized by resistance to Jim Crow laws, erupted in the 1950s. Such laws denied Black Americans equal access to, for instance, public facilities, employment, and voting rights. Out of this context, a movement grew to create a federal conflict resolution agency. 'Black congressional members argued that "mediation" ... not be in the agency's title, reflecting a long-time wariness that the function of dispute resolution is as a vehicle of maintaining the status quo, rather than for change.'[7] In President Kennedy's 1963 address to Congress, he stated that an essential component of advancing Civil Rights would be the establishment of 'an independent Community Relations Service.'[8] The civil rights movement culminated in

---

3 29 USC Ch. 12: Department of Labor (1913).

4 Title 29, Chapter 7, Subchapter II, United States Code Section 1. [§151.]; see also, Max M. Kampelman 'The United States Conciliation Service' (1947) 31 Minn. L. Rev. 680.

5 Labor Management Relations Act of 1947.

6 29 USCA § 172(a)(d); see also, Joseph F. Finnegan, 'Federal Mediation: How It Works' (1959) 9 DePaul L. Rev. 1.

7 Grande Lum, 'The History of Community Mediation Uncovered: The Department of Justice's Community Relations Service' (2024) 30 Dispute Resolution Magazine 16, 16–17.

8 John Fitzgerald Kennedy, *Message from the President of the United States Relative to Civil Rights* (US Government Printing Office, 1963) 11.

President Johnson signing the Civil Rights Act of 1964, which, in part, created the Community Relations Service (CRS).[9]

Known as 'America's Peacemakers,' CRS was tasked with assisting communities in 'resolving disputes, disagreements, or difficulties' related to discrimination based on 'race, color, or national origin.'[10] Independence, as noted by Kennedy, established a layer of separation between CRS mediators and the law enforcement functions of the DOJ, enhancing their credibility in engagements with communities and institutional actors. Furthermore, CRS relies upon statutory confidentiality in performing its duties to enhance trust and gain entry with parties who are reluctant to engage with 'Feds' (federal law enforcement). Mediators 'who shall make public in any manner whatever any information in violation of this subsection, shall be deemed guilty of a misdemeanor,' and, 'fined not more than $1,000 or imprisoned not more than one year.'[11] Functionally, CRS demands that its mediators build trust with communities in conflict. To build trust, CRS acts as a third party neutral, defined by independence, confidentiality, and a non-law enforcement mandate.[12]

Following the establishment of CRS, community mediation centers emerged in response to social conflict. Modeled after CRS, these grassroots mediation centers overwhelmingly employed neutral mediators as well.[13] Throughout the first half-century of mediation's development, neutrality was consistently defined as a cornerstone principle of mediator conduct. Labor and civil rights disputes were routinely creating intense divisions, and neutrality (or independence) demonstrated federal mediators' credibility and mitigated perceptions that they might have a particular interest in resolving the conflict.

8.3 FOUNDATIONS OF MEDIATOR NEUTRALITY

In the 1970s, civil court dockets were overflowing and court-connected mediation programs represented a desirable avenue to unload some of the caseload.

---

[9] 42 USC 2000g-1, 2000g-2(b); see also Bertram Levine & Grande Lum, *America's Peacemakers: The Community Relations Service and Civil Rights* (new ed. University of Missouri Press, 2020) 31–32, 98–99 (CRS was originally created as a federal mechanism for conflict resolution within the Department of Commerce. In 1966, President Lyndon Johnson signed an Executive Order to transfer CRS from the Department of Commerce to the Department of Justice).

[10] Levine & Lum (n 9).

[11] 42 USC 2000g-2.

[12] Community Relations Service <https://www.justice.gov/crs> accessed 15 November 2024.

[13] Tim Hedeen & Patrick G. McCoy, 'Community Mediation and the Court System: Ties that Bind' (2007) 17 Conflict Resolution Quarterly 351.

Mediation was touted as adaptable enough to be used in any civil dispute. Witnessing this trend, scholars set out to prove the importance of neutrality by defining it, which proved difficult. Most definitions of neutrality describe mediators as in the middle, independent, disinterested, unbiased, impartial, equidistant, abstaining from judgment, seeking fairness, for both sides and for neither.

While mediation blossomed, guidelines and standards emerged to highlight best practices and set minimum expectations for mediator competence and ethics. The discussion that preceded the adoption of statutory obligations and guidelines for mediators confirmed the importance of mediator neutrality, while also questioning whether it must be an unassailable trait of all mediators.

Scholarship from this period inspired debate regarding the place of neutrality in mediation. James Laue and Gerald Cormick differentiate mediation from other types of conflict intervention, specifically focusing on the ethical issues raised by mediator neutrality.[14] They define mediation as a process in which mediators 'assist the parties in reaching a mutually satisfactory settlement of their differences.'[15] Laue and Cormick write that merely by intervening in a conflict, mediators are not neutral, as they are advocating for a certain system of resolution.[16] The pair center their theory of conflict intervention by asking whether 'the intervention contribute[s] to the ability of relatively powerless individuals and groups in the situation to determine their own destinies to the greatest extent consistent with the common good.'[17] This question, according to Laue and Cormick, raises important issues of freedom, justice, power, and equity, which are primary concerns in all systems of conflict intervention, including mediation. Using case studies, they modeled instances in which mediators may abandon a neutral posture and pursue an advocacy role.[18]

Mediation's historic roots in labor and civil rights disputes informed early scholarship and standards of conduct for mediators, particularly regarding their neutral posture. Examining mediator neutrality in other contexts, scholars and practitioners raised concerns that the ill-defined concept hindered durable and efficient outcomes.

---

14 James Laue & Gerald Cormick, 'The Ethics of Intervention in Community Disputes' in Gordon Bermant, Herbert C. Kelman, and Donald P. Warwick (eds), *The Ethics of Social Intervention* (Hemisphere 1978) 212–217. (Apart from mediation, they identify four other types of conflict intervention: (1) activist intervention; (2) advocate intervention; (3) researcher intervention; and (4) enforcer intervention.)

15 ibid 214.

16 ibid 216–217.

17 ibid 217–218.

18 ibid 225.

A. The Neutrality Debate: Part I

Not all mediators embody a neutral posture. In 1981, Lawrence Susskind noticed a trend in environmental mediation which inspired his article in the Vermont Law Review titled, *Environmental Mediation and the Accountability Problem*.[19] Susskind questioned the necessity of mediator neutrality and opened the door for further exploration.

In labor disputes, interests are negotiated collectively through representatives of the union and management. Environmental disputes present unique challenges; the impacts of resolution are difficult to predict and may be exacerbated over time and space.[20] Susskind identified an approach to environmental mediation that de-prioritizes neutrality in favor of accountability for reaching a durable and comprehensive agreement.[21] To frame his appeal, Susskind proposed that mediators ought to ensure that: (1) interests of parties not directly involved in the mediation are adequately represented and protected; (2) agreements are as fair, just, equitable, and stable as possible; and (3) agreements are clear to the community-at-large and set constructive precedents.[22] Susskind's criteria for mediator accountability track Laue and Cormick's central question for mediators – namely, in what instances should a mediator act as an advocate? Susskind narrowly tailored his observations to the environmental context and was careful not to suggest that mediators should abandon neutrality altogether.

Replying to Susskind, Joseph Stulberg identified mediators as one type of intervener and distinguished them from other interveners like law enforcement, judges and magistrates, schoolteachers, administrators and councilors, and countless others.[23] Surely, Stulberg reasoned, each of those professions requires *mediation skills* to accomplish their goals. However, incorporating the defining principles of mediation into their job description would obstruct

[19] Lawrence Susskind, 'Environmental Mediation and the Accountability Problem' 6 VT. L. Rev. 1 (1981).

[20] ibid 39–41 (describing the potential for spillover and long-term impacts with disparate impacts on unrepresented or marginalized groups).

[21] ibid 39–41 (illustrating mediator accountability with three multilateral case studies in which mediators inserted themselves to achieve a durable and comprehensive agreement; these mediators applied deep knowledge of environmental concerns and regulatory processes, expressed personal views about the scope and content of emerging proposals, and used momentum to pressure holdouts).

[22] ibid 16–18.

[23] Joseph B. Stulberg, 'The Theory and Practice of Mediation: A Reply to Professor Susskind' (1981) 6 Vt. L. Rev. 85, 87–88.

their primary professional responsibilities.[24] Stulberg took the position that, while Susskind's intervener (mediator-advocate) might be desirable to certain parties in environmental disputes, this type of dispute resolution should not be defined as mediation.

Stulberg describes a mediator's primary duty as that of a listener offering perspectives that have not received adequate consideration. Mediators, though, are more than passive participants.[25] Stulberg proposes that mediators faced with an impasse should 'forcefully identify' the costs associated with continuing in the conflict and refrain from chastising parties as unreasonable, unfair, or negotiating in bad faith.[26]

Responding directly to Susskind, Stulberg illustrates how mediators with a neutral posture might respond to agreements that are contrary to important principles of public policy or morality:

The mediator should press the parties to examine whether or not they believe that: (1) they would be acting in compliance with the law or with principles they would be willing, as rational agents, to universalize; (2) their activities will be acceptable to their respective constituencies and not overturned by public authorities; and (3) in the short and long run, their proposed actions are not contrary to their own self-interest.[27]

If the parties are not swayed by these appeals and serious ethical concerns remain, the mediator should refuse further assistance and withdraw from the process.[28] Ultimately, Stulberg concludes that mediator neutrality is paramount to the process and must not be compromised.[29]

Much of the debate between Susskind and Stulberg revolved around definitions. Susskind sought to redefine the mediator's duties broadly and Stulberg countered that processes facilitated by a non-neutral third party cannot be construed as mediation. Agreeable definitions of both mediation and neutrality are central to exploring their compatibility. In their 1981 articles, neither Susskind nor Stulberg offered a concise definition of neutrality. The next two decades saw literature on the topic focus specifically on searching for mutually agreeable definitions of both mediation and neutrality.

24 ibid 88.
25 ibid 91–92.
26 ibid 105.
27 ibid 116.
28 ibid 115–116.
29 ibid 111–112.

B. Constructing Neutrality

In their spate of articles published in 1991, Sara Cobb and Janet Rifkin identified Foucault's framework of discursive practice (storytelling) as being both an ideological match and pragmatic approach for mediation practice.[30] Their writing pointed to the explosion in the use of mediation to resolve civil disputes and the relative dearth of empirical studies of mediation.

Specifically targeting the neutrality discourse, Cobb and Rifkin found that neutrality is 'understood and invoked as a stronghold against bias.'[31] However, they also found that, in practice, neutrality often functions like folklore; it is based on a rhetoric of 'tacit local understandings' of power and conflict,[32] and the rhetoric contributes to reinforcing these same tacit understandings.[33] Neutrality, then, is both transparent and opaque: transparent in that it operates on widely held beliefs and opaque because the literature focuses on neutrality's place in mediation, rather than what it means to be neutral.

In a series of interviews with mediators, Cobb and Rifkin found that, when asked to define neutrality, they routinely referenced two distinct concepts:

(1) impartiality – behavior devoid of ideological process, which ensures against mediator biases;[34] and
(2) equidistance – a stance representing that neither side is favored nor disfavored.[35]

---

[30] Sara Cobb & Janet Rifkin, 'Practice and Paradox: Deconstructing Neutrality in Mediation' (1991) 16 L. & Soc. Inq. 35; see also Sara Cobb & Janet Rifkin, 'Neutrality as Discursive Practice: The Construction and Transformation of Narratives in Community Mediation' (1991) 11 Studies in Law, Politics, and Society 69; and see Janet Rifkin, Jonathan Millen, and Sara Cobb, 'Toward a New Discourse for Mediation: A Critique of Neutrality' (1991) 9 Med. Q. 151.

[31] ibid. Rifkin, Millen, and Cobb, 'Toward a New Discourse for Mediation: A Critique of Neutrality' (1991) 9 Med. Q. 151.

[32] Cobb & Rifkin, 'Practice and Paradox' (n 30) 37.

[33] ibid.

[34] ibid 41–43 (discussing that, when asked to define neutrality, 14 out of 15 mediators relied on 'impartiality' and pointed back to the concept as a tool to challenge mediator biases; the very nature of challenging one's own unconscious biases is paradoxical and unlikely to produce a consistent measure of one's neutrality or impartiality).

[35] ibid 43–45 (explaining the differences between the psychological biases addressed by the neutrality-as-impartiality perspective and the proximate biases addressed by neutrality-as-equidistance).

By examining the ways in which mediators practice storytelling, Cobb and Rifkin introduced a third, competing definition – neutrality as a practice in discourse that disrupts marginalization.[36] This approach shifts the mediator's responsibility to remain neutral from an ill-defined concept of impartial equidistance to assisting the disputants in co-creating an agreeable and inclusive narrative.[37]

Building on Cobb and Rifkin's work, Gibson, Thompson, and Bazerman write that regardless of which form neutrality takes, it is essential that mediators understand how they might embody a neutral posture.[38] Further, they opine that professional organizations are overemphasizing the role of mediator neutrality, while simultaneously mystifying prescriptive guidance for mediators seeking a neutral posture. They argue that a maximal view of neutrality leads to inefficient and inequitable outcomes. Instead, the trio suggests that mediators provide symmetric prescriptive advice to disputants – an equity approach to maintaining equidistance.[39]

C. Institutional Neutrality

As community mediation centers and court-connected mediation programs spread across the US, professional standards for mediators were simultaneously enacted. One of the earliest organizations to provide standards for mediators, The Society of Professionals in Dispute Resolution (SPIDR) used the word 'neutral' 35 times without describing what constitutes neutral behavior and technique.[40] Laue, having spent time as a civil rights advocate and a CRS mediator, criticized the over-reliance on neutrality. Laue argued that '[a]ll intervention alters the power configuration among the parties, thus all conflict intervention is advocacy. There are no neutrals.'[41] Laue explained that all

---

36 Cobb & Rifkin, 'Neutrality as Discursive Practice' (n 30) 87; see also Isabelle Gunning, 'Diversity Issues in Mediation: Controlling Negative Cultural Myths' (1995) 1 J. of Disp. Res. 55.

37 Cobb & Rifkin, 'Practice and Paradox' (n 30) 61.

38 Kevin Gibson, Leah Thompson, and Max H. Bazerman, 'Shortcomings of Neutrality in Mediation: Solutions Based on Rationality' (1996) 12 Neg. J. 69.

39 ibid 69–70; see also Laue & Cormick (n 14) 223–225 (discussing 'proportional empowerment').

40 James Laue, 'Dispute Resolution Forum' (National Institute for Dispute Resolution, 1987) 12.

41 James H. Laue, 'The Emergence and Institutionalization of Third Party Roles in Conflict', in D.J.D. Sandole and I. Sandole-Staroste (eds), *Conflict Management and Problem Solving: Interpersonal to International Applications* (Frances Pinter and New York University Press, 1987) 20.

mediators are advocates and thus, to a degree, embody the mediator-advocate posture. Mediators advocate for a certain party, for a certain outcome, or for a specific process that will lead to resolution.[42] For Laue, though, it was less important whether mediators were defined as neutrals, and more important for the field to clarify the ethical standards of mediators and enforcement mechanisms for ethics violations.

In 1992, the Center for Dispute Settlement and The Institute for Judicial Administration co-authored the National Standards for Court-Connected Mediation Programs (National Standards). The National Standards declined to refer to mediators as neutrals, as SPIDR had done. Instead, they referenced the ethical duty of mediator 'impartiality,' defined as the duty to remain free from 'favoritism or bias.'[43] Likewise, the Model Standards of Conduct for Mediators (Model Standards) took a similar approach to the National Standards requiring withdrawal from mediators unable to maintain impartiality.[44]

Similarly, the Uniform Mediation Act (UMA), published in 2001, also spurned reference to mediator neutrality.[45] Since the UMA is intended as a resource for codifying mediator standards, its authors opined that impartiality could expose mediators to 'unwarranted' civil suits from disgruntled parties.[46] Furthermore, the UMA indicates that statutory neutrality is unworkable as it could be challenged based on recent developments in cognitive psychology related to 'hidden biases,' 'attributional distortions of judgment,' and 'inclinations that are the product of social learning and professional culturation.'[47] The UMA also preserved non-neutrality in certain instances, such as in the domestic context in which mediators may act as advocates to protect the interests of children.[48] Thus, the UMA discouraged codifying neutrality or impartiality and expressly referred to instances favoring Laue's mediator-advocate posture.[49]

---

42 ibid.

43 National Standards for Court-Connected Mediation Programs (1992) Section 8.0 Ethical Standards for Mediators.

44 Model Standards of Conduct for Mediators (2005) Standard II (C).

45 Uniform Mediation Act (2001, amended 2003) Section 9(g) Mediator impartiality. The UMA bracketed [Section 9(g)] to signal the ongoing debate regarding mediator neutrality and that it 'need not be part of a Uniform Act.'

46 ibid.

47 ibid.

48 ibid.

49 For instance, Ohio adopted the UMA and codified the requirement that mediators uphold impartiality in Ohio Revised Code Section 2710.08(G), but also specifically allowed parties to waive impartiality after disclosing conflicts of interest.

Mediation reached a new stage in its professionalization. The standards created an important baseline 'upon which further discussion can take place.'[50] The ongoing debate about mediator neutrality impacted the professional sphere. Mediation organizations, courts, and regulatory agencies became responsible for training mediators to meet the newly adopted standards of conduct. Regardless of neutrality's exclusion from many of the widely accepted standards for defining mediator conduct, most mediators continued to uphold a neutral posture as one of their defining characteristics.[51]

8.4 EVOLUTION OF MEDIATOR NEUTRALITY

In an interview for the Civil Rights Mediation Oral History Project, former CRS mediator Wallace Warfield challenged the idea that mediators should be expected to uphold a neutral posture.[52] In the 2000 interview, Warfield summarized his experiences mediating civil rights conflicts and highlighted the need for a clear sense of what it means to be neutral amid 'very complex social issues,' such as identity.[53] Warfield explained that going into a community in conflict and describing yourself as 'neutral' was unrealistic. Most city leaders would be 'smart enough to know that you weren't going to be neutral.'[54] Instead, 'they were more concerned with questions like, "Can you help us?"'[55] To Warfield, that meant acting courageously and telling parties, 'Listen, you're not really negotiating in good faith. If you really want to get something out of this issue, then you need to sort of change your pattern of negotiation.'[56] In this interview, Warfield acknowledged that owing to CRS's mandate, their mediators' very presence indicated an evaluation as to whether civil rights concerns had been implicated, compromising strict neutrality.

In his 2004 book titled, *Beyond Neutrality*, Bernard Mayer proposed that strict adherence to mediator neutrality was stunting the profession.[57] Ethical guidelines related to neutrality framed it as an aspirational intent, rather than

---

50 ibid (n 40).

51 Katherine V.W. Stone, *Private Justice: The Law of Alternative Dispute Resolution* (Foundation Press, 2000) 33, 41.

52 Civil Rights Mediation: Oral History Project, Interview with Wallace Warfield (23 May 2000) <https://www.civilrightsmediation.org/interviews/Wally_Warfield.shtml> accessed 15 November 2024.

53 ibid.

54 ibid.

55 ibid.

56 ibid.

57 Bernard Mayer, *Beyond Neutrality: Confronting the Crisis in Conflict Resolution* (Jossey-Bass, 2004).

a skill, practice, or behavior.[58] Mayer points out that mediators 'tend to rely on a neutral stance to obtain trust and credibility.'[59] But to Mayer, strict adherence to neutrality discouraged a close inspection of the ideological agenda of mediation.[60]

The roots of mediator neutrality emerged from an Anglo approach to conflict that is biased towards resolution, which he argues is related to the field's relative domination by disillusioned lawyers.[61] In many cultural settings, mediators espousing neutrality may be looked at as suspect or unserious.[62] Mayer writes that mediation holds 'underlying assumptions … about what people want in conflict [which] may reflect the class, ethnicity, and privileged status of the dominant groups in our field.'[63] Most mediators have normative, persuasive, emotional, or psychological power over the process.[64] Mayer finds that adherence to neutrality obfuscates mediation stances that are decidedly non-neutral, preventing the field from maximizing its potential.[65]

Mayer envisions a vast, relatively untouched horizon beyond neutrality, in which mediators develop trust, rapport, and credibility through more authentic expressions centered away from approaches biased toward resolution. A strict focus on resolution might foreclose opportunities to examine more fundamental or precipitating issues.[66] Alternatively, Mayer proposes that mediators

58 ibid 30.

59 ibid 17; see also Nancy Rogers and Richard Salem, *A Student's Guide to Mediation and the Law* (M. Bender, 1987) 7–39 (discussing that mediator impartiality is the basis upon which trust is built).

60 Mayer (n 57) 105.

61 ibid 6.

62 ibid 110–111 (describing the Navajo tradition of searching for common ground with the mediator at the beginning of the process).

63 ibid, 6; see also Leah Wing, 'Whither Neutrality? Mediation in the Twenty-First Century' in Mary Adams Trujillo, S.Y. Bowland, Linda James Myers, Philip M. Richards, and Beth Roy (eds), *Re-centering Culture and Knowledge in Conflict Resolution Practice* (Syracuse University Press, 2008) 93–107 (discussing mediator neutrality and compounding enfranchisement for more powerful parties); and see 'A Conversation with Hasshan Batts' in Mary Adams Trujillo, S.Y. Bowland, Linda James Myers, Philip M. Richards, and Beth Roy (eds), *Re-Centering Culture and Knowledge in Conflict Resolution Practice* (Syracuse University Press, 2008) 215–227 (addressing the dominance of 'Eurocentric' mediation models as not 'reality based' and leading communities of color to view mediation as 'a part of the system' and a 'tool of oppression'; mediators who give identity the same power as any other issue in mediation can build trust).

64 Mayer (n 57) 108.

65 ibid 108–113.

66 ibid 119–120.

pursue 'conflict engagement,' thereby promoting constructive conflict development.[67] By exploring mediation's potential beyond the confines of neutrality, Mayer opened the door for scholars and practitioners to probe the topic with renewed rigor.

A. Neutrality, Implicit Bias, and Mediation

In her seminal article discussing implicit bias, Carol Izumi sought to pin down the contours of mediator neutrality.[68] Izumi examined neutrality by weaving in the lessons from implicit bias research.[69] Echoing Cobb, Rifkin, and Mayer, Izumi described mediator neutrality as 'nebulous,' lacking a clear definition and prescriptive advice for mediators seeking to develop as neutrals.[70] Izumi argues that implicit biases will thwart even the most well-intentioned mediator from achieving a neutral stance. Rather than deter mediators from aspiring to an unachievable neutral posture, Izumi challenges mediators to examine their own implicit biases and develop skills that will, in turn, contribute to their ability to act as neutrals.

Izumi deconstructed neutrality, first finding that it exists on a sliding scale in which mediators act 'more' or 'less' neutral, instead of 'neutral' or 'not neutral.' Digging deeper, Izumi identified that neutrality consists of internal and external components which intersect with bias reduction strategies. Internal neutrality is the 'state of being aware of the operation of biases towards the disputants and working to minimize it.'[71] While external neutrality consists of 'freedom from bias or favoritism in the way the mediation is conducted.'[72]

Izumi finds that internal neutrality is accomplished by 'minimizing the operation of biased mental processes'[73] through 'intention, attention, and effort.'[74] Offering three practical suggestions, Izumi encourages mediators to improve internal neutrality by: (1) reflecting on and acknowledging individual

67 ibid 3, 158–178.

68 Izumi (n 2).

69 ibid 88 (citing to Anthony G. Greenwald & Linda Hamilton Krieger 'Implicit Bias: Scientific Foundations' (2006) 94 Cal. L. Rev. 945, 954–55 (defining implicit bias as unconscious mental processes that inform stereotyping and the formation of judgments, while motivating actions).

70 Izumi (n 2) 77.

71 ibid 122.

72 ibid.

73 ibid 141.

74 ibid (citing Patricia G. Devine 'Stereotypes and Prejudice: Their Automatic and Controlled Components' (1989) 56 J. Personality & Soc. Psych. 5, 16).

biases (e.g. bias transparency, self-correction, and real-time adjustments);[75] (2) discussing salient racial or cultural dynamics (e.g. practice addressing identity and lived experience in the course of the mediation);[76] and (3) regularly incorporating mindfulness mediation (e.g. bringing active attention to thoughts, feelings and bodily sensations under stressful conditions).[77]

External neutrality is achieved by 'conducting an outwardly even process, eliminating conflicts of interest that may arise from proprietary, monetary, relational, and other interests, and abstaining from advocating or pressing for a particular outcome.'[78] Izumi directs that mediators can develop their external neutrality by incorporating five distinct considerations into their practice: (1) mindful process management and mediator communication (e.g. eliminating maneuvers that are designed to influence outcomes);[79] (2) sensitivity and humility about language, narratives, and cultural myths (e.g. examination of metaphors and euphemisms);[80] (3) conscious awareness to reflexivity and role play for exposure to other lived experiences (e.g. attention to how process sequencing impacts narrative building);[81] (4) a co-mediation model with an effort to match the mediators' and parties' identities;[82] and (5) a transformative approach focused on procedural justice (e.g. maximizing party self-determination by eliminating agreement bias).[83]

This groundbreaking article filled gaps with prescriptive advice for mediators seeking to uphold a neutral stance and counteract implicit biases. Izumi's neutrality assessment criteria and methods for reflective practice played a crucial role in advancing mediator neutrality beyond theory and into practice. Yet the debate over mediator neutrality remained unsettled.

---

75 Izumi (n 2) 141–146.

76 ibid 146–151.

77 ibid 151–152.

78 ibid 123.

79 ibid 123–125.

80 ibid 126–131.

81 ibid 131–136 (quoting Susan Douglas 'Questions of Mediator Neutrality and Researcher Objectivity:

Examining Reflexivity as a Response' (2009) 20 Aus. Disp. Res. J. 56, 65 (defining reflexivity as 'a rejection of mediator neutrality' and 'an acknowledgement of the impact of mediator subjectivity and a means of addressing that subjectivity in practice')).

82 Izumi (n 2) 136–139.

83 ibid 139–141.

B. The Neutrality Debate: Part II

In 2011, 30 years after the initial exchange between Stulberg and Susskind, Marquette Law School organized a panel discussion on neutrality between the pair and Mayer. As the field grew, each of their approaches to mediator neutrality gained support.

During the panel discussion, Susskind expanded his vision of the mediator-advocate, pointing out how various conflicts ranging from human rights to corporate litigation operate similarly.[84] Susskind also revised the elements of a quality mediated outcome, for which mediators are accountable, to include fairness, efficiency, stability, and *wisdom*.[85] The added element of wisdom directs mediators to focus their efforts on producing high-quality outcomes by pushing parties to make fully informed decisions.[86]

Mediators regularly proselytize that a good process produces a good outcome, although mediators decline to define the components of a good outcome.[87] For Susskind, this is unacceptable and raises the question, 'how can I justify people participating in a mediation process unless I can make a case that the process I am suggesting has a chance of producing good outcome?'[88] Susskind concludes that mediators should redirect parties away from suboptimal outcomes and back towards outcomes that promote fairness, efficiency, stability, and wisdom.

Replying, Stulberg reiterated his framework of mediation as a 'justice event,'[89] analogizing the different perspectives on neutrality to procedural justice.[90] Stulberg finds that Susskind's vision of procedural justice in mediation is not so far off from his own, with two important exceptions. First, Stulberg counters Susskind's proposition that mediators account for inefficient or low-quality outcomes.[91] To Stulberg, mediators are primarily process focused and not necessarily substance experts capable of insuring against issues with

84 Bernard Mayer, Joseph B. Stulberg, Lawrence Susskind, and John Lande, 'Panel Discussion – Core Values of Dispute Resolution: Is Neutrality Necessary?' (2012) 95 Marq. L. Rev. 805, 809.

85 ibid 816.

86 ibid 817.

87 ibid 816.

88 ibid 817.

89 Joseph B. Stulberg, 'Must a Mediator Be Neutral? You'd Better Believe It!' (2012) 95 Marq. L. Rev 829, 830–833 (describing mediation as a process of promoting and displaying justice by 'non-violently securing or advancing individual dignity and freedom').

90 ibid 844–848.

91 Mayer, Stulberg, Susskind, and Lande (n 84) 819.

Pareto-optimality or spillover across time and space.[92] Second, Stulberg argues against Susskind's suggestion that mediators abandon neutrality to produce a 'wise' outcome.[93] From Stulberg's perspective, entrusting mediators to produce wise outcomes corrodes mediation's commitment to democratic principles, like self-determination.[94]

Adding a new flavor to the debate, Mayer presented neutrality as a source of identity representing a mediator's fundamental purpose, knowledge base, and social impact.[95] Mediation is powerful both as an agent of social change and social control.[96] However, neutrality may find natural alignment with powerful parties and dominant perspectives.[97] Through this framing, Mayer asserts that mediator neutrality holds serious social and political implications which might reinforce existing power structures.[98]

Mayer weaves in examples from environmental and family mediation, supporting the notion that process transparency preserves party autonomy for non-neutral mediators.[99] Mayer might ask mediators to consider the following: do I claim to be neutral? If yes, what does that mean and how will it change the process? If no, why not and what alternative postures might the parties accept? A mediator who is self-aware and able to clearly articulate their purpose and posture will generate the best process regardless of neutrality.[100]

While the intervening years did not produce consensus, the second debate illuminated important considerations for the next wave of scholars examining mediator neutrality.

---

92 Stulberg (n 89) 847–848 (citing Susskind (n 19) 17 (discussing that Pareto-optimal issues arise when groups struggle to identify avenues for providing mutual benefit in distributing resources or outcomes)).

93 Mayer, Stulberg, Susskind, and Lande (n 84) 818.

94 Stulberg (n 89) 848.

95 Bernie Mayer, 'What We Talk About When We Talk About Neutrality: A Commentary on the Susskind-Stulberg Debate' (2012) 95 Marq. L. Rev. 859.

96 ibid 870.

97 ibid 870.

98 ibid 868–870.

99 Mayer, Stulberg, Susskind, and Lande (n 84) 812–816.

100 ibid 819–820.

8.5 STRUCTURAL RACISM, COLORBLINDNESS, AND MEDIATOR NEUTRALITY

Structural racism is pervasive in American institutions.[101] The historical narrative of the American legal system has pernicious roots in the Three-Fifths Compromise, chattel slavery, Jim Crow laws, mass incarceration, the attack on civil rights victories, and implicit and explicit bias.[102] As Stulberg suggests, mediation is a justice event first and foremost.[103] Mediation, though, emerging as an alternative to the courts, replicated many of the same structural inequities based on race, gender identity, and sexual orientation, among other inalienable qualities targeted for prejudice and discrimination.[104]

In a 2017 article, Izumi argued that implicit bias manifests in mediation in four main ways: in-group bias;[105] ascribing negative traits to people of color;[106] racial anxiety;[107] and normative ambiguity allowing mediators to rationalize their biases.[108] Izumi concluded that '[n]eutrality in practice is illusory because

---

101 Frank Dukes and Selena Cozart, 'Rethinking Systems Design for Racial Justice & Equity: "We Don't Want Any of That Neutrality" and Other Lessons from Mediating Race and Equity' (2023) 38 Oh. St. J. on Dis. Res. 341 (citing Apoorva Mandavilli, 'Medical Journals Blind to Racism as Health Crisis, Critics Say' (N.Y. Times, 2 June 2021)); see generally Ibram X. Kendi, *Stamped from the Beginning: The Definitive History of Racist Ideas in America* (Nation Books 2016).

102 See generally Michelle Alexander, *The New Jim Crow: Mass Incarceration in the Age of Colorblindness* (New Press, 2020); see also, Julian Maxwell Hayter, 'Civil rights legislation sparked powerful backlash that's still shaping American politics' (PBS, 16 February 2023) <https://www.pbs.org/wnet/preserving-democracy/2023/02/16/civil-rights-legislation-sparked-powerful-backlash-thats-still-shaping-american-politics/> accessed 15 November 2024.

103 Stulberg (n 89) 830–833.

104 Wing (n 63).

105 Carol Izumi, 'Implicit Bias and Prejudice in Mediation' (2017) 70 SMU L. Rev. 681, 687 (discussing spontaneous mediator actions, such as eye contact, seating and room arrangement, blinking, smiling, and facial expressions, which all have the potential to contribute to real or perceived bias, disadvantaging people who are not identified with the in-group).

106 ibid 687.

107 ibid 688 (explaining that racial anxiety manifests in people of color fearing discrimination and hostile treatment, while 'white individuals may fear being perceived as racist and being treated with distrust').

108 ibid 689–90 (explaining that mediation operates with unclear normative expectations for appropriate behavior, which allows discriminatory actions to be attributed to neutrality).

of the operation of implicit bias.'[109] Neutral mediators who fail to account for implicit bias reinforce structural racism leading to less favorable outcomes for disadvantaged parties.[110]

Critiques of mediator neutrality emerged from the racial justice movement. On May 25, 2020, Minneapolis, Minnesota police officers murdered George Floyd, a Black man allegedly in possession of a counterfeit $20 bill. Whitney Benns was interviewed by Dispute Resolution Magazine in October 2020. Her remarks reinvigorated scholarship on mediator neutrality by framing it as a tool for protecting existing 'power paradigms.'[111] Describing her training, Benns learned that 'you ought to be "neutral" if you are going to be helpful to the parties.'[112] Echoing Warfield, Benns disagreed:

> Spoiler alert: I think that's mostly bullshit. You are always implicated in the substantive outcome and impact – period. Instead, we need to ask: how am I connected to this conflict? In what ways am I connected to these parties? And what is that going to mean about how I show up and am accountable to this process and these people?[113]

Striking a similar chord, co-mediators Frank Dukes and Selina Cozart recounted their reminders to parties that they were neutral facilitators, to which one mediation party exclaimed, 'we don't want any of that neutrality!'[114] Dukes and Cozart identify that the source of this party's disdain for neutrality stemmed from white supremacy culture, a pervasive, enduring, and often covert feature of American society.[115] As a helpful comparison, Dukes and Cozart liken white supremacy culture to an addiction and breaking the addiction

---

109 ibid 685.

110 ibid 691 (recommending extensive training in the elimination of bias for mediators, citing that 1 hour is vastly insufficient); see e.g. David Hoffman & Helen Winter, 'Follow the Science: Proven Strategies for reducing Unconscious Bias' (2022) 28 Harv. Neg. L. Rev. 1.

111 Alonzo Emery, 'A Conversation with Whitney Benns, Educator, Facilitator, and Emotional Labor Organizer' (4 June 2021) 27 Dispute Resolution Magazine.

112 ibid 14.

113 ibid.

114 Dukes and Cozart (n 101) 363.

115 ibid 363 (citing Tema Okun, White Supremacy Culture, 'Dismantling Racism: White Supremacy Culture' (1999) <https://www.whitesupremacyculture.info/uploads/4/3/5/7/43579015/okun_-_whitesup_culture.pdf> accessed on 15 November 2024 (defining white supremacy culture as the social construct which 'assigns value and roles to human beings based on their proximity to the standard of whiteness')).

requires engaging in conflict.[116] Building on Mayer's theory of 'constructive conflict engagement,' Dukes and Cozart stress that mediators should not be neutral as to whether an outcome reinforces white supremacy culture and prolongs or adds harm.[117]

Sharon Press and Ellen Deason identify neutrality and colorblindness as sharing an ideological approach to engaging with a multicultural society.[118] They quote Layla Saad, '[c]olorblindness is a particularly insidious way for people with white privilege to pretend that their privilege is fictitious.'[119] Colorblindness manifests in neutral mediators by: (1) controlling and reconstructing the dominant narrative;[120] (2) reinforcing implicit stereotypes;[121] (3) providing cover for white silence;[122] and (4) shrouding the limitations of Western mediation styles.[123] Deason and Press point to court-connected mediation programs and the legal profession more broadly, as the gatekeepers of mediation.[124] Echoing Susskind's argument that mediation should offer parties a better alternative to the courts, Press and Deason admonish against accepting that the 'white way of doing things' is the right way of doing things.[125]

In a 2023 article, Isabelle Gunning challenged the dispute resolution community to commit to social justice by abolishing structural racism in mediation.[126] Gunning proposes that mediators generate norms through 'justice from below,' seeking prosocial outcomes for individuals and communities.[127] In a footnote, Gunning posits that 'mediators need to move in conscious ways towards how trust is actually built rather than relying solely on unexamined notions of neutrality and impartiality to ensure that we as mediators can be

---

116 Dukes and Cozart (n 101) 362.

117 ibid 364.

118 Sharon Press and Ellen E. Deason, 'Mediation: Embedded Assumptions of Whiteness?' (2021) Faculty Scholarship, 453 (citing Layla F. Saad, *Me and White Supremacy: Combat Racism, Change the World, and Become a Good Ancestor* (Sourcebooks 2020) (defining colorblindness as the idea that one does not see color or notice race)).

119 Saad (n 118) 80.

120 Press and Deason (n 118) 466–70.

121 ibid 470–73.

122 ibid 473–477.

123 ibid 477–481.

124 ibid 485.

125 ibid 498 (citing Trina Grillo, 'The Mediation Alternative: Process Dangers for Women' (1991) 100 YALE L.J. 1545, 1579.

126 Isabelle Gunning, 'Justice for All in Mediation: What the Pandemic, Racial Justice Movement, and the Recognition of Structural Racism Calls us to do as Mediators' (2022) 68 Was. U. J.L. & Pol'y 36.

127 ibid 53–54.

"fair" and "just" to all comers.'[128] Gunning concludes by challenging mediators to weigh their attachment to neutrality against their commitment to values of anti-racism and social justice.[129] Examining neutrality through the lens of the 2020 racial justice movement exposed the limitations of absolute and strict adherence to mediator neutrality.

8.6 CONCLUSION: THE FUTURE OF NEUTRALITY IN MEDIATION

Mediators and scholars are committed to exploring the possibilities of mediation beyond neutrality. Joined by co-author Jacqueline Font-Guzman, Mayer expanded upon the case for pursuing constructive conflict engagement.[130] Mayer and Font-Guzman argue that neutrality contributes to conflict avoidance, whereas constructively expanding conflict enhances social cohesion through disrupting avoidant tendencies.[131] They relate mediator neutrality, impartiality, and independence to the 'devil's bargain we make to maintain our privileged position in exchange for supporting the status quo.'[132] Meanwhile parties really want their mediator to be a source of 'fairness, transparency, competence, moral clarity, and authenticity … By substituting neutrality for a commitment to promoting justice and equality, we fall into the neutrality trap.'[133]

The Neutrality Trap constructs a vision of mediation separate from neutrality, instead pursuing social cohesion through constructive conflict engagement – 'good trouble, necessary trouble.'[134] In August 2022, Mayer and Font-Guzman engaged in a three-part written exchange with Heidi and Guy Burgess.[135] The

---

128 ibid 56 in fn 66 (citing Fania E. Davis, *The Little Book of Race and Restorative Justice: Black Lives, Healing and US Social Transformation* (Good Books 2019) 19 (examining the role that restorative justice can play in influencing mediators to confront white supremacy culture)).

129 Gunning (126) 47 (quoting Robert Baruch Bush, 'Mediation and Social Justice: Risks and Opportunities' (2012) 27 OH. St. J. on Disp. Res. 1, 33 ('the use of mediation may inevitably undermine the goal of social justice')).

130 Bernard S. Mayer and Jacqueline Font-Guzman, *The Neutrality Trap: Disrupting and Connecting for Social Change* (Wiley 2022).

131 ibid 112–119.

132 ibid 30.

133 ibid.

134 ibid 169.

135 Guy Burgess and Heidi Burgess, 'Introducing a Discussion with Bernie Mayer and Jackie Font-Guzmán about Hyper-Polarization, Neutrality, and Oppression' (Beyond Intractability, 24 August 2022) <https://www.beyondintractability.org/crq-bi-hyper-polarization-discussion/mayer-font-discussion-intro>

Burgesses assert that neutrality can assuage polarization, while Font-Guzman and Mayer push back by framing neutrality as a driver of polarization. The group concludes that fundamental differences in worldview contribute to their respective perspectives on neutrality.

The DC Mediation & Dispute Resolution Institute organized a year-end conference themed Neutrality Trap: The Danger of Staying Silent in December 2023. Kenneth Cloke delivered the keynote address in which he framed neutrality as a defense against 'the vicarious trauma of the conflict resolver.'[136] Cloke analogized neutrality to the place 'we go in order to emotionally retreat, to compartmentalize our pain, to create a kind of shield made out of apathy, avoidance, and indifference.'[137] When mediators are met with messy, complex, and heart-wrenching pain or emotional expression, neutrality 'saps the soul, weakens the spirit, it strips of joy. It confines us to an isolated little room far from the messy, complex, upsetting chaos of human pain and suffering. But equally far from intimacy, caring, emotional intelligence, moral responsibility, love, genuine reconciliation, and what I think of as the magic of mediation.'[138]

The Magic in Mediation is the title of Cloke's 2023 book which explores the untapped power of mediation through an interdisciplinary lens.[139] Cloke explains that mediation is a way of existing in and engaging with the world. He challenges mediators to express genuine empathy for the people in conflict, validate their emotional experiences, and hold space for parties to co-create a shared vision for the future.

Gunning, Press, and Deason continue to analyze issues related to mediation, race, power, and neutrality. Their forthcoming articles look back at US history

---

accessed 25 October 2024; Jacqueline N. Font-Guzman and Bernard Mayer, 'The False Flag of Hyper-Polarization: A Response to Guy and Heidi Burgess' Critique of The Neutrality Trap' (Beyond Intractability, 24 August 2022) <https://www.beyondintractability.org/crq-bi-hyper-polarization-discussion/font-mayer-post1> accessed 25 October 2024; Heidi Burgess and Guy Burgess, 'Not a False Flag, a More Effective Strategy for Fighting Oppression: the Burgesses Respond to Jackie Font-Guzmán and Bernie Mayer' (Beyond Intractability, 26 August 2024) <https://www.beyondintractability.org/crq-bi-hyper-polarization-discussion/burgess-elephant> accessed 25 October 2024; (the Burgesses elevate hyperpolarization in the US as the primary reason for preserving neutrality. Mayer and Font-Guzman explain that dismantling oppression guides their approach).

[136] Kenneth Cloke, 'Neutrality Trap: The Danger of Staying Silent – Part 1' (End-of-year virtual conference, December 2023) <https://www.youtube.com/watch?v=3dXrBvHR-qM> accessed 25 October 2024.

[137] ibid.

[138] ibid.

[139] Kenneth Cloke, The Magic in Mediation: A Search for Symmetries, Metaphors and Scale-Free Practices (Goodmedia Press, 2023).

and the concept of neutrality and impartiality, examine current understandings of neutrality and impartiality, and propose a theoretical construct for neutrality with implications for mediators. Their ongoing focus on countering racism in mediation promises to continue expanding mediators' awareness of the context in which they intervene.

Before neutrality was fully articulated, it was used as a rhetorical exercise in striving towards objectivity. Emerging from roots in labor and civil rights disputes, mediator neutrality serves as an important practical tool for building trust. As mediation developed and professionalized, neutrality lost some luster. Social justice values such as equity and anti-racism challenged the integrity of maintaining a neutral posture. A common Palestinian protest sign reads, 'I hate a neutral a** b****,' harkening back to Black congressional leaders' concerns that mediation carries negative associations for groups without proximity to power.[140] As Benns notes, 'I don't want someone "neutral" as to whether my life and the lives of people who look like me and the people I am in solidarity with are deserving of dignity and preservation … You are picking a side. And there is absolutely nothing neutral about that.'[141] Viewing mediation through a social justice lens, the process shifts from a resolution-driven, facilitated dialogue among players invited to 'the table' to a change-driven approach of conflict engagement, narrative construction, and reflexivity.

Since their inception, institutions and court-connected programs engaged in the debates over the necessity of mediator neutrality. Still, most court-connected programs replicate and recommit to some form of neutrality.[142] Guidance, assessment, and training on mediator neutrality remain inconsistent and lack the detail necessary to promote mediator development.[143]

Questions about mediator neutrality persist and call for deeper consideration.[144] Mediators examining their own posture might reflect on the following:

140 A Google search of the phrase, without censure, will yield dozens of results, as well as t-shirts with the phrase printed on the front.

141 Emery (n 111) 17.

142 See e.g. Paul Haire, 'Considerations of Neutrality and Impartiality in ADR' (Nevada Lawyer April 2017) 24 (concluding that mediators create trust in their process by demonstrating a clear understanding of their neutral posture); see also Press and Deason (n 118) 481 (finding only one US court-connected mediation program administering culturally defined mediation approaches).

143 Ellen Waldman, 'Values, Models, and Codes' in Ellen Waldman (ed.) *Mediation Ethics: Cases and Commentaries* (Jossey-Bass, 2011) 10–16.

144 See Alfini, James J., et al., *Mediation in an Evolving World: Theory and Practice. United States* (Carolina Academic Press, 2024) (Chapters 7 and 8 provide a deeper exploration of race, justice, power, and mediator neutrality).

- In what ways can mediators be accountable for producing quality outcomes, as defined by Susskind?
- Is neutrality akin to colorblindness? Specifically, how might mediator neutrality play a role in upholding white supremacy culture?
- Can mediators seeking to uphold a neutral posture effectively incorporate racial justice, anti-racism, and equity considerations into their process?
- In which contexts might it be advantageous for mediators to employ a neutral or non-neutral posture?
- In trust-building, are authenticity and transparency sufficient replacements for a neutral posture?

Considerations for administrators of court-connected programs and professional organizations include:

- In what ways do lawyers and professional organizations gatekeep mediation?
- Identify how a mediation program's emphasis on neutrality could reinforce structural inequity.
- How can courts and professional organizations incorporate non-neutral mediation approaches?
- How will mediator training programs incorporate prescriptive advice and exercises to instruct and assess neutral and non-neutral postures?
- Will various jurisdictions adopt mediation legislation that permits both neutral and non-neutral mediators?

9. The Singapore Convention on Mediation: Five years on

Bryan Clark and Viktoriia Hamaiunova

9.1 INTRODUCTION

The United Nations Convention on International Settlement Agreements Resulting from Mediation 2018 ('The Singapore Convention on Mediation', hereinafter 'Convention') is a significant multilateral treaty in the field of international commercial mediation. After some four years in gestation, in December 2018, the United Nations General Assembly passed a resolution to adopt the Convention. The Convention was formally signed in Singapore on 7 September 2019 by 46 countries (including the USA and China). It has been widely heralded as a game changer that has the potential to boost the use of mediation in the international commercial space significantly by underpinning the practice with a unified form of settlement enforcement across jurisdictions. There has been a plethora of writing about the Convention. Much of this commentary has been very positive.[1] In short, the dominant view that emerges from the literature is that the Convention takes significant steps in fixing the 'problem' of the lack of enforceability in cross-border, commercial mediated outcomes while also lending the process greater publicity and credibility. Notwithstanding this positive appraisal, there have been some dissenting voices focusing on the lack of practical need for the Convention, drafting

[1] For example, see Eunice Chua, 'The Singapore Convention on Mediation – a Brighter Future for Asian Dispute Resolution' (2019) 9 Asian Journal of International Law 195; Gary Birnberg, 'Singapore Convention brings big Changes for Litigators and Arbitrators' (JAMS, 5 August 2019); Haris Meidanis, 'International Enforcement of Mediated Settlements: Two and a Half Models – why and how to Enforce Internationally Mediated Settlement Agreements' (2019) 85(1) Arbitration (London) 49; Robert Butlien, 'The Singapore Convention on Mediation: A Brave New World for International Commercial Mediation' (2020), 46 Brook J Int'l L 183.

concerns that might limit its effectiveness and potential unintended consequences arising from its implementation.[2]

Against this backdrop, this chapter reflects on the first five years of the Convention.[3] We briefly examine the Convention's underlying basis and main provisions before reviewing its uptake in terms of both States' signing of the Convention and how ratification has led to the enshrinement of its provisions into domestic systems. We are interested in whether there has been a growth in international commercial mediation (and other forms of mediation) over the past five years and to what extent such developments can be tied to the Convention. Looking to its future impact, we discuss some potential problems in the Convention's drafting that may militate against its impact and some variation in implementation that we are already seeing in different domestic regimes that have ratified the Convention as well as potential dangers arising from its implementation. In all of this, we recognise that the Convention is still in its infancy and its effects remain to be gauged as it is further cemented into the international commercial mediation arena. In part, this chapter draws on recent empirical evidence regarding the utility of the Convention conducted by one of the authors drawn from interviews with international commercial mediators.[4]

9.2 THE TERMS OF THE CONVENTION

9.2.1 Definitional Issues

Prior to examining its provisions, we note that the Convention, as a product of intensive political discussion, is inevitably an instrument of compromise.

[2] Bryan Clark and Tania Sourdin, 'The Singapore Convention: A Solution in Search of a Problem?' (2020) 71(3) Northern Ireland Legal Quarterly 2; Sherby & Co., Advs., The Singapore Convention: The Emperor's New Clothes of International Dispute Resolution, https://www.sherby.co.il/page/the-singapore-convention-theemperors-new-clothes-of-international-dispute-resolution/; David J Stute, 'The Singapore Convention: Not Much There There' (2021) 3(1) Journal of the Institute of Transnational Arbitration 32–58; Migle Zukauskaite, 'Enforcement of Mediated Settlement Agreements' (2019) 111 Teise 205, 211–214; Masood Ahmed, 'Reflections on the UNCITRAL Convention on the Enforcement of Mediation Settlement Agreements and Model Law' (2019) Lloyd's Maritime and Commercial Law Quarterly 259.

[3] Since its signing in Singapore.

[4] For full findings see B. Clark and T. Sourdin, 'Views from the Coal Face: the Development of International Commercial Mediation', (2025) 76(2) Northern Ireland Legal Quarterly 277–309.

The 2018 United Nations General Assembly Resolution emphasised the need for 'the adoption of a convention … that is acceptable to States *with different legal, social and economic systems*'.[5] This approach is reflected in the drafting which leaves a range of issues couched in flexible language. It is also important to note that the Convention applies in a direct sense at least to only a relatively small sliver of dispute resolution activities – settlement agreements arising from international commercial mediation.[6] In terms of how such agreements are defined, Article 1 provides that the Convention applies 'to an agreement resulting from mediation and concluded in writing by parties to resolve a commercial dispute ("settlement agreement") which, at the time of its conclusion, is international'. Article 1 further links the definition of 'international' to the settlement agreement (rather than the subject of the dispute). So for an agreement to be international: '(a) At least two parties to the settlement agreement have their places of business in different States; or (b) The State in which the parties to the settlement agreement have their places of business is different from either (i) The State in which a substantial part of the obligations under the settlement agreement is performed; or (ii) The State which the subject matter of the settlement agreement is most closely connected.'

The term 'commercial' is not defined in the Convention. Reference to this expression can be found, however, in Article 1 of the revised Model Law where 'commercial' is widely defined as 'matters arising from all relationships of a commercial nature, whether contractual or not', including but not limited to, 'any trade transaction for the supply or exchange of goods or services; distribution agreement; commercial representation or agency; factoring; leasing; construction of works, consulting; engineering; licensing; investment; financing; banking; insurance; exploitation agreement or concession; joint venture and other forms of industrial or business cooperation; carriage of goods or passengers by air, sea, rail, or road'.[7] It has been noted by Ferz and Tsuvina, however, that this definition would not be binding in States that have not adopted the Model Law.[8] Nonetheless, they point to general acceptance of a

---

5 Resolution A/RES/73/198, 1 https://documents-dds-ny.un.org/doc/UNDOC/GEN/N18/456/53/PDF/N1845653.pdf?OpenElement.

6 Although, as we note below, it may have wider impacts on the mediation field.

7 UNCITRAL Model Law on International Commercial Mediation and International Settlement Agreements Resulting from Mediation (2018) available at UNCITRAL Model Law on International Commercial Mediation and International Settlement Agreements Resulting from Mediation with Guide to Enactment and Use (2018).

8 S. Ferz and T. Tsuvina, 'The Singapore Convention on Mediation: National Implementation Practices and EU Prospects' in O. Quirico and K. Williams (eds)

wide definition for the term 'commercial' in this setting and in particular, one that would encompass investor–state disputes (as suggested by the fact that the Convention includes the possibility of signatories determining that its terms shall not apply to States or State entities).[9]

Despite the potentially wide application of the term 'commercial', certain disputes are specifically excluded from the scope of the Convention. According to Article 1(2), the Convention does not apply to settlement agreements '(a) Concluded to resolve a dispute arising from transactions engaged in by one of the parties ... for personal, family or household purposes; (b) Relating to family, inheritance or employment law.' Although some commentators have lamented the exclusion of such dispute areas as an opportunity lost,[10] these matters were specifically excluded given the sensitivities that might surround their inclusion, given the different cultural norms that apply to these issues across signatory States that might impact enforcement. Furthermore, Article 1(3)(a) provides that the Convention shall not apply to settlement agreements: '(i) That have been approved by a court or concluded in the course of proceedings before a court; and (ii) That are enforceable as a judgement in the State of the court.' Similarly, Article 1(3)(b) excludes 'Settlement agreements that have been recorded and enforceable as an arbitral award.' Again, definitional questions arise here. There remains some uncertainty, for example, as to the extent that agreements reached in the shadow of ongoing litigation will be covered by the Convention.[11]

Bilateral negotiated agreements are excluded from the Convention. Settlements must arise from mediation. The term 'mediation' is afforded a wide definition to encapsulate a range of processes, irrespective of the domestic term used to describe them, in which 'parties attempt to reach an amicable settlement of their dispute with the assistance of a third person ... lacking the authority to impose a solution upon the parties'.[12] Any settlement agreement must be recorded in writing. Under Article 2(2), this is defined as being recorded in 'any form', specifically encompassing an agreement found in

---

The European Union and the Evolving Architectures of International Economic Agreements (2023, Singapore: Springer) at 307.

[9] Ibid at 307–308. Reservations are discussed below at para 9.2.3.

[10] See, for example, Migle Zukauskaite, 'Enforcement of Mediated Settlement Agreements' (2019) 111 Teise 205, 211–214.

[11] See for example the discussion of interaction with 'Tomlin Orders' in the England and Wales civil justice system in the UK consultation response to the Singapore Convention: Ministry of Justice, *Government response to the Consultation on the United Nations Convention on International Settlement Agreements Resulting from Mediation* (New York 2018) at paras 6.16, 6.17.

[12] Article 2(3).

'electronic communication' such as email correspondence. A party seeking to rely on the mediated agreement must also evidence its existence. Thus, the agreement must be signed by the parties.[13] There must also be proof that the agreement stemmed from mediation. This can be achieved in accordance with Article 4(1)(b) by: (i) the mediator's signature on the settlement agreement; (ii) a document signed by the mediator indicating that the mediation was carried out; (iii) an attestation by the institution that administered the mediation; or (iv) in the absence of (i), (ii) or (iii), any other evidence acceptable to the competent authority. Article 4(2) makes special provision meeting the requirements for signature in respect of electronic communication. One issue that remains unclear is how settlements reached at some point after the cessation of formal mediation (as is not uncommon) are treated under the Convention. Recent research has found mediation in this space developing into a more fluid, interactive process commonly encompassing post-mediation discussions beyond the main mediation event, which may help ensure flexibility in terms of when agreements are deemed to have arisen from mediation.[14]

9.2.2 Grounds for Refusal of Relief

Article 5 provides for a range of grounds under which the enforceability of mediated agreements may be challenged. Some of these grounds are familiar and follow those found in the New York Convention. By dint of Article 5(1), these include: incapacity; when the agreement is null and void, inoperative, or incapable of being performed; that the agreement is not binding or not final according to its terms; that it has been subsequently modified; that the obligations have been performed or are not clear or comprehensible; and that relief would be contrary to the terms of the settlement agreement.[15] Under Article 5(2), exceptions are also provided for where granting relief would be contrary to public policy, or the subject matter is not capable of settlement by mediation of the competent authority. These grounds for refusing relief echo challenges faced by states with weak sovereignty, where internal groups may undermine international agreements,[16] potentially compromising the Singapore Convention's effectiveness in such contexts. In terms of the public

---

[13] Article 4(1)(a).

[14] B. Clark and T. Sourdin, 'Necessity the Mother of Invention? International Commercial Mediators' Views on Online Mediation' (2024) Mediation Theory and Practice 8(1), 53–70.

[15] For example, where the parties specifically exclude enforcement under the Convention in their settlement agreement.

[16] See Wolford, S. and Rider, T.J., *Weak Sovereignty and Interstate War. International Theory*, 1–25 (2024, Cambridge University Press).

policy exceptions, which may of course vary across different regimes in which enforcement may be sought, it is expected that given the commercial focus of the Convention, these caveats may in practice be narrow.

Further grounds of relief pertain to the conduct of the mediator. Specifically, challenges may be brought where there has been either a 'serious breach of mediator standards'[17] or 'a failure by the mediator to disclose to parties circumstances that raise justifiable doubts as to the mediator's impartiality or independence'.[18] These exceptions have been the subject of much academic debate and raise a range of uncertainties. We discuss these issues below at section 9.6.

9.2.3 Reservations

Two possible reservations are included in Article 8. States may stipulate that the Convention shall apply 'only to the extent that the parties to the settlement agreement have agreed to the application of the Convention'.[19] Signatories may also stipulate that the Convention shall not apply to government agencies or persons acting on behalf of such agencies.[20] These are controversial issues that we discuss below at section 9.5.2.

9.2.4 Operational Issues

In terms of providing enforceability of mediated settlement agreements, the Convention operates as both 'sword' and 'shield'. Thus, under Article 3(1) the terms of the Convention may be used as a way in which to enforce mediated outcomes. By dint of Article 3(2) the Convention may be used as a means of resisting legal action by another on the basis that the dispute has already been resolved.

Unusually, the Convention is non-reciprocal in nature. Mediated agreements under the Convention may be enforced in any State in which the treaty is in force, regardless of the country of origin, which may be seen as helpful in expanding its reach in its early days. There is no requirement for a review of the settlement agreement in the country of origin. Relatedly, no attempt is made to define the 'seat' of the mediation. For practical reasons, this is understandable given that it may be hard to identify a seat, especially if the

---

17 Article 5(e).
18 Article 5(f).
19 Article 8(1)(b).
20 Article 8(1)(a).

mediation takes place online, although it may give rise to complications in determining relevant rules for refusing relief in Article 5.[21]

9.3 THE UNDERLYING RATIONALE FOR THE CONVENTION

Undoubtedly, prior to the introduction of the Convention, there was a widespread view suggesting a potential problem with the enforceability of international mediation settlement agreements. In particular, empirical evidence suggested the need for an instrument that would do for mediation what the New York Convention did for international commercial arbitration.[22] The voracity of this evidence has been questioned, however, on the basis that this sentiment may arise largely from lawyers and relatively uninformed parties, that such views do not reflect the experience of the durability of mediated settlements on the ground, that it conflates the consensual nature of mediation with adjudicative processes such as arbitration, and that there may be significant regional differences.[23]

More recent empirical research into the views and experiences of international commercial mediators around party adherence to mediated outcomes and the potential impact of the Convention has added to the literature base. These findings show little evidence that the problem that the Convention seeks to fix is a real one, at least in the eyes of mediators who generally reported that non-enforcement of settlements brokered is a very rare occurrence in their experience.[24] The mediators pointed to the fact that, unlike the case with imposed court judgments and arbitral awards, in their experience parties were far less likely to depart from agreements reached in mediation. In terms of why this was the case, interviewees pointed to the voluntary nature of settlement formation and the ownership that parties might experience in respect of those agreements. They also referenced the internal terms of settlements, including the use of securities and performance bonds, which often rendered them self-enforcing. Additionally, some mediators also pointed to the relative ease

---

[21] Discussed at para 9.6.1.

[22] Including S.I. Strong, 'Realizing Rationality: An Empirical Assessment of International Commercial Mediation' [2016] 73 Washington and Lee Law Review 1973; David Weiss and Michael Griffiths, 'Report on International Mediation and Enforcement Mechanisms' (Institute for Dispute Resolution IDR (NJCU) School of Business, UNCITRAL Working Group II (Dispute Settlement) 2017); Herbert Smith Freehills and PWC, 'Global Pound Conference Series: Global Trends and Regional Differences' (Global Pound Conference Series 2018).

[23] Clark and Sourdin *supra* n. 2.

[24] Clark and Sourdin *supra* n. 2.

of using 'med-arb' approaches, which would allow the parties to register their agreement as a consent award and take advantage of the framework provided by the New York Convention. Mediators also pointed to the important role of the mediator in ensuring that agreements reached are realistic and durable.

Notwithstanding this, we should recall other, more general potential impacts of the new Convention. As referenced in the discussions leading up to the Convention's formulation,[25] it was acknowledged that the Convention might not be used in practice that much, but its inception would provide confidence for potential users that enforcement could be expedited if necessary as well as providing more publicity and legitimacy for the mediation process. Such views have been prominent also in the literature.[26] The recent study of international commercial mediators found mediators often stating that although the issue did not commonly arise in practice, there did exist a perception of a problem with enforcement stifling use amongst the uninitiated.[27] Equally, most interviewees supported the Convention as granting mediation a greater profile, and also rendering it more legitimate in the eyes of would-be users and their lawyers.[28] In this there was a sense of the Convention appealing to lawyers and others more comfortable with formal modes of dispute resolution by imbuing mediation with some of this traditional, juridical colour.

9.4 THE CURRENT STATE OF PLAY

The Convention enjoyed an auspicious beginning, initially signed by a relatively large number of jurisdictions from different parts of the world, far outstripping the initial 24 signatories to the New York Convention on international commercial arbitration. There has been a steady trickle of signatories since. At the time of writing, the number of signatory States has swelled to 57, amounting to over half of world GDP, with high-profile countries such as India, the UK and Australia joining the fold.[29]

---

[25] See Timothy Schnabel, 'The Singapore Convention on Mediation: A Framework for the Cross-border Recognition and Enforcement of Mediated Settlements' (2019) 19 Pepperdine Dispute Resolution Law Journal 1, at 4.

[26] Veronika Vanisova, 'Current Issues in International Commercial Mediation: Short Note on the Nature of Agreement Resulting from Mediation in Light of the Singapore Convention' Research Paper No. 2019/11/5 (Charles University in Prague Faculty of Law 2019); Karl Mackie, 'Another Historic Step for Mediation' (LinkedIn Pulse, 8 August 2019).

[27] Clark and Sourdin *supra* n. 4.

[28] Ibid.

[29] See About the Convention | Singapore Convention on Mediation, https://www.singaporeconvention.org/jurisdictions.

9.4.1 Limited Ratifications

There have thus far been only 14 ratifications, however, in which the terms of the Convention have been brought into force into States' domestic law. Important economies including the USA, China, the UK and India have not yet ratified. Moreover, neither the European Union ('EU') nor any EU member states have signed the Convention. Hence, any direct effect of the Convention can be said to be limited at present.[30] Indeed, at the time of writing, we can find no reported case law and no record of actual use of the Convention to enforce mediated agreements. This reluctance may partly be explained by the strategic interests of these powers, as they carefully evaluate how the Convention aligns with their existing legal frameworks and international commitments. In a multipolar world, the ratification of international treaties more and more becomes subject to the political and economic interests of major players.[31] Entering the international arena amidst evolving geopolitical dynamics, the Singapore Convention faces the strategic influence of major powers, who may encourage or impede its ratification to protect their interests, thereby shaping the future landscape of global dispute resolution.

It has been argued, however, that the recent ratification of Japan is a 'watershed moment' in the Convention's journey.[32] Japan is arguably the most important country economically to bring the terms of the Convention into its domestic regime. As one commentator has put it, '[w]ith the prospect of thousands of Japanese multinational companies doing business across the globe soon having the opportunity to avail themselves of the Singapore Convention in resolving their international disputes, other global economic powerhouses will soon be compelled to decide if they will follow suit.'[33] While it remains to be seen if that will be the case, certainly the stated desires of States signing up to the Convention suggest that a primary motive is to become established as a recognised central of international mediation. Competition in this regard will be keen.[34]

---

[30] The relevant provisions are in force in 13 of those countries, with Sri Lanka's domestic provisions set to come into force in late August 2024.

[31] See Christina J. Schneider and Johannes Urpelainen, 'Distributional Conflict Between Powerful States and International Treaty Ratification'. *International Studies Quarterly* 57.1 (2013): 13–27 at 14–19.

[32] With Japan's Ratification, the Singapore Mediation Convention Gains International Momentum | Paul Hastings LLP.

[33] Ibid.

[34] We discuss the rationale behind States' engagement with the Convention at para 9.5.1.

In terms of why ratifications are currently limited, to do so may take time and political will. The requirement of States dealing with the implications of COVID-19 may also have led to delays in this regard.[35] There are different ways to embed the terms of the Convention into domestic law. For common law countries, this will likely entail legislating around existing court rules, and for civil law countries, amending relevant civil codes. Some countries are likely to take the opportunity to make provision more broadly for mediation as part of their ratifying legislative initiatives. For the UK, ratification still seems a distant prospect. A complicating factor for the UK lies in the fact that the relevant court rules would require amending across the different internal home jurisdictions, requiring cooperation from the devolved administrations. Any amendments to court procedures could not be laid before the UK Parliament until after relevant legislation has been enacted in the devolved administrations. And then the Convention would not come into force in the UK until six months after the UK government had deposited its instrument of ratification with the UN Headquarters in New York.[36]

9.4.2 The Case of the EU

One notable absentee from those rallying behind the cause of the Convention is the EU. Neither the EU as a bloc nor any EU countries have signed the Convention thus far. The EU is very supportive of mediation development and participated in the discussions leading up to the Conventions. The Singapore Convention can be viewed as troublesome for the EU, however. It has been argued that these stumbling blocks can be split into two categories: 'formal' and 'substantive'[37] with the former representing legal complexities and the latter arising from the philosophical underpinnings of mediation.

In terms of the former, the first issue to be determined is whether it would be appropriate for the EU to sign up as a bloc or allow individual countries to do so.[38] The Convention specifically makes provision for its signing by 'regional

---

35 I. Apter and R.B. Davis 'Chronicle of the Singapore Convention: An Insider View' in G. Palao (ed.) *The Singapore Convention on Mediation* (2022, Edward Elgar) at 38.

36 Government response to the Consultation on the United Nations Convention on International Settlement Agreements Resulting from Mediation (New York, 2018) – GOV.UK (www.gov.uk) at 6.13.

37 S. Ferz and T. Tsuvina, *supra* n. 8 at p. 310.

38 For a discussion see Joséphine Hage Chahine, Ettore M. Lombardi, David Lutran, and Catherine Peulvé, 'The Acceleration of the Development of International Business Mediation after the Singapore Convention' (2021) 32(4) European Business Law Review 769.

economic integration organizations' such as the EU.[39] Certainly the EU would seem to have competency to sign, and such an approach would help to standardise the implementation throughout the bloc. However, how the Convention might interact with existing provisions relative to mediation such as the EU Directive 2008/52/EC on specific aspects of mediation in civil and commercial matters (hereinafter 'Mediation Directive') may be problematic. The Mediation Directive does allow for the enforceability of cross-border mediated agreements within the EU but only at the behest of the parties to the settlement agreement.[40] Moreover, under the EU Directive, mediated settlements gain enforceability by dint of their approval by a court or other competent authority or conversion into an 'authentic' instrument.[41] In contrast, absent a reservation applying the Convention only at the behest of parties, the settlement agreement is automatically binding in signatory States. Furthermore, there may be difficulties in the imposition by the EU of a 'hard' instrument such as the Convention on Member States in a field where interventions are typically made by 'soft law' measures, leaving significant discretion in terms of implementation to states.[42] In terms of the disparity in approach taken between the Mediation Directive and the Convention, there is scope for the dissonance to be accounted for, in that for intra-EU issues, the terms of the Directive could be given priority but that for engagements between actors in EU states and those in non-EU countries, or involving non-EU parties seeking enforcement in the EU, then the Convention's terms would be operable.[43]

In terms of 'substantive' barriers, Ferz and Tsuvina point to the significant variation in mediation standards across different EU countries which may militate against the uniformity that the Convention seeks to foster. They also point to the issue of further 'juridification' of mediation raised by the Convention

---

39 Article 12.

40 Article 6.1 of the Mediation Directive holds that Member States shall 'ensure that it is possible for the parties of mediation, or for one of them with the explicit consent of the others, to request that the content of a written agreement resulting from mediation be made enforceable'.

41 Article 6.2.

42 See the discussion by Dr Rimantas Simaitis at the European Centre for Dispute Resolution, Report on 'Roundtable on the Position of the European Union on the Singapore Convention on Mediation' organised on 18 June 2021 by the European Law Institute Slovenian hub and the Forum for International Conciliation and Arbitration, available at Okrogla Miza o Stališču Evropske Unije o Singapurski Konvenciji o Mediaciji | Evropski center za reševanje sporov – ECDR.

43 See the discussion by Dr Norel Rosner at the European Centre for Dispute Resolution (ibid).

which may hamper the qualitative benefits of the process, and which may find resistance within EU states.[44]

9.5 WILL THE CONVENTION LEAD TO GROWTH IN INTERNATIONAL COMMERCIAL MEDIATION?

As we have discussed, the signalling impact of the Convention is perhaps its most important function. At this juncture, it is difficult to point to any concrete impacts of the Convention beyond greater academic and professional interest and discussion. While the catalytic impact of the New York Convention is often held up as a harbinger of positivity for mediation, one other notable comparator is the European Mediation Directive. Even though this development led to significant legislative developments in many EU jurisdictions relative to both cross-border and domestic mediation, it has been argued that its impact thus far has been patchy in terms of growing mediation across European jurisdictions, even if there has been marked growth in some jurisdictions such as Italy.[45] International commercial mediation does at least appear to be on the rise in different parts of the world.[46] However, recent research has suggested that international commercial mediation is still underused and there remain significant barriers to be overcome to grow the field.[47]

---

[44] Ferz and Tsuvina *supra* n. 8.

[45] See for example, C.R. Chereji, Mediation in the European Union: The Directive 2008/52/EC and its Effects on National Legislations, Conflict Studies Quarterly Issue 15, April 2016, pp. 3–16; Kumar, Ashish, EU Directive on Mediation: Assessing the Development and Challenges (May 20, 2017). Contemporary Developments in International Law: Some Random Reflections Satyam Law International (1st edn, 2017) pp. 112–126; David J. Stute, 'The Singapore Convention: Not Much There, There' (2021) 3(1) Journal of the Institute of Transnational Arbitration 32.

[46] K. Taylor, 'Rising Global Demand for International Dispute Resolution: Trends and Perspectives' Jams ADR Insights, 17 July 2024 available at Rising Global Demand for International Dispute Resolution Trends and Perspectives | JAMS Mediation, Arbitration, ADR Services (jamsadr.com); I. Castro et al., 'Recent Trends in WIPO Arbitration and Mediation' Global Arbitration Review, 24 May 2024 available at Recent Trends in WIPO Arbitration and Mediation – Global Arbitration Review; Global Times, 'China Accelerates International Commercial Mediation Cooperation, Helping Domestic and Foreign Companies Resolve Disputes', 5 January 2024.

[47] Clark and Sourdin *supra* n. 4.

9.5.1 The Influence of Major Players

The support of major economies lent to the Convention may be influential. It is known that participation of major powers, especially as initiators or signatories, may accelerate the spread of treaties and may encourage others to follow.[48] Many of those States who signed the Convention are already very active in the mediation sphere, so engagement with this new instrument would seem a natural consequence of that, rather than representing a new shift into the mediation field. Moreover, the rationale behind the signing of States to the Convention may be largely self-serving. For example, reading the UK government's response to the Consultation on whether to join the Convention,[49] where it confirmed its intention to become a party, we can see that the primary rationale to sign up was to cement its own reputation in the field: 'The Government has concluded that it is the right time for the UK to become a Party to the Singapore Convention on Mediation, *as a clear signal to our international partners that the UK is committed to maintaining and strengthening its position as a centre for dispute resolution and to promote the UK's flourishing legal and mediation sectors.*'[50] Furthermore, signing would lead to 'reinforcing and potentially increasing the UK's attractiveness as a respected jurisdiction for international dispute resolution',[51] as well as serving to 'reaffirm the UK's intention to build upon its long history of leadership in international law-making fora such as the UN and the Hague Conference on Private International Law'[52] There is, however, also some consideration found in the response that the Convention will help grow mediation more broadly: 'The uniform framework for the effective recognition and enforcement of international mediated settlement agreements, which the Convention provides, will increase confidence to trade across borders and between different legal jurisdictions,

---

[48] Ki Eun Ryu, *Dynamics of International Treaty Diffusion* (2020, The University of Iowa).

[49] Consultation Paper on the United Nations Convention on International Settlement Agreements Resulting for Mediation (New York, 2018) 2022, available at Consultation on the United Nations Convention on International Settlement Agreements Resulting from Mediation (2018, New York) (the 'Singapore Convention on Mediation') (publishing.service.gov.uk).

[50] UK Government response available at Government response to the Consultation on the United Nations Convention on International Settlement Agreements Resulting from Mediation (2018, New York) (www.gov.uk) para 6.1 (emphasis added).

[51] Para 6.4.

[52] Para 6.6.

by providing a clear and expedited process for resolving commercial disputes through mediation.'[53]

Similarly, in terms of Japan's ratification of the Convention, self-interest seems largely at its core. It has been remarked that 'Japan's decision to ratify the Convention was predicated on its belief that promoting the use of mediation in international commercial disputes will help attract foreign investment at the domestic level and encourage Japanese companies to expand overseas. These objectives will, in turn, not only help Japan establish a stronger position in the international community with respect to the resolution of international commercial disputes, but potentially help to stimulate Japan's economic development.'[54]

Whether these developments will in fact drive significant growth of mediation still remain to be seen. Certainly, it is known that participation of major powers, especially as initiators or signatories, may accelerate the spread of treaties and may encourage others to follow.[55] Nadja Alexander has pointed to the issue of 'status quo' bias which might limit the impact that the Convention may have, in which actors remain with tried and tested modes of dispute resolution.[56] The cultural preferences of lawyers and clients for traditional means of dispute resolution are well known. Moreover, recent research into the views of international commercial mediators has suggested that significant barriers to the use of mediation in the international commercial sphere remain, including a default preference for arbitration, ignorance of and resistance to mediation by disputants and their lawyers, cultural barriers in some localities, and concerns over standards and the quality of mediators.[57]

One area of particular optimism is the investor–state dispute setting. The traditional use of arbitration in this setting has become heavily criticised in this space and the Singapore Convention is seen as a boon to the growth of mediation.[58] New rules have recently been enacted to govern mediation in this space.[59] The availability of reservation, absenting public bodies from its

---

53 Para 6.3.

54 With Japan's Ratification, the Singapore Mediation Convention Gains International Momentum | Paul Hastings LLP.

55 Ki Eun Ryu, *Dynamics of International Treaty Diffusion* (2020, The University of Iowa).

56 Nadia Alexander, 'The Singapore Convention: What Happens After the Ink has Dried?' (2020) 30(2) American Review of International Arbitration 236–237.

57 Clark and Sourdin *supra* n. 4.

58 Nadja Alexander et al., *International Dispute Resolution Survey* (SIDRA Final Report, 2nd edn, 2022).

59 See for example, the mediation rules developed by the International Centre for the Settlement of Investment Disputes (ICSID) at Mediation | ICSID (worldbank

provisions, may limit the Convention's effectiveness in this regard somewhat, however. Moreover, mediation may still entail significant challenges in the investor–state setting for a raft of reasons, including issues around confidentiality, political sensitivities, public accountability of settlements, and concerns over the supply of appropriately qualified mediators.[60]

9.5.2 Enforcing Common Provisions Across Jurisdictions

How the terms of the Convention are implemented in different domestic regimes and how consistent such approaches are may go some way to influencing the effectiveness of the Convention in practice. Uniformity in application is likely to be patchy given the great diversity in legal systems and existing approaches to mediation regulation found across jurisdictions. Reforms that do not align with the established legal traditions of the society are likely to remain ineffective, regardless of their formal status in the legal system.[61]

9.5.3 Reservations

Reservations under Article 8 have already been signalled by some jurisdictions, meaning that either the Convention shall not apply to public entities or shall only apply to the extent that parties to mediated settlement agreements specify that to be the case. So, for example, of the countries that have ratified the Convention, Belarus, Georgia, Kazakhstan and Saudi Arabia have disapplied the provision to public entities, and Georgia and Japan have rendered the Convention applicable only in circumstances in which parties have expressly consented to this in their settlement agreement.[62] Interestingly, the New York Convention provides no avenue for the making of such reservations. While their inclusion may have been necessary to gain the support of all States, we posit that the Singapore Convention's inclusion of reservations may lead to a weakening of its effectiveness. In respect of rendering the Convention

---

.org).

60 James M. Claxton, 'Compelling Parties to Mediate Investor State Disputes: No Pressure, No Diamonds?' (2020) 20(1) Pepperdine Dispute Resolution Law Journal, 78; Ignacio de la Rasilla, '"The Greatest Victory?" Challenges and Opportunities in for Mediation in Investor State Dispute Settlement' (2023) 38(1) ICSID Review, 169.

61 Viktoriia Hamaiunova, 'Influence of Implicit and Visible Legal Cultures on Modernisation of Judicial Systems in European Countries' (2023) 9 Athens JL 653–666 at 660.

62 Other countries, such as Iran, have indicated on signing that they will make reservations.

applicable only where disputing parties expressly consent to this, although accepting that this is consonant with party autonomy, it has been suggested that this may lead to uneven application and also 'afford the opportunity to more dominant parties to coerce their counterparty to opt into the terms of the Convention or otherwise to ensure that they can follow the most advantageous approach to pursuing or resisting enforcement of the [settlement agreement].'[63] As we note above, absenting public bodies from the regime may hold negative consequences, in particular for investor–state mediation.

9.5.4 Variations in Domestic Implementation

Beyond the issue of reservations, we are already seeing distinct variances in approach in terms of domestic application in those countries that have ratified the Convention. This is likely to herald an uneven application of the Convention and increase levels of uncertainty. So, for example, in Belarus, the domestic legislative rules anticipate the enforcement regime applying to a narrower set of activities than specified in the Convention. While the definition of mediation in the Convention focuses upon processes in which decision makers lack the authority to impose outcomes,[64] Article 15-1(1) of the Belarusian Mediation Law provides that an international mediation agreement is 'an agreement reached as a result of a procedure whereby the parties achieve the settlement of a dispute with the participation of a third party (parties) who do not have the authority to propose specific resolution options to the parties'.[65] This stems from the Rules of Mediation Procedure approved by the resolution of the Council of Ministers of the Republic of Belarus dated 28 December 2013 No. 1150, which prohibits mediators from expressing on their own initiative specific proposals to the parties to resolve the existing dispute. This significantly narrows the definition of mediation to preclude those processes in which mediators may take a more evaluative or directive approach. These are, of course, very common mediation approaches in many jurisdictions.

In Ecuador, where the terms of the Convention are brought into domestic law via the General Organic Code of Processes,[66] for the settlement agreement

[63] B. Clark and T. Sourdin, *supra* n. 2 at 485. It should be noted that given that under Article 5(1)(d) enforcement under the Convention of a settlement may be challenged as being contrary to its own terms, parties already have the scope to specifically exclude Convention enforcement in their agreement.

[64] See infra, para 9.2.1.

[65] See Залесский, Д. А. 'Приведение законодательства Республики Беларусь в соответствие с Сингапурской конвенцией о медиации' (2022).

[66] Available at Sro506.indd (https://www.funcionjudicial.gob.ec/pdf/CODIGO%20ORGANICO%20GENERAL%20DE%20PROCESOS.pdf).

to be enforceable, it must comply with the formalities required for it to be considered authentic *in the State of origin.* As we have alluded to above, the Convention does not attempt to define a mediation 'seat' and the State of origin in cross-border mediation may in practice be difficult to define. Similarly, in its empowering legislation,[67] Nigeria has limited the application of the Convention to mediation agreements arising from jurisdictions which are also signatories to the Convention, thus reinserting reciprocity and requiring the identification of a mediation 'seat'.

In Qatar, pursuant to Article 24 of the Mediation Law, to be enforceable, the settlement agreement must be in writing and signed by the parties and the mediator(s).[68] The Convention allows alternatives to the signing of the agreement by the mediator, and it is known that mediators may be reluctant to do so.

In Japan, under Article 3 para (v), relief may be granted where 'the mediator has breached laws, regulations or any other rules applicable to the mediator or to the mediation implemented by the mediator pursuant to an agreement between the parties (limited to those unrelated to public order), and the fact constituting the breach is serious and affects the conclusion of the international settlement agreement'.[69] This requirement differs from the equivalent provision in the Convention which specifically links any breach to the decision of a party to enter into the settlement agreement, thus potentially widening the scope for challenge in Japan.[70] Kazakhstan also treats grounds of relief differently from those set out in the Convention.[71]

As more countries ratify, it will be important to continue to monitor variances that occur between the different regimes' approaches to enforcement.

---

[67] Arbitration and Mediation Act 2023, s 87.

[68] 'Qatar Law No. 20/2021 on the Issuance of the Law on Mediation in the Settlement of Civil and Commercial Disputes' (the 'Mediation Law') issued on 4 November 2021.

[69] An English translation has been drawn from 調停による国際的な和解合意に関する国際連合条約の実施に関する法律 – 日本語/英語 – 日本法令外国語訳DBシステム (japaneselawtranslation.go.jp).

[70] See infra para 9.6.1.

[71] For a discussion of the differences here in respect of Kazakhstan see Чимаров, Николай Сергеевич, and Сергей Юрьевич Чимаров. 'Институт медиации в законодательстве Республики Казахстан: перспективы региональной адаптации' (2023) 17.3(45) *ЕВРАЗИЙСКАЯ ИНТЕГРАЦИЯ: экономика, право, политика* 120–128.

9.6 POTENTIAL RISKS

9.6.1 Mediation Standards and Challenges under Article 5(1)(e)

The matter of commonality of mediation standards has gained a sharper focus given the introduction of the Convention which seeks to have application across a broad range of different jurisdictions. Bodies such as the International Mediation Institute have sought to establish common international mediation standards.[72] Collaborations have also taken place between different standard setting bodies.[73] Recent empirical research has found that international commercial mediators broadly believe, however, that there is a limit to the extent that standards could or should be put on a common footing across jurisdictions. While some were in favour of developing greater assurance in professional standards across different jurisdictions, they pointed to the significant differences around mediation practice norms across the globe as well as different party expectations of mediation and mediator conduct.[74] In some jurisdictions, for example, caucusing is routine, but this practice is not commonly found in others. Mediators may be expected to be more authoritative or evaluative in some settings but not in others. Process pluralism is an established feature of mediation, indeed as specifically recognised by the wide definition afforded to the term in the Convention.[75]

Against this backdrop of variation and uncertainty, much of the adverse commentary about the Convention has arisen around the prospect of uneven interpretations of mediator standards in different jurisdictions amidst the possibilities of challenges to settlements based on mediator misconduct under Article 5(1)(e). Some commentators have argued that this provision represents a danger to mediated agreements as it may concentrate parties' minds on the possibility of challenges.[76] Recent interviews with international commercial

[72] See IMI – Driving transparency and high competency standards in mediation, worldwide (imimediation.org).

[73] On the Singapore International Mediation Institute's initiative, four international mediation organisations, namely the Asia Mediation Centre, the Instituto de Certificacao e Formacao de Mediadores Lusófonos, the International Dispute Resolution & Risk Management Institute and the Institut Français de Certification des Médiateurs, have signed a Memorandum of Understanding to create an Alliance for Mediation Standards.

[74] Clark and Sourdin *supra* n. 4.

[75] Article 2(3).

[76] Clark and Sourdin *supra* n. 2; Dorcas Quek Anderson, 'A Matter of Interpretation? Understanding and Applying Mediation Standards for the

mediators also found a minority expressing such fears.[77] Other commentators have pointed, however, to the high bar the Convention sets with the need for the party seeking that relief to prove serious breaches of mediator conduct without which parties would not have entered into the mediated settlement.[78] What 'serious' means in this context is unclear and in terms of establishing that the breach vitiated the party's consent, 'the standard of proof may differ across jurisdictions, depending on prevailing judicial attitude towards mediation and the policy of supporting mediated settlements'.[79]

One further complicating factor is that a court from one jurisdiction shall be required to judge the standard of conduct of a mediator drawn from a different jurisdiction. As we have noted, expected standards of mediation conduct may vary considerably across borders. Furthermore, it is not clear upon what basis mediators shall be judged. The parties may of course specify the appropriate law or regulations in their settlement agreement which one might expect courts would recognise. In the absence of this, Joel Lee has recently addressed this question and proposed a non-comprehensive list of reference points for which the relevant standards might be established, including the established standards of the jurisdiction in which enforcement was being sought, the standards specified in the agreement to mediate, the standards as indicated by the mediator, the standards applicable to the mediator by their associated mediation organisation, or the standards as established by independent standards bodies.[80]

Cross-border Enforcement of Mediated Settlement Agreements' (2020) Conflict Resolution Quarterly 38, 27.

[77] Clark and Sourdin *supra* n. 4. On the other hand, it has been argued that the lack of a 'set aside' provision in the state of origin of the mediated settlement is a 'seemingly endless opportunity to litigate the validity and enforceability of a mediated settlement in one jurisdiction after another [where the other party has assets]' – at David J. Stute and Alexis N. Wansac, 'The Singapore Convention: Not Much There' (2021) 3(1) ITA in Review 32 at 46.

[78] Karl Mackie, 'Another Historic Step for Mediation' (LinkedIn Pulse, 8 August 2019) https://www.linkedin.com/pulse/another-historic-step-mediation-karl-mackie-cbe/.

[79] Valerie Lim An Qi, 'Operationalising Article 5(1)(e) of the Singapore Convention' (2024) Contemporary Issues in Mediation at 4.

[80] Joel Lee, Seminar Singapore Convention Week 2023 – Event Details – Ensuring Quality in Cross-Border Mediation: The Place of Standards. For a derailed discussion of some of these issues see Ben Köhler, 'Blaming the Middleman? Refusal of Relief for Mediator Misconduct under the Singapore Convention' (2023) 19(1) Journal of Private International Law 42–66.

While we wait for these provisions to be tested in practice, the uncertainties inherent here may undermine confidence in the Convention.[81] Other grey areas around circumstances where courts may refuse to grant relief (and refuse to enforce settlements) include Article 5.1(c)(ii) which holds that the court in which enforcement is sought may refuse to grant relief if the party requesting it 'furnishes … proof that ... the obligations in the settlement agreement ... [a]re not clear or comprehensible'. As has been noted, 'settlement agreements are indeed contracts, they may, despite the settling parties' (or mediator's) best efforts and intentions, employ language that is ambiguous and so require interpretation to arrive at their intended meaning … Does this mean that, in the event that language in a mediated settlement agreement is found by the competent authority to be ambiguous, the competent authority should simply refuse to enforce it, even though the ambiguity is capable of being resolved?'[82]

9.6.2 Confidentiality

An associated issue that arises from the potential for challenges is the extent to which the confidentiality of mediation – one of the central attributes of the process – becomes eroded. With significant differences relative to confidentiality and privilege across different jurisdictions, we may see very different approaches taken, increasing levels of uncertainty for disputing parties.[83] The Convention itself is silent on the issues of confidentiality and without prejudice rules, leaving it to national regimes to determine. An associated issue is to what extent any new approaches adopted for international commercial mediated settlements, perhaps based on the Model Law, are extended to domestic mediation in ratifying jurisdictions. It has been noted, for example, that the way in which confidentiality and privilege operate in the UK is quite different to the rules set out in the Model Law on Mediation and thus represents an opportunity to provide much-needed reform more broadly. [84] As more States

---

[81] It should also be noted that these grounds are 'permissive', meaning that a court may decide nonetheless to grant relief even where grounds under s 5 are proven.

[82] Anthony Ullman and Diora M Ziyaeva, 'The Singapore Convention and its Potential Impact on Mediation in the Americas' (2021) Global Arbitration Review 1–12.

[83] See the discussion in Qi *supra* n. 79 at 5–7.

[84] See Herbert Smith Freehills, 'The UK will Join the Singapore Convention: So What Now?' 6 March 2023 available at The UK will join the Singapore Convention – so what now? | Herbert Smith Freehills | Global law firm. https://www.hsfkramer.com/notes/adr/2023-03/the-uk-will-join-the-singapore-convention-so-what-now/

ratify the Convention, it will be interesting to see if there is any confluence of rules around confidentiality and privilege.

9.7 CONCLUSION

This chapter has focused on the Singapore Convention and reviewed its impact over the five years since the signing ceremony. Clearly, the Convention represents an impressive achievement in bringing together an enforcement regime for international commercial mediation that is able to span a range of different jurisdictions and different legal and mediation landscapes. While its empirical basis – the real need for a new enforcement regime in this setting – can be questioned, it has undeniably served to help put mediation on the map, assuaging the doubters and creating more legitimacy for the mediation process in the minds of would-be users and their lawyers. To what extent the Convention is leading to a growth in mediation in the international commercial space remains unclear. Barriers to uptake in this setting remain and may require different approaches to surmount.

While the range of signatories is impressive, ratifications have been relatively slow, meaning any direct impact of the Convention has not yet been felt. Politically, ratifications take time and will. Legally, such processes may be complex. The addition of more major economies to the list of ratifying States may have a catalytic effect in encouraging others to follow suit and render the Convention more meaningful in a practical sense. If the EU can find a way to accommodate the Convention within its existing legislative framework, that would be a major fillip for the Convention's prospects.

As a product of political compromise, the Convention was always destined to leave a range of issues clouded in uncertainty and leave much of the detail to be provided by domestic enforcement regimes. In terms of those countries that have ratified, a number have made reservations, potentially diluting the potential impact of the Convention. Moreover, there have been some marked differences in the ratifying States' respective enforcement regimes, at times around the fringes, but in other cases, contrary to the core approach of the Convention (e.g. around reciprocity). Such variances may create further uncertainties for potential users.

Finally, there remain significant doubts around the application of the grounds for refusing relief, especially in respect of mediator misconduct, how these are likely to be perceived by different courts internationally and the implications this may hold for confidentiality in the mediation process.

Given the nascent stage of the Convention currently, it is too soon to cast judgement on its efficacy. Time will tell if the Convention secures its aims, will do more good than damage to mediation, or survives in its current formulation.

10. The use of mediation for art disputes: A survey of 'bespoke' international mediation schemes

Debbie De Girolamo

INTRODUCTION

In this chapter, the focus is on the cultural heritage and cultural property dispute (broadly referred to herein as the 'art dispute') and various international mediation schemes established to promote the use of mediation for their resolution. The art law literature has discussed the relevance of mediation as an appropriate dispute resolution process for such disputes and supports it as a way to achieve a certain justice for claimants whose claims may not be suitable for litigation.[1] Alongside this discussion in the literature, international bodies have established mediation schemes that cater specifically to the art dispute, such as the Intergovernmental Committee for Promoting the Return of Cultural Property to its Countries of Origin or its Restitution in Case of Illicit Appropriation (ICPRCP), established under the auspices of UNESCO and the specific sector alternative dispute resolution (ADR) services offered by the World Intellectual Property Organization (WIPO).[2] While mediation is

[1] See for example, De Girolamo D, 'ADR, Cultural Heritage and Intellectual Property: A Continuum of Dispute Resolution Processes' in Stamatoudi I (ed.), *Research Handbook on Intellectual Property and Cultural Heritage* (Edward Elgar Publishing 2022); Chechi A, 'Alternative Dispute Settlement Mechanisms' in Francesco Francioni and Ana Filipa Vrdoljak (eds), *The Oxford Handbook of International Cultural Heritage Law* (OUP 2020) 718; Cornu M and MA Renold, 'New Developments in the Restitution of Cultural Property: Alternative Means of Dispute Resolution' (2010) 17 IJCP 1.

[2] Statutes of the Intergovernmental Committee for Promoting the Return of Cultural Property to its Countries of Origin or its Restitution in Case of Illicit Appropriation (ICPRCP) (adopted 27 November 1978, amended 4 November 2010) <https://unesdoc.unesco.org/ark:/48223/pf0000145960> accessed 7 January

generally known to be a flexible process that can be applicable to varying types of disputes, these schemes were developed specifically for the art dispute and tailored in various ways to meet its specific characteristics and needs. They suggest that the usual mediation procedures for civil and commercial cases such as offered by domestic mediation service providers or court-connected schemes[3] may not be sufficient for the art dispute, requiring a more bespoke mediation process.

This chapter will explore these schemes in terms of what they offer the art dispute that may not be offered by the typical mediation process often discussed in the literature.[4] To do so, it will first discuss the nature of the art dispute to situate the relevance of ADR processes to it, and in particular, the mediation process and its suitability to these disputes. This aims to provide an understanding of why international organisations treat the art dispute as one that requires particular consideration when it comes to creating an ADR process suitable for it. They see mediation as a viable process for resolution by offering mediation services within a particular framework that seeks to add value for these disputes.

The chapter will then examine art dispute-related mediation schemes offered by three such organisations, noting features that respond specifically to the nature of the art dispute. In its final section, the chapter will consider the benefits of and the remaining challenges facing the mediation of the art dispute offered by these schemes. It will conclude that mediation's flexibility to adjust its process in order to meet the demands of the art dispute reflects the versatility of the process to meet the demands of a dispute, and one that

---

2025; WIPO Alternative Dispute Resolution (ADR) for Art and Cultural Heritage <https://www.wipo.int/amc/en/center/specific-sectors/art/> accessed 7 January 2025.

[3] For examples of typical mediation processes offered by domestic mediation service providers, see Centre for Effective Dispute Resolution Model Mediation Procedure at <https://learn.cedr.com/hubfs/Model%20Documents/Mediation%20Guidelines%20and%20Procedures/Model-Mediation-Procedure-July-2023.pdf> accessed 9 January 2025; and IPOS Mediation Model Mediation Procedure at <https://mediate.co.uk/wp-content/uploads/2021/06/IPOS-Model-Mediation-Procedure-Final-June-2021.pdf> accessed 9 January 2025. For examples of court-connected mediation schemes, see the mandatory mediation rule of the Ontario civil justice system which sets out the requirements of the procedure: Rules of Civil Procedure, RRO 1990, Regulation 194, rule 24.1 under the Courts of Justice Act, RSO 1990, c. C.43 at <https://www.ontario.ca/laws/regulation/900194> accessed January 15, 2025.

[4] See discussion of the mediation process in De Girolamo D, 'The Mediation Process: Challenges to Neutrality and the Delivery of Procedural Justice' (2019) 39(4) OJLS 834.

could be applied more broadly in civil justice to strengthen its capacity to respond to the nature of the dispute being mediated. Often, mediation in civil justice generally offers mediation in a one-size-fits-all category when it comes to commercial and civil disputes.[5] While it is understandable why this may be the case given the broad nature of litigated claims, approaching mediation as a process that can be made more responsive to the needs of the dispute at hand, such as done with the art dispute in the international sphere, is an area for further research and policy development in civil justice where the aim would be to improve its outcomes as a result.

THE ART DISPUTE AND ADR

As discussed elsewhere, the art dispute may have issues found in many commercial disputes such as breach of contract, negligence and breach of warranty which may well be suited to an adjudicative outcome in state courts.[6] For the commercial art dispute such as one that may arise between artist and gallery owner, between gallery owners or between art collector and auction house, the dispute may be no different from any other commercial dispute involving contractual arrangements and business relationships.[7] An example is Sotheby's action against an art dealer who purchased a Keith Haring painting at a Sotheby's auction. The piece had been estimated to bring in between £4 million and £6 million. The painting was purchased at auction for £6.5

5 It is recognised that exceptions exist: for example, in England and Wales separate schemes exist for low-sum claims (i.e. Small Claims Court Mediation Schemes; County Court Mediation Schemes), for appeal claims (the High Court and Court Appeal Mediation Schemes) and for the National Health Service.

6 De Girolamo D, 'Art Disputes and Their Resolution through ADR: A Matter of Creativity Rather than of Brexit Implications' (2017) 22(2) AA&L 143 at 144.

7 See for example, Shonk K, 'Mediation Used in Dispute Resolution Over Art Museums' (PONS Daily Blog, 9 March 2017) at <https://www.pon.harvard.edu/daily/mediation/conflict-managementmediation-used-in-dispute-resolution-over-art-museums/≥ where Shonk describes two disputes dealing with the ownership of museum collections, based on contract (accessed 8 January 2025); Bandle AL, Wallace A and Renold MA, 'Case Banksy Mural – Bioresource, Inc. and 555 Nonprofit Studio/Gallery' Art-Law Centre, University of Geneva at <https://plone.unige.ch/art-adr/cases-affaires/banksy-mural-2013-bioresource-inc-and-555-non-profit-studio-gallery>, which discusses issues of ownership regarding a Banksy mural (accessed 8 January 2025); and see Prowda JB, '15 Minutes on Mediation of Arts Related Disputes' (Stropheus LLC Blog, 2014) at <https://stropheus.com/artist/mediation-in-the-arts/> for a hypothetical example of a contract dispute arising between artist and gallery and how a solution through mediation could lead to creative outcomes.

million. Owing to a subsequent failure to pay, Sotheby's commenced action against the buyer for the deficiency in sale price between the original purchase price and what Sotheby's was able to obtain on its resale after it became clear that the buyer would not complete the transaction. The case involved the usual breach of contract issues such as varying interpretations of agreed terms and mitigation efforts on resale. Sotheby's was successful on summary judgment on both the contractual and mitigation issues.[8]

While the art dispute can carry with it many of the elements of commercial issues, it is situated within a market that has its own idiosyncrasies: privacy and confidentiality are primary principles by which transactions often occur; contractual formalities may be discarded to the peril of parties; relationships are guarded; and ownership and authenticity of objects may be unclear or difficult to establish.[9]

Further, not all art disputes are confined to general commercial issues: the disputes may be about the protection and preservation of cultural heritage or they could involve restitution claims involving looted objects or human remains. Here, examples could include protection of heritage sites during armed conflict under the auspices of various international instruments such as the Hague Convention for the Protection of Cultural Property in the Event of Armed Conflict and the UNESCO Convention Concerning the Protection of the World Cultural and Natural Heritage;[10] the restitution claims of art dealer

---

8 Adam G, 'Anatole Shagalov must pay Sotheby's £2m for Keith Haring painting, judge rules' (*The ArtNewspaper*, 3 July 2020) at <https://www.theartnewspaper.com/news/anatole-shagalov-must-pay-sotheby-s-usd2m-for-keith-haring-painting-judge-rules> accessed 8 January 2025.

9 For a summary discussion about various art disputes and the particular issues raised by them, see Palmer N, *Art, Adventure and Advocacy: Contracts, Claims and Controversies in the World of Cultural Property* (Institute of Art & Law 2015).

10 Hague Convention for the Protection of Cultural Property in the Event of Armed Conflict 1954 at <https://www.unesco.org/en/legal-affairs/convention-protection-cultural-property-event-armed-conflict-regulations-execution-convention?hub=415> accessed January 2025; First Protocol to the Hague Convention for the Protection of Cultural Property in the Event of Armed Conflict 1954 at https://www.unesco.org/en/heritage-armed-conflicts/convention-and-protocols/first-protocol#:~:text=The%20First%20Protocol%20regulates%20the,of%20retention%20of%20cultural%20property accessed 15 January 2025; UNESCO Convention Concerning the Protection of the World Cultural and

Natural Heritage, 1972 at https://whc.unesco.org/archive/convention-en.pdf> accessed 15 January 15, 2025;

UNESCO's Operational Guidelines for the Implementation of the World Heritage

Max Stern for the return of property looted by the Nazis in the 1930s;[11] and the return of Tasmanian human remains from the Natural History Museum in London.[12] Ethics, morality, cultural identity, sovereignty, ideas of non-Western concepts of ownership, reconciliation and punishment can impact the disputes. Indigenous repatriation claims illustrate disputes having many of these elements, such as the repatriation claim of the Inuvialuit for return of an Inuit kayak in the possession of the Vatican.[13] Disputes can cross political, historical, legal, social and philosophical boundaries, and can involve domestic and international actors: a good example here is the dispute between Greece, the United Kingdom and the British Museum about the Parthenon Marbles.[14] Actors can be individuals, regional communities, nation-states, private organisations and public institutions. Resolution may not rest solely on legal entitlement (particularly where claims face legal barriers to proceeding such as limitation periods and lack of evidential proof regarding ownership);[15] in fact, often the dispute is not determined through legal entitlement, but through a recognition of moral obligations or acknowledgements of party interests and priorities.[16]

Convention, 24 September 2023 at <https://whc.unesco.org/en/guidelines/> accessed 15 January 15, 2025.

11 De Girolamo D, 'The Max Stern Art Restitution Project: A Case Study of Restitution Claims involving Museum Holdings' in Ruth Redmond-Cooper (ed.) *Museums and the Holocaust* (2nd edn, The Institute of Art and Law 2021).

12 Palmer N, *Art, Adventure and Advocacy: Contracts, Claims and Controversies in the World of Cultural Property* (Institute of Art & Law 2015) at 60–62.

13 De Girolamo D, 'ADR and the Indigenous Repatriation Claim: Exploring Sources of Conflict and Processes for Resolution' in Ulp J, Vigneron S and Domince AM (eds), *Research Handbook on Art, Culture and Heritage* (Edward Elgar Publishing 2026); Prazmowska-Marcinowska K, 'Repatriation of Indigenous Peoples' Cultural Property: Could Alternative Dispute Resolution Be a Solution? Lessons Learned from the G'psgolox Totem Pole and the Maaso Kova Case' (2022) 8(2) SA&CLR 135.

14 See generally, Herman A, *The Parthenon Marbles Dispute: Heritage, Law, Politics* (Hart 2023).

15 This is often seen with claimants seeking a return of family artworks looted under Nazi policies and state acts. Spoliation panels have been established in the UK and in Europe dealing with such claims, where guiding principles for determination include consideration of legal and non-legal factors. For a discussion about the UK Spoliation Panel, see Woodhead C, 'Putting into Place Solutions for Nazi Era Dispossessions of Cultural Objects: The UK Experience' (2016) 23 IJCP 385.

16 De Girolamo D, 'The Conflation of Morality and "the Fair and Just Solution" in the Determination of Restitution Claims Involving Nazi-Looted Art: An Unsatisfactory Premise in Need of Change' (2019) 26(4) IJCP 357.

MEDIATION AND THE ART DISPUTE

Mediation can be suitable for the art dispute given its ability to craft creative solutions, overcome legal and non-legal barriers to resolution and to focus on interests rather than strict legal rights in coming to resolution, which is particularly important where the law may impose barriers for a party. It is also as private and confidential as the parties require, as well as fast and efficient. Its focus on communication, too, offers opportunities for reconciliation and acknowledgement, often issues underlying an art dispute. Examples of successful mediations in the cultural property field include a mediation involving two Swiss Cantons (Zurich and St Gallen) who each claimed ownership over religious objects (a celestial globe and manuscripts) removed during religious wars, and a mediation over the loss of artworks due to a fire destroying a warehouse where the artworks had been stored.[17]

International organisations have recognised the relevance of mediation as a way to resolve cultural property or heritage disputes, and in their mediation rules of procedure, have tailored those rules specifically with the art dispute in mind. For example, UNESCO's ICPRCP offers mediation and conciliation services to its member states for disputes relating to the restitution or repatriation of cultural property.[18] Under its mediation rules, mediators are to have expertise in the subject matter of the dispute so that the complexities of the art dispute are readily understood (which is not necessarily typical of mediation procedures for civil and commercial disputes).[19] Furthermore, its rules

---

17 Bandle AL, Contel R and Renold MA, 'Case Ancient Manuscripts and Globe – Saint-Gall and Zurich' Platform ArThemis <http://unige.ch/art-adr>, Art-Law Centre, University of Geneva <https://plone.unige.ch/art-adr/cases-affaires/ancient-manuscripts-and-globe-saint-gall-and-zurich> accessed 10 January 2025 (the settlement reached was made public); Bandle AL, Contel R and Renold MA, 'Case Warehouse Fire – Gillian Ayres et al. and Momart', Platform ArThemis (http://unige.ch/art-adr), Art-Law Centre, University of Geneva, November 2018 <https://plone.unige.ch/art-adr/cases-affaires/warehouse-fire-2013-gillian-ayres-et-al-and-momart?searchterm=Ayres> accessed 10 January 2025 (the settlement agreement was not made public but reports refer to a cash settlement).

18 UNESCO, Rules of Procedure for Mediation and Conciliation, in accordance with article 4, paragraph 1 of the Statutes of the Intergovernmental Committee for Promoting the Return of Cultural Property to its Countries of Origin or its Restitution in Case of Illicit Appropriation (ICPRCP), CLT-2010/CONF.203/COM.16/7 (ICPRCP Mediation and Conciliation Rules), established in 1978 under the auspices of the 1970 UNESCO Convention at <https://unesdoc.unesco.org/ark:/48223/pf0000192534_eng> accessed January 16, 2025.

19 ICPRCP Mediation and Conciliation Rules, article 2.2; compare to International Chamber of Commerce (ICC) Mediation Rules, article 5 and Centre

require that international law and recognized principles are given due recognition in reaching an 'amicable and just solution' (also not usually required to be observed in mediations).[20] The ICPRCP mediation rules also offer investigatory powers to mediators to determine facts (again not a typical authority given to a mediator, but which can be relevant in art disputes where facts can be in issue).[21] This brief discussion of the ICPRCP mediation rules is an introduction to the type of alterations made to a mediation process to better suit the cultural art dispute. These rules will be further explored below together with those offered by two other organisations which seek to offer mediation assistance to parties involved in these disputes.

MEDIATION RULES AND PROCEDURES FOR THE ART DISPUTE: THREE INTERNATIONAL SCHEMES

This section will explore approaches taken by three international organisations which expressly acknowledge the relevance of mediation for the art and cultural heritage dispute and offer differentiated procedural provisions for these disputes. The differentiation varies from organisation to organisation. The three organisations include one applying to member states established pursuant to an international instrument requiring state ratification, one also established pursuant to an international instrument but accessible to private actors, and the third, a domestically established, private, not-for-profit organisation for private actors, primarily. They are UNESCO's ICPRCP Rules of Procedure for Mediation and Conciliation (the ICPRCP Mediation Rules, introduced in the section above),[22] WIPO's Mediation Rules,[23] and the Court of Arbitration for Art (CAfA) Mediation Rules.[24] Each will be discussed in turn.[25]

---

for Effective Dispute Resolution (CEDR) Model Mediation Procedure, paragraph 3.

[20] ICPRCP Mediation and Conciliation Rules, article 3.4; compare with ICC Mediation Rules, article 7 and CEDR Model Mediation Procedure, paragraphs 1, 7 and 9.

[21] ICPRCP Mediation and Conciliation Rules, article 8.3; for comparison, see generally ICC Mediation Rules and CEDR Model Mediation Procedure.

[22] ICPRCP Rules of Procedure for Mediation and Conciliation at <https://unesdoc.unesco.org/ark:/48223/pf0000192534_eng> accessed 16 January 2025.

[23] WIPO Mediation Rules at <https://www.wipo.int/amc/en/mediation/rules> accessed January 16, 2025.

[24] Court of Arbitration for Art (CAfA) Mediation Rules, 2019 at <https://www.cafa.world/docs/CAfA%20Mediation%20Rules.pdf> accessed 16 January 2025.

[25] It should be noted that the Milan Chamber of Commerce offers a mediation service, and as part of that service, it encourages the use of its mediation rules for art disputes. Its art dispute arm is referred to as ADR Arte; see <https://www

(a) ICPRCP Mediation Rules

The ICPRCP is a permanent intergovernmental committee created under the auspices of UNESCO in 1978, initially to act as an advisor and educator about cultural property claims that fell outside the scope of its 1970 Convention on the Means of Prohibiting and Preventing the Illicit Import, Export and Transfer of Ownership of Cultural Property (the 1970 Convention), particularly with respect to claims dealing with cultural property illicitly removed from countries of origin prior to its coming into force.[26] Mediation and conciliation services were introduced in 2005 and formalised in 2010 to encourage parties to resolve art and cultural heritage disputes collaboratively, emphasising mutual understanding and consensual solutions that respect the cultural significance of the disputed object while supporting international efforts to protect cultural heritage.[27]

.camera-arbitrale.it/en/mediation/art-related-disputes/activation-and-procedure.php?id=662> accessed 15 January 2025. While ADR Arte refers to art disputes, the rules for art disputes are its general rules for all disputes, and there do not appear to be any specific guidelines for art disputes as offered by WIPO. As a result, its rules have not been included for exploration in this chapter.

[26] UNESCO Convention on the Means of Prohibiting and Preventing the Illicit Import, Export and Transfer of Ownership of Cultural Property, 14 November 1970, 823 UNTS 231 (1970 UNESCO Convention); see Article 7, which sets out the aim of the Convention to prevent illicit trafficking and facilitate the recovery or restitution of cultural property for its member states. Claims under the 1970 Convention can only be brought for cultural property stolen or illicitly exported after a member's ratification date; generally, therefore, pre-1970 losses are not caught by the Convention, nor are losses not defined by the Convention (i.e. non-inventoried objects as required by the Convention).

[27] UNESCO, Rules of Procedure for Mediation and Conciliation, in accordance with Article 4, paragraph 1 of the Statutes of the Intergovernmental Committee for Promoting the Return of Cultural Property to its Countries of Origin or its Restitution in Case of Illicit Appropriation (ICPRCP), CLT-2010/CONF.203/COM.16/7 (ICPRCP Mediation and Conciliation Rules), established in 1978 under the auspices of the 1970 UNESCO Convention at <https://unesdoc.unesco.org/ark:/48223/pf0000192534_eng>; Introduction of Mediation and Conciliation Services to ICPRCP Remit, February 2005, Recommendations 3 and 4 at <https://unesdoc.unesco.org/ark:/48223/pf0000140529>; Adoption of the ICPRCP's Rules of Procedure, September 2010, Recommendation 4 at <https://unesdoc.unesco.org/ark:/48223/pf0000189639> accessed January 2025; see also general discussion at <https://www.unesco.org/en/fight-illicit-trafficking/return-and-restitution> accessed 16 January 2025.

The ICPRCP's Mediation Rules provide a detailed framework for mediation, including the processes for entering into mediation on mutual consent (Articles 4 and 6); appointment of mediators (Articles 2(6), 3(4) and 7); party attendance at the mediation (Article 4(4)); details as to how the mediation sessions are conducted and the role of the mediator during the session (Article 8); and the possible outcomes of the mediation (Article 10). Other key provisions address costs (Article 11), confidentiality (Article 8) and time expectations (Articles 8(9) and 8(10)). Many of these procedural provisions are not unusual and are generally found in generic mediation rules; those that depart from the usual are discussed below.

Mediation is defined under these rules as a process where 'an outside party intervenes to bring [parties] together and to assist them in reaching an amicable solution of their dispute with respect to the restitution or return of cultural property' (Article 2(1)). Here, the focus is clearly stated – these rules are about the return of cultural property. Further, the mediation is to be 'conducted in conditions of confidentiality and in accordance with the general principles of fairness, impartiality and good faith' (Article 3(2)) and the mediator is to 'participate with a view to facilitating an amicable and just solution or settlement of the dispute having due regard to international law and recognized principles' (Article 3(4)). What is interesting about these provisions regarding the principles underlying the conduct of mediations is the specific reference to 'fairness', 'good faith' and 'just solutions'. These are not the usual principles by which commercial mediations may be conducted, and in fact, these principles can give rise to debate as to their definitional boundaries as well as the nature of imposed obligations on the mediator and parties with respect to process issues and outcomes reached.

Further, the law is placed squarely within the mediation by reference to the requirement that law and 'recognised' principles (definition unclear) must be considered in coming to a resolution. Mediation's unique selling point is often its creativity of solutions, which may not be available at law. These unusual provisions may be explained by the complexities of the dispute at hand: claims for the return of cultural property can involve issues of cultural identity, sovereignty, looting, concepts of ownership, and religious and geopolitical aspects that call for parties to take into consideration these additional principles.

A primary feature of the ICPRCP's Mediation Rules is the clear preference for mediators who are knowledgeable about restitution of cultural property disputes. A mediation under the ICPRCP rules 'shall require the involvement of one or more individuals who shall act as mediators, chosen by the Parties preferably among independent experts on the return and restitution of cultural property.' (Article 2(2)). To assist the ICPRCP in formulating a list of expert mediators, the ICPRCP encourages its member states to nominate two mediators with cultural heritage experience to the list (Article 2(6)). Further, where the ICPRCP is requested to select a mediator by the parties (rather than parties agreeing to a mediator between themselves), Article 7(3) requires that a mediator's 'expertise in the field of restitution and/or their knowledge with regard to the nature of the dispute or the specificity of the cultural property at stake' must be taken into account in the selection process.

This reference to subject-matter knowledge in two of the ICPRCP articles moves away from a traditional view that mediators do not require substantive knowledge of the subject matter in dispute; that they are procedural experts of the process.[28] Such a requirement can provide a level of comfort to those parties who have complex art disputes that necessitate an understanding of the workings of the art market, for example. ICPRCP's specialisation in cultural property and cultural heritage as a UNESCO instrument supports the importance of this requirement of expertise on the part of a mediator under its rules and arguably highlights a recognition of a need for such expertise for these types of disputes.[29]

Another interesting provision, and also unusual from a perspective of a traditional model, is Article 8(3), which empowers mediators to conduct their own independent inquiries and research to determine facts or verify information. In the normal course, while mediators are responsible for guiding the process, their decisions about process are subject to parties' consent. This provision seems to reduce the capacity for parties to make process decisions by giving mediators the ability to act independently of the parties and take such steps as they think appropriate to gain knowledge of the dispute. It should also be noted that the ICPRCP Mediation Rules have an accessibility barrier: the mediation services of the ICPRCP are restricted to member and associate

---

[28] This is particularly relevant to facilitative mediation where the third-party intervenor is not conducting an advisory or evaluative role for the parties, which necessitates an understanding of the legal issues in dispute for effective interventions; see for example, Moore CW, *The Mediation Process: Practical Strategies for Resolving Conflict Fourth Edition* (Jossey-Bass 2014) at 46–59.

[29] Pursuant to Article 1 of the Constitution of the United Nations Educational, Scientific & Cultural Organisation, 1945 (UNESCO Constitution), UNESCO's main task is 'to contribute to peace and security by promoting collaboration among nations through education, science and culture'. It achieves this mission in a variety of ways such as introducing specific legal instruments to protect cultural heritage such as the 1970 UNESCO Convention, designating and protecting World Heritage Sites, promoting intangible cultural heritage through legal instruments such as its Convention for the Safeguarding of the Intangible Cultural Heritage, 2003, advising on cultural policy development, facilitating international cultural exchanges, and raising awareness of the importance of cultural heritage and diversity.

member states (who may represent private and public institutions or the interests of their nationals: Article 4(1)(2)).

(b) The World Intellectual Property Organisation Mediation Rules

WIPO is an intergovernmental organisation established by the WIPO Convention in 1967, entered into force in 1970 and became a specialised agency of the United Nations in 1974.[30] Through its Arbitration and Mediation Centre (WIPO ADR Centre), WIPO offers mediation, arbitration and expert determination services for disputes in the art and cultural heritage sector. While WIPO applies its general mediation rules to art and cultural heritage disputes (WIPO Mediation Rules), it provides tailored guidance and subject-matter mediator expertise through its sector specific guidance for the art and cultural heritage dispute, ADR for Art & Cultural Heritage (WIPO Art Dispute Guidance), in order to better serve the particular needs of the disputes as well as promote the effectiveness of mediation for these disputes.[31]

First, many of the provisions of the WIPO Mediation Rules are the usual provisions found in mediation procedure rules dealing with the commencement of the process (Articles 3–6, with the exception of Article 4(b), more fully discussed below), conduct at the mediation, the role of the mediator (Articles 9, 10 and 12), confidentiality (Articles 15–18), termination (Articles 19–21) and costs (Articles 22, 23 and 25).

The WIPO Mediation Rules give the WIPO ADR Centre a more proactive role in the administration of the mediation early in the process: for example, according to Article 4(b), following a party's submission of a request to mediate, the Centre may, at the request of one of the parties, appoint a neutral to assist the parties in considering mediation. Further, where the parties, who have agreed to conduct a mediation under the WIPO Mediation Rules, cannot agree on the selection of a mediator, the Centre will appoint the mediator, having regard to all the circumstances of the dispute (Article 7(a)(v) and (b)). Under the WIPO Mediation Rules, the mediator appears to be provided with extended authority in terms of the mediator's process: Article 14(a) states that a mediator may promote settlement in any manner they think appropriate.

---

30 WIPO Convention, 1967; see <https://www.wipo.int/treaties/en/convention/> accessed 17 January 2025.

31 WIPO Mediation Rules at <https://www.wipo.int/amc/en/mediation/rules> accessed 16 January 2025; WIPO Alternative Dispute Resolution (ADR) for Art & Cultural Heritage (WIPO Art Dispute Guidance) at <https://www.wipo.int/amc/en/center/specific-sectors/art/#:~:text=for%20court%20litigation.-,Art%20and%20Cultural%20Heritage%20Disputes,-Art%20and%20cultural> accessed 20 January 2025.

Further, in Article 14(b), the mediator is explicitly provided with the guidance to offer proposals to the parties in the event that the parties cannot come to a resolution in mediation: the mediator may propose other processes that would be appropriate for the parties including expert determination, arbitration, and last offers of settlement arbitration.

Art and cultural heritage disputes are specifically distinguished through the WIPO Art Dispute Guidance, mentioned above. Most relevant is WIPO's maintenance of a list of neutrals with expertise in art and cultural heritage for the WIPO ADR Centre's mediations, arbitrations and expert determination processes. It is also prepared to adapt its processes to better meet the needs of the parties and the dispute: 'Where appropriate in light of the needs of the relevant stakeholders, the WIPO [ADR] Centre provides guidance in the establishment of adapted ADR frameworks, including fees and clauses, and provides administrative services thereunder.'[32] Furthermore, the Centre offers educational training with procedure and contract issues relating to the art dispute, including 'advice on the drafting and adaptation of ADR clauses in art and cultural heritage related contracts and submission agreements, as well as helping to bring disputing parties to ADR'.[33] WIPO is also prepared to organise and deliver mediation workshops on request.[34]

The above information is provided on a dedicated webpage detailing WIPO's ADR services for the art and cultural heritage sector, including information about its caseload and examples of the disputes it has administered.[35] This, together with its past collaborations with the International Council of Museums (ICOM)[36] and its programme on genetic resources, traditional knowledge and

---

32 WIPO Art Dispute Guidance at <https://www.wipo.int/amc/en/center/specific-sectors/art/#:~:text=for%20court%20litigation.-,Art%20and%20Cultural%20Heritage%20Disputes,-Art%20and%20cultural> accessed January 2025; also, WIPO has advised that there is flexibility to adjust administrative costs where stakeholders do not have the resources necessary to undertake mediation and meet WIPO fees (discussion with WIPO legal officer on 13 January 2025; notes on file with the author).

33 WIPO Art Dispute Guidance at <https://www.wipo.int/amc/en/center/specific-sectors/art/#:~:text=for%20court%20litigation.-,Art%20and%20Cultural%20Heritage%20Disputes,-Art%20and%20cultural> accessed 20 January 2025.

34 WIPO Art Dispute Guidance at <https://www.wipo.int/amc/en/center/specific-sectors/art/#:~:text=for%20court%20litigation.-,Art%20and%20Cultural%20Heritage%20Disputes,-Art%20and%20cultural> accessed 20 January 2025.

35 WIPO Art Dispute Guidance at <https://www.wipo.int/amc/en/center/specific-sectors/art/#:~:text=for%20court%20litigation.-,Art%20and%20Cultural%20Heritage%20Disputes,-Art%20and%20cultural> accessed 20 January 2025.

36 While the WIPO Art Dispute Guidance refers to ICOM collaboration, in the past, this collaboration manifested in ICOM-WIPO Mediation Rules offering

traditional cultural expressions, the latter of which culminates with the WIPO Treaty on Intellectual Property, Genetic Resources and Associated Traditional Knowledge adopted by its members in May 2024, further illustrates WIPO's commitment to the cultural heritage sector.[37] WIPO's work in these areas solidify its expertise and promotes support for its resolution processes as ones which are administered by experts in the field and which offer flexibility for effective handling of art and cultural heritage disputes.

(c) The Court of Arbitration for Art

The Court of Arbitration for Art (CAfA) was created by the Netherlands Arbitration Institute and Authentication in Art in Holland to address challenges associated with art and cultural heritage disputes by offering mediation and arbitration services tailored to those disputes.[38] In particular, CAfA sees a need for mediators to be resolution professionals and experts qualified to resolve disputes including those dealing with collectors, art market professionals, historians, museums and financial institutions.[39] The range of disputes is broad, including authenticity disputes, restitution claims, copyright issues and other issues of the art market.[40] The *raison d'être* of CAfA is the art dispute, and accordingly, it has some unique provisions in its administration of the mediation process and its rules, in addition to standard provisions dealing with the commencement of mediation (Articles 3 and 5), conduct of the

---

a mediation framework administered by WIPO, which included an obligation on parties and the mediator to have regard to ICOM's Code of Ethics for Museums (former article 13(a) of the ICOM-WIPO Mediation Rules). According to WIPO, these rules were discontinued sometime in 2022 when WIPO came to the view that its mediation rules with the ADR sector-specific guidance were appropriate for the art and cultural heritage dispute (discussion with WIPO legal officer on 13 January 2025; notes on file with author).

37 For information about the programme, see at <https://www.wipo.int/en/web/traditional-knowledge> accessed 21 January 2025; and for information about the Treaty, see <https://www.wipo.int/en/web/traditional-knowledge/wipo-treaty-on-ip-gr-and-associated-tk> accessed 21 January 2025.

38 The Court of Arbitration for Art (CAfA) at <https://www.cafa.world/cafa/about_us/> accessed 21 January 2025.

39 Article 1(4) of the Explanatory Notes for the CAfA Mediation Rules at <https://www.cafa.world/docs/CAfA%20Mediation%20Rules.pdf> accessed 21 January 2025.

40 For a discussion about CAfA, see for example, Kadhim N, 'Arbitration in the Art World and the Court of Arbitration for Art: Heading towards a More Effective Resolution of Arts Disputes' (2019) 24 AA&L 223.

mediation (Article 6), termination (Article 7), confidentiality (Article 10) and costs (Article 9) (CAfA Mediation Rules).

The Court of Arbitration for Art veers from the standard with Article 4 which deals with the selection of the mediator. Similar to the WIPO Art Dispute Guidance, the mediator must have expertise in matters dealing with art and cultural heritage. Unlike the WIPO Art Dispute Guidance, the CAfA rules are quite specific on the existence of CAfA's pool of qualified neutrals and the selection of the mediator from that pool. Specifically, Article 4 requires the parties to select a mediator from CAfA's list of approved mediators, unless CAfA agrees otherwise. If parties cannot agree on a mediator from CAfA's list, CAfA will then proceed to select a mediator according to its procedure under Article 4(3). Another relevant provision to the art and cultural heritage dispute is found in Article 4(7), which provides for the appointment of experts to assist the mediator and parties, and where issues involve forensic science and provenance, the expert is to be selected from CAfA's pool of qualified experts.

The CAfA website sets out the qualifications required of its mediators and experts who apply for appointment to CAfA's pool of mediators and experts. The applications are reviewed and determined by CAfA's Selection Committee according to the following established criteria (the arbitrator criteria are set out since the mediator criteria subsume them):

Arbitrator criteria

1. (Formerly) admitted private practice lawyers, judges, law professors.
2. Five years of significant experience in at least one relevant field, including (without limitation):
   (a) authenticity;
   (b) chain of title of art or cultural property (including heritage/patrimony/restitution);
   (c) purchase and sale of works of art through private sale and/or auction;
   (d) copyright in the field of art;
   (e) insurance of fine art or cultural property;
   (f) museum exhibition and loan agreements;
   (g) loan agreements (non-museum);
   (h) UNESCO;
   (i) taxation, trusts, estates & succession;
   (j) import/export regulations; and/or
   (k) international arbitration.

Mediator criteria

1. Same criteria as arbitrators.
2. Five years of significant experience as a mediator.

3. Advanced mediation training or certification from mediation organisations such as the International Mediation Institute and/or membership in the roster of recognised ADR providers or the Court ADR Program.[41]

Article 2 of the Explanatory Notes to CAfA's Mediation Rules sets out the nature of the mediator and expert pool:

> 2.1 The Mediator Pool is composed of international mediators with demonstrated experience in art law disputes and/or international mediation.
>
> 2.2 The Expert Pool is composed of international materials analysts/forensic scientists, and art historians/provenance researchers qualified, among other things, to analyze and document art objects, most often for authentication purposes. Art authenticity is typically understood to be evaluated according to standards of connoisseurship, provenance research, and forensic science. While relevant connoisseurs or scholars of a particular artist or a particular type of art objects or collectibles must be approached on a case-by-case basis, experts in the fields of provenance and forensic science can analyze objects of art more generally. As an alternative to having disputing parties retain their own respective experts in these particular fields, with such experts then advocating for their side, the CAfA Mediation Rules shall offer the Expert Pool to provide the exclusive analysis and professional opinion on these subjects.[42]

The CAfA Mediation Rules have a couple of additional quirks which illustrate the arbitral underpinnings of CAfA: Article 8 provides that a settlement reached at mediation can be converted to an arbitral award and become enforceable as such; and Article 15 stipulates that a mediation conducted under the rules will be referred to arbitration in the event that the parties do not settle. The former provides an added benefit to parties to change the nature of the settlement from an enforceable agreement to an enforceable arbitral award. The latter provides the parties with a further resolution process in the event of failure at the mediation, giving them a further opportunity for a resolution, albeit one that is not consensual in outcome.

---

[41] CAfA Selection Criteria for Arbitrators and Mediators at <https://cafa.world/docs/2018%20CAfA%20Selection%20Criteria%20Arbitrators%20and%20Mediators.pdf> accessed 21 January 2025.

[42] Article 2 of the Explanatory Notes for the CAfA Mediation Rules at <https://www.cafa.world/docs/CAfA%20Mediation%20Rules.pdf> accessed 21 January 2025.

THE RULES: A DISCUSSION

The surveyed mediation schemes offer parties an opportunity to address topics and issues particular to the art and cultural heritage dispute. These could include: (1) addressing the legal limitations in assessing the merits of the dispute; (2) accommodating specific cultural traditions underlying the dispute; (3) recognising a broader historical narrative requiring inquiry into the circumstances under which a cultural object was acquired, particularly with respect to looted or stolen objects; (4) understanding the intangible value of the cultural object in dispute such as its relationship to the cultural identity of a community; and (5) addressing legal, ethical and intergovernmental issues that may impact resolution.

One of the key advantages of these mediation schemes is that they situate the mediation within a specialised milieu which increases the opportunity to effectively respond to challenges posed by the dispute. While judges adjudicate a wide array of legal issues – including those involving technical or specialised subject areas – the distinct nature of the art dispute often introduces complexities that may exceed the scope of general judicial expertise, such as definitional and authenticity claims.[43] This is where mediators with specific expertise in the field become relevant for these disputes. Their knowledge of and experience with the art dispute can help direct their facilitation of issues such as provenance, authenticity, or restitution more effectively; the sources of conflict underlying the art dispute are more readily understood by such mediators and thus they are better able to guide parties to resolution by responding specifically to the intricacies of the conflict and its barriers to resolution.

Each of the rules under consideration has been designed (ICPRCP, CAfA) or adapted (WIPO) to cater to the needs of art and cultural heritage stakeholders such as states, cultural institutions, private collectors, regional communities, auction houses and art dealers. These mechanisms offer varying degrees of mediator involvement, allowing parties to select mediators with profiles that best suit their dispute. For example, mediators can range from legal experts having international art law experience to art historians to experts with experience in restitution claims.[44] Such mediators may be familiar with the unique

---

[43] See for example, Paintin I, 'The Art of Connoisseurship through Judicial Eyes: The Law of Negligence and Fine Art Attribution' (2015) 20 AAL 101; Holland J, 'The Approach of the English Court to Connoisseurship, Provenance and Technical Analysis' (2012) 17 AAL Law 365.

[44] ICPRCP Mediation Rules, Articles 2(2) and 7(3) at <https://unesdoc.unesco.org/ark:/48223/pf0000192534_eng> accessed 16 January 2025; CAfA Selection Criteria for Arbitrators and Mediators at <https://cafa.world/docs/2018%20CAfA%20Selection%20Criteria%20Arbitrators%20and%20Mediators.pdf>

pressures and priorities of the art and cultural heritage market, such as reputational concerns, the need to preserve ongoing relationships, and a requirement for confidentiality in a market which prizes privacy.

Additionally, as noted above, the ICPRCP Mediation Rules offer additional provisions which are not usually found in generally applicable mediation rules such as the principles by which a mediation is to be conducted: the application of general principles of fairness and good faith (Article 3(2)); and a requirement to facilitate a just solution that takes into account international law and recognised principles (Article 3(4)). The CAfA Mediation Rules offer access to a pool of experts in forensic science and provenance where a dispute involves such issues (Article 4(7)). Such provisions further acknowledge the multi-layered issues that can define an art dispute involving, for example, cross-border issues, proof of authenticity or ownership, protection of cultural identity or defence of human rights.

The schemes also offer some extended authority for mediators: the ICPRCP Mediation Rules allow mediators to conduct their own independent inquiries and research to determine facts (Article 8(3)). The WIPO Mediation Rules give the mediator authority to promote settlement in any manner they deem appropriate and to offer proposals to the parties (Article 14(a)). Schemes also provide access to complementary ADR methods, such as conciliation (ICPRCP) or arbitration (CAfA, WIPO) or good offices (ICPRCP, WIPO), which can give parties options to modify or escalate the process if mediation alone cannot achieve a resolution agreeable to all parties.

Through these provisions, ICPRCP, WIPO and CAfA seek to improve mediation processes for a particular type of dispute by addressing certain specific needs of the art dispute. While these provisions seek to improve the process for its users, there is still room for improvement, however.

Despite the special provisions for the art dispute discussed in this chapter, the main disadvantage of all mediation processes still exists: mediation relies on the consent of all parties to initiate the process. While the consensual nature of mediation is often seen as a strength – fostering empowering, collaborative and voluntary solutions – it can also present significant challenges, particularly in contentious or emotionally charged disputes such as those involving cultural property and heritage issues. Such disputes may stem from long and complex histories marked by deeply entrenched positions, strained relations,

---

accessed 21 January 2025; Article 2.1 of the Explanatory Notes for the CAfA Mediation Rules at <https://www.cafa.world/docs/CAfA%20Mediation%20Rules.pdf> accessed 21 January 2025; WIPO Art Dispute Guidance at <https://www.wipo.int/amc/en/center/specific-sectors/art/#:~:text=for%20court%20litigation.-,Art%20and%20Cultural%20Heritage%20Disputes,-Art%20and%20cultural> accessed January 20, 2025.

miscommunication, mistrust or even hostility between the parties, all of which can make resolution appear impossible even if the parties agree to engage in the process at first instance. The lack of prevalent use of mediation in this sphere seems to attest to the difficulty of getting parties to the mediation table. For example, as at May 2024, the ICPRCP reported that its mediation rules have not yet been used, despite having been formalised between 2005 and 2010.[45] WIPO has advised that it has conducted a handful of mediations in recent years.[46] With respect to CAfA mediations, as at the time of writing, no information could be found as to mediations conducted pursuant to CAfA Mediation Rules.[47]

Another challenge deals with power imbalances. Despite the provisions in the ICPRCP Mediation Rules and the WIPO Mediation Rules (and its WIPO Art Dispute Guidance) regarding the conduct of the mediation (for example, to be conducted in fairness; promotion of settlement in any manner), mediation may not adequately address power disparities between the parties, whether financial, political or social in nature.[48] For example, although mediation is

---

45 See ICPRCP Session Report, 'Presentation of the tools necessary to simplify the use of mediation and
conciliation procedures' 29–31 May 2024 at <https://unesdoc.unesco.org/ark:/48223/pf0000389425_eng> accessed 13 January 2025. In order to promote mediation, the Report refers to changes made to the ICPRCP Mediation Rules website to help parties with the decision to request mediation.

46 A representative of WIPO advised on 13 January 2025 that a review of its mediation case load found that about six disputes have been mediated through WIPO's services over the years. These involved restitution, authenticity, title and copyright disputes; notes on file with author.

47 It should be noted that the Milan Chamber of Commerce, ADR Arte, has reported that between 2015 and 2017, 32 mediations took place using their rules (out of 935 mediations conducted). ADR Arte lists the types of disputes as involving contract, inheritance and property disputes; for these statistics, see <https://www.camera-arbitrale.it/upload/documenti/statistiche/adr-art-facts-figures-2015–2017.pdf> accessed January 2025; ADR Arte also released a report dated 2018; however, the statistical reporting is not clear and therefore is not reported here (see <https://www.camera-arbitrale.it/upload/documenti/statistiche/adr-art-facts-figures-2018.pdf> accessed 2 February 2025).

48 There is debate in the literature as to whether a mediator should make interventions that would address power imbalances that become evident between parties during a mediation. This issue involves consideration of the role of mediators, the extent of the impartiality and neutrality requirements often found in mediation procedures, and mediator interventions (whether they should be directive, facilitative, evaluative, for example). See Moffitt ML and Bordone RC, The Handbook of Dispute Resolution (Jossey-Bass 2005) at 309–316.

less costly than litigation, the financial and logistical demands of participating in a specialised mediation process can still burden smaller stakeholders, such as Indigenous communities or smaller cultural institutions, which may not be able to access the mechanisms to initiate the process or resources to effectively participate in the process, once initiated. These parties may struggle to cover fees or travel costs, or access the necessary legal and technical expertise, limiting their ability to fully engage in the process.[49]

The confidential nature of mediation, while advantageous in preserving privacy (an important consideration for many stakeholders in the art dispute), presents another challenge. The emphasis on confidentiality in these schemes can result in a lack of transparency about its process and public accountability about its outcome. This is particularly problematic for disputes involving cultural heritage of national or international significance where public interest in the resolution process and outcome is high. Confidentiality can create the perception that decisions are being made without public oversight or input, potentially undermining the legitimacy of the resolution.

Linked to party desire for confidentiality and protection of party privacy is the argument that mediation does not contribute to the development of legal precedents or publicly accessible guidelines for similar cases. This limitation means that future parties facing similar disputes cannot rely on established frameworks or outcomes for guidance. In the realm of art disputes, where legal and ethical questions are evolving, the absence of precedential value can perpetuate uncertainty and exacerbate power and resource imbalances. This is supported by the lack of information readily available regarding the use of mediation by parties with the three mediation organisations examined in this chapter.[50]

These issues involving power imbalances, lack of transparency of process and outcome, and lack of process accessibility suggest that further specialised provisions are needed to improve the process for the art dispute.[51] While

---

[49] It is noted that WIPO ADR Centre advised that it is flexible with its fees when a party suffers hardship in meeting the administrative costs of the process (discussion with WIPO on 13 January 2025; notes on file with author).

[50] In notes 45, 46 and 47 above, reference was made to the lack of mediations initiated through these three schemes. For the mediations conducted by the WIPO, disclosed in a private communication, the details of the mediations were scarce and the information is not publicly available. Even for the Milan Chamber of Commerce ADR Arte mediations, also referenced in note 47, the information about the mediations that is publicly available is also scarce, offering only categories of the nature of the dispute and statistics about outcomes.

[51] The challenges enumerated here have been discussed in the mediation literature generally; see for example, Spencer D and Brogan M, Mediation Law and

these mediation schemes recognise the specific nature of the art dispute by the implementation of particular provisions such as those discussed in this chapter, challenges remain and should be addressed to continue to improve the process for these disputes. The lack of data available in the literature about the nature of the process conducted in the art and cultural heritage field impedes further development of bespoke rules for these disputes. This is an area ripe for further research, one which requires access to conducted mediations as well as to interested stakeholders, and which, given the private nature of the market, can be difficult to access.

In conclusion, this chapter illustrates the ways in which a particular field, the art law field, has taken steps to ameliorate the mediation process for its users so that it can better respond to the art dispute. It has targeted mediation as a process that can assist parties with their resolution and seeks to promote it by responding to particular needs of the parties in these disputes. This exploration suggests that adapting the mediation process to meet distinct aspects of the art dispute is seen to add value to the process for its stakeholders. In a related fashion, the chapter also raises the question of whether this adaptability should be applied more broadly: stakeholders of other types of disputes may benefit from more bespoke mediation processes, particularly when the process is integrated with a state's civil justice framework and the delivery of the outcome is connected to issues of access to justice and justice delivery.[52]

Further, while this chapter has discussed the ways in which the art law field has adapted mediation processes to encourage the use of mediation through what it sees to be bespoke processes for the art dispute, this chapter also recognises that there is more to do to 'bespokevise' the process further to address the process challenges of mediation which continue to exist for art dispute stakeholders. By doing so, it also highlights the challenges which continue to underpin mediation processes generally which are situated within the nature of mediation as a consensual, informal, non-rule-based, confidential process. A more adaptive mediation process that takes into account the nature of a dispute not only may improve the process for stakeholders, but may also address

---

Practice (CUP 2006) at 120–124; Palmer M and Roberts S, *Dispute Processes: ADR and the Primary Forms of Dispute Resolution*, 3rd edn (CUP 2020); Frenkel DN and Stark JH, The Practice of Mediation (Wolters Kluwer 2010) at 289–321.

[52] For discussion about mediation in civil justice and views about the delivery of justice, see for example, De Girolamo D & Spenser Underhill D, 'ADR and the Civil Courts – A Very British Type of Justice. The Legacy of the Woolf Reforms in 2022' (2022) 4(1) AC 129 and De Girolamo D, 'Sen, Justice and the Private Realm of Dispute Resolution' (2018) 14(3) IJLC 353.

challenges that appear embedded within the process and impact its attraction to potential users.

ACKNOWLEDGMENTS

I am grateful to Karla C.M. Checa and Lauren E. Gowler for their research assistance and to the editors of this collection for their support throughout.

11. New trends in mediation in Brazilian law

Antonio Cabral

11.1 INTRODUCTION: THE GROWTH OF MEDIATION AND ADR IN BRAZIL AND LATIN AMERICA

In recent decades, the growth of alternative dispute resolution (ADR) in Latin America is undeniable. Various legal systems have adopted public policies to foster dispute resolution proceedings that could present an alternative path to the adjudication of conflicts by the judiciary. Instead of encouraging the resolution of disputes by imperative decisions, with a focus on judicial authority, one can clearly see the strengthening of consensual methods of conflict management such as conciliation, mediation, and more recently collaborative law and dispute boards.[1]

A next step in this evolution has been a more detailed and extensive regulation of some of these proceedings. The introduction of rules for these types of procedure in statutes, or at least general norms enabling the parties to adopt and contractually design procedures for the resolution of their disputes, is not only crucial for establishing due process standards, but also contributes to publicise ADR, to increase professionals' knowledge of these methods and to drive innovation in dispute resolution. All of these have been observed in some jurisdictions at least for a few of the most practised conflict resolution mechanisms such as arbitration.

Mediation has only gained academic attention in more recent times, greater focus in public policies, and more prominence in legislative reforms. While some jurisdictions in Latin America still suffer from the lack of regulation, government neglect (few state investments) and the cultural difficulties of a

[1] See several references to various jurisdictions in Antonio Cabral, Consensual Dispute Resolution, *in* Burkhard Hess, Margaret Woo, Loïc Cadiet and Enrique Vallines (eds). *Comparative Procedural Law and Justice*, Part XV.1, p. 3 ff, available at https://www.cplj.org/download, accessed 4 July 2025.

community still reliant on litigation, others have made significant progress in the past decade, as is the case with the Brazilian legal system.

The aim of this chapter is to present the latest developments of mediation, as well as future prospects of mediation in Brazil. We shall see that the growth of mediation in the Brazilian legal system is as a result of recently enacted regulations and public policies that are boosting this form of ADR. This context will allow for some reflections on the role that mediation will take in the future considering the general framework of dispute resolution.

11.2 PUBLIC POLICY TO ENCOURAGE SETTLEMENTS AND AGREEMENTS: THE ROLE OF THE BRAZILIAN NATIONAL COUNCIL OF JUSTICE

In Brazil, incentives for the development of consensual dispute resolution mechanisms come not only from the private sector, but also and above all from public policies. In 2010, the Brazilian National Council of Justice – the administrative body that deals with court management and court administration in the country – issued Resolution 125, designed to organise a national policy for the proper handling of conflicts of interest within the judiciary. The goal was to break with the tradition that used to favour a culture of litigation (of fierce and ruthless judicial combat as the prime form of dispute resolution, which in Brazil has led to excessive belligerence and the exaggerated judicialisation of conflicts, resulting in an overwhelming number of cases brought before the judiciary) and to replace it with a culture of consensual dispute resolution. To this end, the regulation provided for the qualification and training of civil servants, conciliators and mediators, as well as specific statistical monitoring.

An important structural change brought about by Resolution 125/2010 was the provision for court-connected or court-annexed mediation. According to the legal norm, courts were obliged to create structures or units to promote mediation and conciliation in judicial procedures already commenced before a court. Resolution 125/2010 of the National Council of Justice organised the so-called 'judicial conflict resolution centres' in each court, where mediation and conciliation are carried out within the judiciary, but by accredited mediators and conciliators, not judges.

11.3 OTHER MILESTONES IN LEGISLATIVE DEVELOPMENT: THE CODE OF CIVIL PROCEDURE AND THE MEDIATION ACT 2015

There have been numerous legislative reforms that are worth mentioning in describing the evolution of mediation in the Brazilian legal system. The two major changes were the Code of Civil Procedure (CCP)[2] and the Mediation Act (statute No. 13,140),[3] both enacted in 2015. The CCP was published in March 2015 and came into legal force a year later. The Mediation Act was published on 26 June 2015, but curiously, according to its art. 47, came into legal force 180 days after its official publication, i.e. in December 2015, before the CCP.

The publication of two statutes regulating partially the same subject matter created a potential conflict of norms, which was emphasised by the fact that the Mediation Act did not expressly revoke the CCP in the part that it had regulated mediation. So if the same issue is regulated by different provisions of the two statutes, it is up to legal interpretation to determine if they are incompatible in any way, and to conclude which one should prevail.

Fortunately, there are not many points of divergence between the Code of Civil Procedure and the Mediation Act. Although the Mediation Act has much more detailed rules, both regulations can be combined and integrated, and complement each other.[4]

A. Guidelines to Encourage Consensus and Settlement

Article 3 § 2 of the CCP states, right from its fundamental principles, that 'the State shall promote, whenever possible, the consensual solution of conflicts'. It is understood that this guideline encouraging agreements and settlements is aimed at all of the individuals involved in litigation, not only the parties but all public bodies too, including the court.

In addition to this guideline, art. 3 § 3 of the CCP imposes a legal duty on those involved in a judicial court procedure: it is now the responsibility of magistrates, parties and lawyers, before or in the course of judicial litigation proceedings, to encourage the use of conciliation, mediation and other consensual conflict resolution mechanisms. This includes efforts and investments to train civil servants and other staff, create physical structures, and educate citizens and legal professionals about the advantages, proceedings and alternatives available in the legal system for consensual conflict solving. Furthermore, art. 139, V of the CCP reaffirms and complements the justice system's guideline to foster consensual solutions, imposing on the court not only the power,

---

2 An English (non-official) translation of the Code of Civil Procedure is available at: https://www.academia.edu/34624319/Brazilian_Code_of_Civil_Procedure_Translated_to_English.

3 Available (only in Portuguese) at: https://www.planalto.gov.br/ccivil_03/_ato2015-2018/2015/lei/l13140.htm.

4 I have approached the very few inconsistencies between the two statutes in Antonio Cabral, 'Mediation und Schlichtung nach brasilianischem Recht' (2017) 116 *Zeitschrift für Vergleichende Rechtswissenschaft*, 342–359.

but the duty to promote settlement at any time and at any stage of the proceedings, preferably with the help of conciliators and mediators.

The CCP also provides for the possibility of the parties bringing any out-of-court agreement involving rights of any nature for judicial approval or ratification[5] even if the subject matter of these agreements is different or greater than the claim that was initially filed in court.[6] On the other hand, art. 784, IV of the CCP attributes effects of an extrajudicial enforceable document to the settlement entered into by the Public Prosecutor's Office, the Public Defender, when the agreement is signed by the parties' lawyers or by a mediator accredited by the court.

Based on those guidelines of creating incentives for consensual dispute resolution, various rules and procedures have been structured to help implement this goal sought by the legislator. We shall look into some of them in the next sections.

B. Regulation of the Activity of Mediators and the Mediation Procedure

The CCP provides for an entire chapter on mediation and conciliation.[7] Mediation can take place in judicial dispute resolution centres (court-annexed mediation) or in private mediation chambers.

According to art. 166 of the CCP, mediation must be guided by the principles of party autonomy, orality and informality of the proceeding, independence and impartiality of the mediators, and confidentiality. Confidentiality extends to all information produced in the course of the procedure, the content of which may not be used for any purpose other than that provided for by express decision of the parties. Due to the obligation of secrecy inherent in their functions, mediators (and members of their teams) may not divulge or testify in court about facts or elements arising from the mediation.

In the same sense, the Mediation Act lists guiding principles for mediation which, although not identical, are in line with those provided for in the CCP: party autonomy; orality and informality of the procedure; impartiality of the mediator; equality between the parties; the search for consensus; confidentiality and good faith. Moreover, the ordinary procedure has been structured by the CCP in such a way as to contain an initial stage aimed at negotiating settlements that could bring the dispute to a consensual end. Unless both parties expressly state that they do not want a negotiated solution, the judge

5 CCP art. 515, III; art. 725, VIII, CCP.
6 CCP art. 515 § 2.
7 CCP arts 165–175.

must appoint a hearing to try to reach an agreement[8] at which the parties must attend, under penalty of a fine. In disputes involving family law, the hearing will be compulsory even if both parties say they do not want it.[9]

This obligation to attend the mediation hearing, and the provision of a fine for absence, are legal rules that have been much debated in Brazilian legal literature. The fact is that several provisions of the Mediation Act point to the voluntary nature of mediation, which should only be set up and/or continue if and for as long as the parties wish (see, among other provisions, art. 1, sole paragraph, and art. 2 § 2 of the Mediation Act), points out the impossibility of any penalty for non-attendance at the mediation hearing.

C. Mediation Involving Public Administration Bodies

Contrary to the previous tradition that depicted cases involving state bodies as the realm of *ordre public*, of authority and imperativeness, of the invariable presence of public interests, and therefore unfit to be solved by the parties themselves, a clearly broadening trend in the Brazilian legal system has been the expansion of mediation to cases of public interest, those in which a public body or administrative entity is involved.

The CCP provides for the mandatory installation of administrative chambers for conciliation and mediation.[10] The public administration, in all federal spheres (Union, States, and Municipalities) must create specific conciliation and mediation chambers, which will have attributions related to the consensual resolution of conflicts involving public bodies and entities. At the federal level, an example of this is the Federal Public Administration Mediation and Conciliation Chamber, organised by the Federal Advocate General's Office, which between 2018 and 2023 resolved 143 cases worth around 40 billion US dollars.

Other subsequent statutory reforms followed the same tendency and have expanded the possibilities for mediation in areas of the law that were thought to be incapable of serving for conflict resolution. Nowadays, for example, the public administration is allowed to submit disputes involving expropriation to mediation.[11]

---

8 CCP art. 334.

9 CCP art. 695.

10 CCP art. 174.

11 Art.10-B of Statutory-Decree 3365/41.

D. Procedural Agreements: Negotiation About Procedure

The possibilities for the parties to modify by contract the formalities of court litigation procedures have always been a very controversial issue, mainly because of the tradition that considered litigation as embedded with strong public interests. This orthodox approach used to restrict party autonomy in civil procedure, preventing the disputants from contracting to deviate from default statutory provisions. The subject of procedural agreements was treated very timidly by legal scholars and whenever mentioned, the theme generated a strong rejection. This resistance resulted from a long-term approach to judicial processes as a state matter, influencing the conceptual analysis of several instruments of procedural law through a strong public interest perspective.

However, over the past two decades, there has been a worldwide tendency in favour of contractualisation of civil litigation.[12] Many jurisdictions allow the parties to enter into 'procedural agreements' or 'procedural contracts', i.e. contracts to shape the formalities of court procedures, something once envisaged only for arbitration, but now a visible trend also for litigation.[13]

In Brazil, procedural contracts have been consistently used as a tool for shifting or modifying statutory provisions, and the subject has reached a very sophisticated and unusual stage of evolution with the enactment of the CCP.[14] On one hand, the Brazilian CCP expressly provides for several types of procedural agreements, such as forum selection clauses;[15] agreement to extend or reduce deadlines;[16] agreement for stay of the proceeding;[17] joint expert appointment;[18] agreement to set a procedural timetable;[19] agreement to

[12] Anna Nylund and Antonio Cabral. *Contractualisation of Civil Litigation* (Intersentia 2023).

[13] Antonio Cabral, 'Procedural Contracts and Agreements: An Introduction to a New Era of Party Autonomy in Litigation', *in* Antonio Cabral and Anna Nylund. *Shaping Civil Litigation Using Procedural Agreements* (Eleven, 2024), 3–23.

[14] Nylund and Cabral, *supra* note 5, where one can see studies from 20 different jurisdictions from the Americas, Europe and Asia.

[15] CCP art. 63 and 781, I.

[16] CCP art. 222 §1.

[17] CCP art. 313, II and 922. During the COVID-19 pandemic, it became common for parties to enter into procedural agreements to suspend proceedings, in light of the need to comply with social isolation measures that would hinder the practice or performance of certain procedural legal acts.

[18] CCP art. 471.

[19] CCP art. 191.

define the rules of burden of proof;[20] agreement for withdrawal of claims and appeals;[21] and agreement about attachable assets.[22]

On the other hand, the newly enacted legislation has general provisions empowering the parties to negotiate about the procedure, as we shall see in detail in the following section.

11.4 ARTICLES 190 AND 200 OF THE BRAZILIAN CODE OF CIVIL PROCEDURE: GENERAL ENABLING NORMS FOR PROCEDURAL CONTRACTS

Among the many normative changes brought by the CCP, especially interesting for the subject of procedural agreements is the novelty of arts 190[23] and 200,[24] both providing for the admissibility of parties' negotiation about the procedure via legal transactions with binding effects on the court. Judges could only oppose or not apply the contractual norm if it presents grounds for invalidity (such as abuse of rights, vulnerability of one of the litigants, bad faith negotiations, etc.).

In light of these general enabling provisions, parties are not limited to what was explicitly regulated by the legislator. The Brazilian legal system is now open to parties' stipulations as a result of the exercise of their party autonomy. Procedural agreements can be designed by the parties even if not specifically provided for in specific statutory norms. Indeed, arts 190 and 200 of the CCP enable the parties to agree upon and waive their procedural legal situations (legal rights, duties, burdens, etc.), or determine by contract the legal rules of

---

[20] CCP art. 373 § 3.

[21] CCP arts 775, 998 and 485 § 5.

[22] CCP art. 833, I.

[23] 'Art. 190. When the action deals with legal rights that permit the resolution of the dispute by the parties themselves, the competent parties can lawfully stipulate changes in the procedure to adapt it to the specific requirements of the lawsuit and to agree upon their procedural legal burden, powers, rights and obligations, before or during the proceedings. Sole paragraph. Whether ex officio or upon request, the judge shall control the validity of the agreements set forth in this article, denying their application only in the case of nullity or inclusion of unconscionable terms in adhesion contracts or in cases where any of the parties is in a manifest position of weakness.'

[24] 'Art. 200. The acts of the parties consisting of unilateral or bilateral declarations of will shall immediately produce the constitution, modification or extinction of procedural rights. Sole paragraph. The discontinuance (withdrawal) of a lawsuit shall only produce effects once it has been ratified by the court.'

judicial proceedings involving their affairs. This possibility stems validly from these general norms and does not depend on any other specific provision.[25]

It is therefore possible to use procedural agreements for various purposes such as: (a) to expedite the procedure, e.g. a waiver of future appeals, so that the case thereby is terminated more quickly with a single first instance trial; (b) define in advance and with more predictability the evidence to be used in a future lawsuit, and rule out certain types of evidence that may increase the costs of the procedure, such as expert examinations; (c) contractually modify standing to sue, transferring to third parties the possibility of litigating in favour of a legal interest (whether or not excluding standing of the original parties to the agreement); (d) suppress legal acts or stages of the procedure, e.g. eliminating judicial hearings, mediation sessions, or certain requests/motions of the parties, all of this in order to make the proceeding simpler and more efficient; (e) change the formalities of the proceeding, for example moving away from orality (establishing a proceeding that is predominantly written), or providing for a maximum number of pages for petitions and motions; (f) avoid the initiation of judicial proceedings under certain conditions; (g) divide the responsibility to pay for certain types of evidence (for example attributing to a party the expenses with expert examinations, witness transportation), or contracting litigation insurance and/or transferring the costs to third parties (third-party litigation funding); and (h) increase penalties for malicious prosecution or contractually define situations that would fit into agreed definitions of bad faith litigation. The list of potential contract configurations is vast.

Shortly after the Code of Civil Procedure came into legal force, practitioners began to increase the use of agreements to shape court proceedings. Clauses to modify statutory provisions and determine the formalities of litigation procedures started to be inserted in contracts more frequently and more intensely than they previously used to be. And so far, case law has reacted in a very

[25] As I observed in another text, this makes substance and procedure intertwine and mingle in contract and settlement negotiations: 'as procedural rules are changeable, it becomes possible for the parties to a legal transaction to exchange substantive legal rights for procedural legal norms, a trade-off between the rules of substantive law and procedural law. A discount can be negotiated in the price of goods or services in exchange for a waiver of appeals (building procedure at a single instance, much faster) or forfeiting an asset's protection in enforcement proceedings (thereby facilitating the selling of the debtor's property in case of breach).' See Antonio Cabral, 'Designing Procedure by Contract: Litigation Agreements in Contemporary Civil Procedure' (2019) 9 (2) *International Journal of Procedural Law*, 375.

receptive manner.[26] Examples of procedural agreements that are not expressly provided for but that can be and frequently are entered into by the parties are covenants not to sue (*pactum de non petendo*), appeal waivers, contractual stipulations about enforcement (regulating means of enforcement, seizure and attachment of assets),[27] agreements about litigation costs,[28] etc.

---

[26] The Superior Court of Justice (short STJ, the second highest tribunal in the country) has precedents holding that procedural agreements create contractual norms, which are binding on the parties and on the court, so judges have to control the agreement and verify its validity. If they cannot find exceptional grounds to invalidate the procedural contract/agreement and decide otherwise, they must apply the rules and formalities provided for in the agreement (STJ-REsp 1738656/RJ, DJe 05/12/2019; REsp n.1.810.444/SP, j.23/02/2021). Not only the Superior Court of Justice, but also in several states of the federation, courts of justice have frequently permitted procedural agreements, ruling on their binding effect over the court, and confirming that the contractually established legal norm derogates statutory provisions. This is the case in the Supreme Courts of the States of Rio de Janeiro (Apelação 0030304-05.2018.8.19.0209, j.01/09/2020; AI n.0061850-89.2019.8.19.0000, j.19/02/2020); Apelação n.0391414-47.2013.8.19.0001, j.17/11/2016; Apelação 0199167-63.2018.8.19.0001, j.08/05/2019), Paraná (Processo 0002809-44.2020.8.16.0000, j.03/08/2020; Processo 0005906-06.2017.8.16.0017, j.06/07/2018), Minas Gerais (Agravo de Instrumento-Cv 1.0000.19.026277-4/001, j.30/07/2019; Apelação Cível n.1.0000.20.036217-6/001, j.24/06/2020; Apelação Cível n. 1.0702.13.006601-3/001, j.10/10/2018), Rio Grande do Sul (Apelação Cível n. 70068728534, j.28/06/2016; Apelação Cível n. 70082573767, j.30/10/2019) and Espírito Santo (Apelação cível n. 0031438–17.2016.8.08.0024, j.21/11/2017), among many others. Moreover, Courts of different regions in the country have also enforced agreements to waive legal terms and deadlines, and redistribute the burden of proof. Supreme Court of the State of Goiás, Apelação cível 5353531-65.2018.8.09.0168, j.10/05/2021; Supreme Court of the State of Paraná, Processo 0005906-06.2017.8.16.0017, j. 06/07/2018; Supreme Court of the State of Rio Grande do Sul, Apelação Cível 70075492462, j.26/10/2017. The research group I lead at the University of Rio de Janeiro State has been conducting empirical research that has found more than 1400 decisions from higher courts and appellate courts, in both federal and state jurisdiction, debating procedural contracts. The findings of this research, although not final, show a very high percentage of judicial deference to parties' stipulations. Courts mostly enforce and validate parties' agreements.

[27] On the vast possibilities of negotiating about enforcement, some of which might seem counter-intuitive in many civil law jurisdictions, see Antonio Cabral and Fredie Didier Jr, 'Procedural Agreements to Shape Enforcement Proceedings' (2022) 27 Zeitschrift für Zivilprozess International, 219 ff.

[28] Antonio Cabral, 'Procedural Contracts about the Costs of Civil Litigation: a Brazilian View in Comparative Perspective', *in* Eva Storskrubb (ed.). *YSEC*

There has therefore been a rapid development of the subject, with a swift application of those agreements in practice and their smooth control by the courts, most decisions allowing considerable leeway for the parties' flexibilisation of court procedures via agreements, even if sometimes submitted to limited control by the judge. Therefore, those intense changes in regulation have been integrated into a feature of the legal system with little dissonance.

11.5 AGREEMENTS TO MEDIATE: CONTRACTUAL STIPULATIONS OVER THE MEDIATION PROCEEDING AND CHOICE OF MEDIATORS

This movement towards an empowerment of the parties to shape and determine the formalities of court litigation procedures has also had an impact on mediation. Along with the protagonism of the litigants to design the procedure came more possibilities to define core aspects of mediation and its relations with litigation.

One very important procedural contract related to mediation is the so called 'agreement to mediate', a contractual provision by which the parties must take the conflict to mediation prior to bringing a lawsuit into state courts. By way of an agreement to mediate, mediation becomes mandatory, and parties are obligated to attend a first mediation session.[29] It is also possible and rather common in practice that the agreement to mediate is followed by a covenant not to sue for as long as the mediation procedure is pending (or at least until the first mediation session).

If parties breach that contractual provision and commence arbitration or file a lawsuit, the judge or arbitrator must stay the procedure until the negotiated deadline or until the parties take the matter to mediation. A sole exception is urgency matters that can be taken to and decided by judges or arbitrators if there is a need to safeguard rights or a risk of perishment of the debated assets or goods.[30]

Parties can also define via agreement the mediation procedure and their interactions with the mediator. Article 166 §4° of the CCP provides that mediation will be conducted as determined by the interested parties, including the rules of the mediation proceeding.

The Mediation Act also lays down some minimum requirements for the agreement to mediate to be valid.[31] The contract must necessarily set out: (1)

Yearbook of Socio-Economic Constitutions: Funding of Justice (Springer 2022), 245–266.

29 Mediation Act art. 2 §1o.

30 Mediation Act art. 26.

31 Mediation Act art. 22.

the maximum and minimum time limit for holding the first mediation session, to be counted from the date of the receipt of the invitation sent by the counterparty; (2) the venue for the first mediation session, which must be a place suitable for a meeting that may involve exchanging confidential information; (3) the criteria for choosing the mediator or mediation team; and (4) the sanctions for non-attendance at the first session.

If the contractual provision is incomplete, failing to fill those requirements, or if there are no specific rules, the parameters set out in the statute apply.[32]

Furthermore, in Brazil the legislation expressly enables the parties to choose the mediator(s) by a procedural contract.[33] By agreement, parties can choose whoever they deem fit to act as a mediator, regardless of being listed in or accredited by the court.[34] The only existing requirements are provided for in the Mediation Act:[35] mediators must be capable and competent individuals that have the confidence of the parties, and they must display expertise in mediation. Expertise should not be measured by affiliation to any sort of entity or association, but rather by personal professional experience and/or by attendance to specific courses.

The contract could regulate fees and duties of the mediator (such as confidentiality), and therefore, must be agreed upon also by the mediators themselves. Obviously, parties cannot unilaterally establish duties and regulate payment for mediators' services without their consent).[36]

One last observation is that courts in Brazil maintain records of accredited mediators, who are obligated to take courses and show capacity to perform their duties. Whenever there is no prior agreement to mediate and a conflict is brought to court, if parties cannot agree upon the name of the mediator, the judge will assign the case to one of the accredited mediators from the court's list. If the case recommends, more than one mediator can be designated.

---

32 Mediation Act art. 22 §2.

33 CCP art. 168.

34 The Mediation Act distinguishes out-of-court mediation and in-court or court-annexed mediation, providing that in the latter parties cannot freely choose the mediator, only among those that are accredited and listed by the court (art. 11). This provision conflicts with the liberty given to the parties by the Code of Civil Procedure to choose the mediator (arts 168, 190 and 200).

35 Mediation Act art. 9.

36 However, the Mediation Act admits that mediation can be volunteer work if the mediator freely decides to give up her remuneration (art. 164 §1° of the CCP).

11.6 STATISTICAL DATA ON MEDIATION

Despite all the structural and normative innovations in the Brazilian legal system over the past 10–15 years, the few empirical data so far show that mediation has not reached the status of other more developed and practised ADR (such as arbitration).

A research study called Mediation in Numbers ('Mediação em Números'), conducted at the Getúlio Vargas Foundation Law School in seven of the most prominent mediation chambers between 2012 and 2022, demonstrated that over the course of the 10 years covered by the collected data, the number of mediations is four times bigger than before, and if one compares the value of claims, it is 80 times higher. The findings are interesting regarding the profile of mediators (gender, age, etc.), the most frequent subject matters involved in mediation, duration of the proceedings, percentage of settlement, etc. However, the same research shows that, if one considers abstract numbers, mediation has been used in very few cases[37] and involves low-value claims considering the huge overload of pending procedures in the Brazilian judiciary.[38] As for court-connected mediation, the latest data show that, by the beginning of 2023, 1,437 mediation centres had been set up in all courts in the country, structures that have almost tripled in eight years of statistical monitoring.

Nevertheless, the National Council of Justice's efforts have only partially achieved the desired goals. Today's statistics show that, although awareness of consensual dispute resolution proceedings has increased, and the number of cases resolved by agreement has grown (has practically doubled in eight years if we follow the historical series), the settlement rate in cases pending in Brazilian courts, in all spheres and competences, has currently stagnated at around 12%.[39] This shows that a lot of other initiatives are needed to obtain better results in terms of consensual conflict resolution.

---

[37] For example, in 2021, there were only 90 overall cases in all seven chambers. In 2020, there were 63.

[38] Brazil has almost 80 million pending litigation procedures in all courts and instances of its 92 tribunals. The findings of the research 'Mediation in Numbers' are available (only in Portuguese) at https://direitosp.fgv.br/noticias/fgv-direito-sp-canal-arbitragem-divulgam-pesquisa-inedita-sobre-numeros-mediacao-no-brasil, accessed 11 November 2024.

[39] Accurate data can be obtained from the yearly report 'Justiça em Números' (Justice in Numbers) edited by the Brazilian Supreme Court. Settlements reach 18% of all pending cases if we consider only the trial stage in the first instance (excluding appeals and enforcement stages). The report is available in English at: https://www.cnj.jus.br/wp-content/uploads/2024/02/justice-in-numbers-2023.pdf.

11.7 TECHNOLOGY AND CONSENUAL DISPUTE RESOLUTION: THE HIGH LEVELS OF DIGITISATION OF THE BRAZILIAN DISPUTE RESOLUTION SYSTEM

Another clearly visible trend in the Brazilian legal system is the growing use of information and communication technology (ICT) in the dispute resolution system. In fact, Brazil has stood out on the international stage as one of the countries that has applied the most technology in this area.

The Brazilian judicial system has high levels of digitisation. Videoconferencing hearings have been frequent and common for at least 10 years, i.e. this practice began well before the Covid-19 pandemic, which allowed the Brazilian judiciary not to have a single day of interruption during the health crisis and social distancing that struck in 2020. From another perspective, for quite some time many courts have fully digitised their case files. Brazil has had electronic procedure systems for over 20 years, and there have been general statutes regulating the e-filing and e-processing of these cases for over 16 years.

There are many courts that function entirely online, the so-called e-courts, cyber courts or online courts, which have been a reality for many years. Online courts usually benefit the parties because they reduce delays and costs associated with an offline court case (for example, travel costs).

More recently, other sophisticated technological applications have also reached the judiciary, such as the use of artificial intelligence in court proceedings, for various types of activities, from case management to decision-making.[40]

A. Online Dispute Resolution: Applications of ICT to Mediation both Out-of-court and in Court-connected Mediation

In this scenario of a growing use of technology in civil justice, many legal systems have been developing the so-called online dispute resolution proceedings or simply ODR. Online dispute resolution involves proceedings that are fully automated, and also those services through which technology facilitates a predominantly face-to-face procedure. In this broader sense, ODR is understood

---

[40] Peter C.H. Chan and Antonio Cabral. 'Digitisation of Judicial Procedure: AI, ODR, Blockchain and E-Justice', in C.H. van Rhee and Margaret Woo (eds). *Civil Procedure Handbook* (Elgar 2025, upcoming); Antonio Cabral, 'Dispute Resolution and Technology in Brazil: Artificial Intelligence, ODR and Online Courts' (2024) 14 *International Journal of Procedural Law*, 235–244.

as the use of online environments to facilitate communications and dispute resolution. Online dispute resolution tools can be useful not only to handle the entire proceeding, but also to ameliorate some aspect or stage of the proceeding instead of managing the whole.[41] In fact, traditional face-to-face ADR borrows applications from ICT to boost its effectiveness by assisting mediators in their traditional procedural settings. In mediation, ODR systems can, for example, target one of a few activities that the mediator would perform (brainstorming, prioritising, options drafting, etc.), and contribute to a more efficient performance of those tasks.[42]

On the other hand, ODR can be complementary to traditional state-run court systems. Online dispute resolution then is a way of providing and exchanging information, which can help resolve conflicts either at the judiciary or at court-annexed settings.

This consolidated use of technological means to resolve disputes in Brazilian law has also led to applications for mediation. Large organisations with offices all over the country have found e-mediation to be helpful in recent years, particularly when it comes to resolving conflicts among coworkers in the workplace. This has been a very useful feature in Brazil because of its immense territory. Online mediation sessions are a reality and can be performed both out of court and within a judicial procedure, or at least in court-annexed or court-connected online platforms.

One interesting example of the use of ICT in court-connected consensual dispute resolution is the project implemented by the Court of Justice of Rio de Janeiro State, which created an online dispute resolution mechanism for cases related to health insurance disputes. The goal is to manage more efficiently court litigation procedures involving consumers and health plan companies. When filing their lawsuit through the electronic system of the court (e-filing), once the plaintiffs fill the e-form and express that the dispute is related to health care insurance, they are directed to a mediation portal, where pop-ups show the percentage of settlement achieved through mediation in such types of cases. The system, therefore, uses an incentive (nudge) that provides adequate

---

[41] Thomas Schultz, Gabrielle Kaufmann-Kohler, Dirk Langer and Vincent Bonnet, 'Online Dispute Resolution: The State of the Art and the Issues', E-com Research Project of the University of Geneva, 2001. On the debate about whether ODR is similar to ADR or has qualitative differences, see Carrie Menkel-Meadow, 'Is ODR ADR? Reflections of an ADR Founder from the 15th ODR Conference' (2016) 3 (1) International Journal on Online Dispute Resolution, 4–7; Colin Rule, 'Is ODR ADR? A Response to Carrie Menkel-Meadow' (2016) 3 (1) International Journal on Online Dispute Resolution, 8 ff.

[42] Ethan Katsh and Janet Rifkin, *Online Dispute Resolution: Resolving Conflicts in Cyberspace* (Jossey-Bass 2001), 28.

information to the plaintiffs and encourages them to choose to follow a mediation procedure. The system then automatically connects the consumer, via electronic chat, with the representatives of the companies, who can immediately offer settlement proposals. If the proposal is accepted, a draft judgement is automatically produced and the case is assigned to a judge for approval (ratification) of the agreement (consent judgment).[43]

B. Distinctions Between e-Mediation and Offline Face-to-face Mediation: Benefits and Disadvantages of ICT Applied to Mediation in Developing Countries

e-Mediation normally presents fewer differences to the offline face-to-face mediation procedures.[44] The most relevant difference of online mediation is that the interaction between the parties takes place fully (a whole virtual environment in a virtual setting) or partially through ICT tools. The application of ICT to mediation proceedings requires a discussion of benefits and drawbacks of its usage. It is crucial to emphasise the distinctions between e-mediation and offline, conventional forms of mediation, even if one acknowledges that ODR offers a number of advantages over face-to-face offline mediation.

One of the major advantages of e-mediation is accessibility. With an increase in connectivity to broadband and wireless networks, communications all over the globe are available at the click of a button. People can access platforms from wherever they are and whenever they want. Therefore, with greater access to technology, access to justice would be strengthened.[45] But this is not a reality for everyone. Especially in a developing country such as Brazil, access to state-of-the-art hardware and broadband internet can be precarious in vast regions, preventing people from attending and/or participating

---

43 http://www.tjrj.jus.br/noticias/noticia/-/visualizar-conteudo/5111210/6137834.

44 Legal scholars observe that some mediation practices that were sometimes seen in offline mediation are not used in e-mediation. For example, co-mediation is not very common online, maybe because of the facilities of asynchronous communication, but there is nothing particular to e-mediation that prohibits that practice or that would speak against it. See Noam Ebner, 'E-Mediation', *in* Mohamed S Abdel Wahab, Ethan Katsh and Daniel Rainey (eds). *Online Dispute Resolution: Theory and Practice: A Treatise on Technology and Dispute Resolution* (Eleven 2012), 397.

45 Mirèze Phillipe, 'Access to Justice Through Online Dispute Resolution is not Science Fiction: A Practitioner's Perspective on the Good, the Bad and the Future', *in* Leonardo Oliveira and Sara Hourani (eds). *Access to Justice in Arbitration: Concept, Context and Practice* (Wolters Kluwer 2020), 229–231.

adequately in online hearings. That diminishes accessibility, which poses a problem in terms of access to justice and fairness in dispute resolution settings.

Another frequently noted advantage of ODR is the enormous cost reduction in conflict solving. Indeed, ODR provides for communications at very low rates, so these online instruments present themselves as cost-efficient methods to deal with disputes. This also relates to the duration of the proceedings. Online dispute resolution instruments usually provide a rapid flow of information and solve disputes faster, and so appear to be more adequate to the speed of online transactions, which cannot always be matched by the duration and rhythm of court litigation and even of traditional ADR. Therefore, ODR contributes to reducing the delay and length of dispute resolution proceedings.[46]

Additionally, ODR enables interested parties to represent themselves, which lowers the expense of employing solicitors and paying their fees. Parties can also negotiate and mediate outside of typical business hours (because they are not required to attend sessions in person). On the one hand, the parties benefit from this cost reduction because it eliminates the need for them to miss work, incurs minimal transportation and childcare costs, and eliminates the need to pay for legal representation – all of which are crucial in low-value disputes where costs are frequently a significant factor.

On the other hand, from the perspective of court administration, it is also highly relevant. In a context in which most countries have a limited budget for their judiciary services, moving to the digital world offers resource economy. [47] Brazil spends a lot of money on its judiciary, and therefore it makes sense in terms of public policy to invest in ODR in general, and in e-mediation specifically.

---

[46] Ethan Katsh, 'ODR: A Look at History. A Few Thoughts About the Present and Some Speculation About the Future', *in* Mohament S Abdel Wahab et al. (eds). *Online Dispute Resolution: Theory and Practice: A Treatise on Technology and Dispute Resolution* (Eleven 2012), 30; James J Prescott and Alexander Sanchez. 'Platform Procedure: Using Technology to Facilitate (Efficient) Civil Settlement', *in* Yun-Chien Chang (ed.). *Selection and Decision in Judicial Process around the World: Empirical Inquiries* (Cambridge University Press 2020), 30, 38.

[47] The use of ICT allows judiciaries to reduce the number of civil servants (and of accredited mediators), or at least redirect them to other activities, since much of the bureaucratic procedural formalities that used to be performed by those persons could be solved automatically by the online systems. This is the case of Brazil, for example, whose judiciary has to deal with an extremely large overload of pending cases; technology was adopted in judiciary services out of a practical necessity. Cf. Antonio Cabral, 'Online Dispute Resolution', *in* Daniel Mitidiero, Antonio Cabral and Paulo Lucon (eds). *Artificial Intelligence and its Impacts on the System of Civil Justice – IAPL Online Conference 2021* (Thomson Reuters Brasil 2023), 61.

Moreover, one of the main characteristics of ODR is the increased degree of asynchronous communication that is offered. This gives parties the time and chance to formulate answers, rephrase messages, and slow down the negotiation or mediation pace, allowing for a more accurate expression of questions, concerns, and remarks. This keeps the process from spiralling out of control, such as when pressure, rage, or threats escalate negotiations. Because the mediator might feel rushed and under pressure to find a solution, and because it would be difficult to control and channel the flow of information, some scholars argue against the use of chat-type interactions (such as instant messaging with real-time synchronous communication).

From a different perspective, ODR is currently among the greatest options for resolving disputes when distance is a barrier. Technology shrinks the world and reduces distances, which is important when travel is either infeasible or too expensive. Online dispute resolution eliminates issues related to displacement, which results in lower travel expenses and quicker dispute resolution· Indeed, ODR provides for logistical facilitation, allowing easy contact and interaction among people. However, it should be noted that whenever there is a risk of encouraging face-to-face communication, or in situations where parties could be in danger of physical or psychological harm if they were to meet, dispute resolution may depend on distance (e.g. domestic violence).

Despite all the pros of ODR, there are also many drawbacks to utilising ICT to settle disputes. Privacy and security, for instance, are always mentioned as one key concern. But in this section I want to limit my approach to some remarks that might be more interesting when speaking about mediation.

First and foremost, communication between the parties involved is essential to dispute resolution. And in online interactions, people communicate and behave differently in many ways. While face-to-face contacts tend to restrain violent behaviour to some degree, there may be an increase in contentiousness and many people feel more inclined to lash out at each other when they are online.[48] On the other hand, without personal encounters, the role of mediators faces additional challenges in the absence of face-to-face interactions. Contextual clues, including non-verbal communication, which mediators and negotiators frequently understand in personal offline discussions, can occasionally be absent from e-mediation procedures.

Another factor to take into account is that personal face-to-face interactions are more intimate and personal, whereas electronic communications are more impersonal, cold, and distant. e-Mediation thus takes place in an environment

---

48 Noam Ebner, 'ODR and Interpersonal Trust', *in* Mohamed S Abdel Wahab et al. (eds). *Online Dispute Resolution: Theory and Practice: A Treatise on Technology and Dispute Resolution* (Eleven 2012), 229.

where trust is weaker. Furthermore, research indicates that while mistrust can lead to defensive, contentious, or competitive behaviour, triggering attitudes such as threats or attacks, forcing parties to withhold information and lock themselves in negotiation positions difficult to withdraw from, empathy, generosity, and rapport promote a more cooperative attitude towards integrative outcomes. Therefore, even if they might be helpful, video conferences cannot completely replace face-to-face contact. Indeed, online processes lack immediacy and empathy, and physical distance transmits a sense of isolation that reduces identification with others. When disputes necessitate a customised strategy and involve human intervention to engage with the parties, such as in family law matters, e-mediation poses challenges. This is also why face-to-face mediation is frequently preferred when it comes to this type of offline dispute resolution.[49]

11.8 CONCLUSION AND FUTURE PERSPECTIVES

Much has changed in the Brazilian legal system with regard to consensual dispute resolution. From a legal culture that almost exclusively favoured adjudicated solutions, the country has evolved in recent decades to develop numerous instruments and structures available to the parties for the consensual resolution of their disputes, many of them related to mediation.

Mediation centres have been set up in every tribunal for court-connected ADR; extensive regulations have been published on mediation, its procedures and formalities, and investments have been made in the training of mediators and practitioners. Legal education at universities has adapted to dedicate more courses and hours to imparting mediation knowledge and techniques to undergraduate students. These measures combined make it possible to acknowledge an improvement in the general portrait of consensual dispute resolution, which has been reflected in the statistics on the termination of court litigation by settlement.

Moreover, the greater flexibility that the Code of Civil Procedure attributed to the judicial court procedure, with wide possibilities for the parties to negotiate on its formalities, has expanded the powers of litigants to establish out-of-court mediation as a prior condition to filing a lawsuit, as well as to choose the mediators and even design the mediation procedure via procedural agreements. This level of party autonomy, which has been consistently backed by favourable decisions and precedents in case law, tends to be increasingly

---

49 Some studies argue that e-mediation is typically not even the first option for online dispute resolution, usually coming after assisted online negotiation. In this sense, see Ebner, 'E-Mediation', *supra* note 44, 376.

consolidated, with mediation being further integrated and reinforced by contractual binding stipulations with other forms of consensual dispute resolution, whether judicial or not (a possible future perspective is the growth of med-arb clauses that combine mediation with arbitration or dispute boards).

Finally, the high levels of digitisation of the Brazilian judicial system, as well as the familiarity of legal professionals with the everyday use of technological tools to resolve disputes, have increased the possibilities of e-mediation in recent years and opened other possible features in conflict management, as seen in the example of coupling court-connected e-mediation in the computerised systems of electronic judicial procedure in matters of health insurance cases.

Yet this shift to ODR requires new developments. First, regulation must account for the problems that digitisation can pose to fundamental guarantees of civil litigation. Due process rights and access to justice must always be on the radar of legislators and policymakers.

On the other side, technology requires new approaches from mediators and judges. Mediators should be familiar with new methods of communication in order to avoid pitfalls and extract the most out of the online environment. As for judges, since ODR provides a wide variety of possible combinations, the idea of a 'multi-door courthouse' should nowadays be thought of as a *'multi-modal'* system, and that calls for a slightly different role of courts. Instead of simply referring a case to mediation, the role of the court would be to 'navigate' the dispute through different procedural instruments in mixed settings, moving from one to the other as circumstances require, also with possibilities to modify the dispute resolution schemes throughout different stages of the conflict.[50]

In this quite interesting and so far fruitful scenario of mediation in Brazil, it still remains unclear if the future evolution of the Brazilian dispute resolution system, with the fusion of all the structural and normative developments of the past years, will effectively contribute to enhancing settlement rates and reducing the (still) immense judicialisation of conflicts.

50 Cabral, Consensual Dispute Resolution, *supra* note 1, 61.

12. The near horizons of digitalised dispute resolution

Tony Guise and Victoria McCloud

This chapter considers the challenge posed to the administration of civil justice by the ever growing demand for dispute resolution. We seek to explain how that challenge is being addressed in England and Wales (E&W) and canvas potential further developments to enhance the experience and reality of justice in that jurisdiction. The authors consider:

- The extent to which digitalisation can provide new scope to produce what *the participants* (and not just judges or normative law) see as 'justice'. The civil justice system of the 21st century puts the user, whether citizen or business, at the heart of its design with the aim of bringing about enduring change.
- Introducing AI into dispute resolution: a gradual feedback and reinforcement approach based upon very rich data. Given a growing population and a finite number of judges, the civil justice system must take advantage of modern, 21st-century technology to overcome the challenge of demand outstripping the supply of resolution services.
- The role and implications of digitalisation in finding a route to reduce the national case backlog in the civil justice system. Having identified ways in which a modern civil justice system can respond to increasing demand, it is necessary to understand how the waiting times for resolutions may be reduced to build a better service in the future.
- How is the private sector to be funded on a sustainable basis to deliver this people-intensive, often mediation-based, service enabled by sophisticated technology? Current civil justice policy envisages the private sector having a primary role in delivering dispute resolution, with court proceedings very much a last resort. How can this private sector solution be funded in a proportionate, affordable way and at the same time enable the private sector to develop a sustainable business model for delivering dispute resolution?

12.1 THE EXTENT TO WHICH DIGITALISATION CAN PROVIDE NEW SCOPE TO PRODUCE WHAT *THE PARTICIPANTS* (AND NOT JUST JUDGES OR NORMATIVE LAW) SEE AS 'JUSTICE'

> Justice? You get justice in the next world, in this world you have the law.[1]

What is this thing called 'Justice'? It is a familiar yet also slippery concept: when we try to pin it down it writhes and wriggles; it seems to defy definition. Perhaps the best stab one can have is to set out a few features one instinctively associates with Justice, as a lawyer or judge:

- *Equality before the law*: 'everyone is equal before the law'. Regardless of their background or other factors, individuals should receive the same rights, protections, and remedies.
- *Rights and protections*: individuals' rights respected and protected. This includes fundamental rights such as freedom of speech, the right to a fair trial, and protection against discrimination, but also more conventional legal rights.
- *Fairness and merits*: Decisions made based on merits, evidence, and law rather than arbitrary factors.
- *Legal remedies*: Legal remedies exist to the extent that the legislature or common law has seen fit to do so (not every wrong has a remedy, in other words).
- *Adjudication and dispute resolution*: The legal system's courts are responsible for adjudicating disputes and ensuring justice alongside other voluntary mechanisms which may be binding or non-binding.

A more intellectual approach is typified by Rawls in his well-known theoretical work on Justice,[2] envisaging that concepts of liberty and equality are reconciled in a form of social justice which informs how not only courts but other elements of society work, or ought to work:

1. Each person is to have an equal right to the most extensive total system of equal basic liberties compatible with a similar system of liberty for all.
2. Social and economic inequalities are to be arranged so that they are both:
   (a) to the greatest benefit of the least advantaged, consistent with the just savings principle; and

---

1 William Gaddis, *A Frolic of His Own* (Poseidon Press 1995).

2 John Rawls, *A Theory of Justice*, revised edn (Harvard University Press 1999).

(b) attached to offices and positions open to all under conditions of fair equality of opportunity.[3]

Other theories of justice, as they say on the TV, are available, such as social contract theory expounded by, among others, Hobbes.[4]

All of this seems to the author (VM) as worthy and idealistic. There is surely nothing *wrong* with either worthiness or idealism. Yet it is lacking a foundation in what one might call 'people's' justice. Many have asked the philosophical questions, but few have asked the ultimate authority on the matter: the people affected by 'justice', whatever it may mean.

In lectures and presentations on the Judicial College's well-known Equal Treatment Bench Book, on which this author (VM) served for a year or so, the position I have outlined is that justice is not something one merely does *to* someone; it is something one does *with* someone. It is a process of applying law but in a real and practical sense which one hopes engages the individual, empowers them rather than excludes them, and perhaps most important of all, is a working and effective system rather than a finely wrought clockwork mechanism with finials and springs and bells, yet which runs painfully slowly and sometimes either stops entirely or provides hopelessly wrong times when the user glances at it in the hope of a simple answer to the equally simple question 'Clock: what time is it?'

Mechanical metaphors aside, whilst we may have a body of rules, of statutes, of courts and processes, of precedent, courts and parliamentary sovereignty, and all the other trappings which a typical view of Diceyan constitutional theory brings with it, arguably what is missing is justice from the standpoint of the practical sovereignty of the citizen when it comes to defining what is and is not 'just' in prevailing social, global and economic circumstances. There is an irony highlighted by Rivka Weill in 'Dicey was not Diceyan'[5] in that, in life, Dicey was a supporter of the use of the referendum as a source of sovereignty of citizens, which has, as the author argues, a certain 'non-Diceyan' flavour about it.

It is apparent to this author and no doubt others that perhaps a fresh approach to notions of 'justice' is needed, which is one born of the 'Woolfian' and 'Jacksonian' concepts of efficient use of resources and efficient justice processes and hence which puts practicality and access to (functioning!) justice at the top of the list of features. It is here where one sees the potential of

---

3 Ibid, at p. 266.

4 Thomas Hobbes, *Leviathan*, Clarendon edn ed. Noel Malcolm (Oxford University Press 2012).

5 R. Weill, 'Dicey Was Not Diceyan', Cambridge Law Journal 62(2), July 2003 p. 474.

an integrated 'cradle to grave' digitised dispute resolution system of the near future. In such a system, as VM envisages it, the pre-court process involving dispute resolution, the packaging of a claim, if there has to be one, into a digital form able efficiently to be received and issued by the court, the process of 'formal justice' (with occasional loops back into dispute resolution on the way), thence to decision making and (importantly) enforcement and resolution of disputes over legal costs, is seen as one sequence, a flow of data and disputes representing real world issues, from inception to outcome in one form or another.

As with the digestive system of any mammal, and as with the court system, what enters at the front may well end up, if it 'goes the distance' to court, coming out of the back – and not at present always to the satisfaction of the court users. Whether what drops out at the end is the golden egg or the horse manure depends on the perspective of the user as to whether going to court actually delivered what *they* regard as 'justice'. If we look at the above 'cradle to grave' model of digitised justice, we can see that it affords the potential for a similarly 'cradle to grave' process of collection of anonymised data which in principle could yield vital information about such matters as:

- why claims settle before claim, or fail to settle, and what factual, legal or other circumstances (such as pragmatism or economics) tend to drive that;
- what factors drive settlement during the process of a claim and how that is typically achieved for different circumstances;
- where claims go to trial, how the outcomes canvassed in negotiation reflect what actually happens in the end, or do not reflect what happens at the end; and
- after trial, whether enforcement is effective and over what timescales, and similarly for how the costs of the litigation stack up when compared with the position the parties were in at the pre-action mediation stages when less by way of expense had been incurred, and whether in the end the outcome is (or to what extent it is) a pyrrhic victory or a heroic failure for any given party.

We can see that this approach requires a truly seismic shift of outlook whereby for the first time the process of confidential, privileged negotiation is, in anonymised and unidentifiable form, actually made available as data for research (and, as VM suggests in section 12.2, other purposes). This is something which VM herself has raised whilst she was practising as a judge, before choosing to take a break, within bodies such as the Civil Justice Council (CJC) and elsewhere such as the European Digitalisation of Justice group, but it is inherently 'heretical' to most lawyers and goes against the grain.

The benefits, however, could be considerable since by following the 'justice process' from cradle to grave, or mouth to back end if one prefers, in addition to the 'mere' gathering of rich data about the drivers of settlement and the forms which it takes, we could implement a process of engaging with participants on a truly enormous scale to find out what they, and their lawyers, perceive to be the 'justness' or otherwise of not only the processes but the outcomes. We could then really get into the fine grain of 'people's justice' and it would be well within the realms of likelihood that we would discover some surprising things: for example, does a party who settles for less than they wanted, but does so quickly and cheaply, see that as a more 'just' outcome than the 'triumphant' litigant getting full damages and interest, at the cost of several years and some unrecovered legal costs? What about the sense of justice of those who lose claims at court or who pay or make concessions when perhaps they did not want to: what is justice for them?

By knowing more about what the 'just' in the justice process means in real, experiential and operationalised ways, the fruits of such work could then be valuable for informing design changes and targeted resourcing to improve and fine-tune the justice system to maximise the extent to which users report 'just' results (see Figure 12.1).

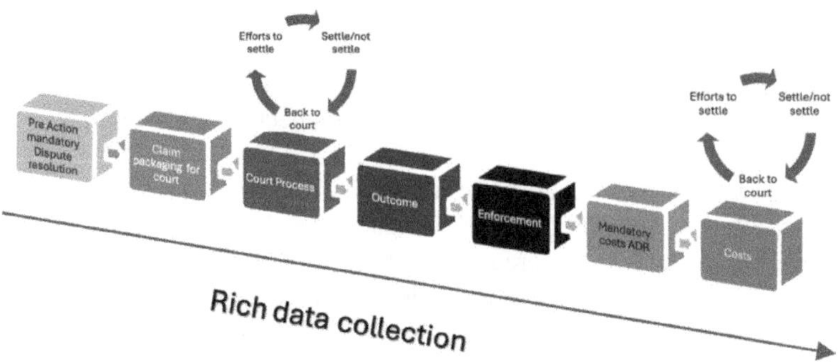

Figure 12.1 *A cradle-to-grave conception of the justice process*

12.2 INTRODUCING AI INTO DISPUTE RESOLUTION: A GRADUAL FEEDBACK AND REINFORCEMENT APPROACH BASED UPON VERY RICH DATA

In the preceding section, VM set out a model of the 'justice process' by which, in principle, the concept of a just outcome or a just process can be examined with empirical data based on users' perceptions and experience of the system, both at different stages of progress and in terms of outcomes and settlements, and what drives them.

In this section, VM takes matters a step (many steps) further and well into what some readers will see as beyond blue sky thinking but which VM prefers to see as an experiment worth doing, by considering how the 'cradle to grave' data collection approach could – in principle but in ways as yet untested – advance the creation of artificial systems proposing settlement terms. Such systems would be able to offer a form of opinion upon the probable outcomes of certain categories of case and therefore to offer suggested forms of settlement with a given level of confidence. It is a simple proposition and, to anyone with experience of essentially hand-coded 'AI' as it was in the 1980s and with efforts to 'write' – by clever coding and a bit of luck – clever programs, it will be dismissed immediately as an impossibility, but bear with me.

A Quick Sketch

Let us imagine that either or both parties in an as yet unissued dispute are (some years hence) able to consult what amounts to an expert AI system trained (over past years) on many thousands of sets of actual rich case data, not manually processed, not interpreted by human eye, not filtered, and which was trained *not only on outcomes where matters go to trial but also on settlements where those take place*, and still further, *how far the ultimate case outcomes (in non-settled cases) differed from predicted outcomes at the start when the system was consulted.*

A Digression

I shall digress at this point, conscious that this is a book about the future of mediation in a new civil justice system, that lawyers are not always fascinated with tech, and that for many the concept, for example, of 'unsupervised learning' rather than an AI process is a dimly remembered time when, as an associate or trainee, they had a rare day when their supervising solicitor or pupil supervisor was away from the office or chambers.

The burgeoning field of artificial Intelligence has garnered significant scholarly attention owing to its transformative potential, much of which has not yet been explored fully. At the heart of AI lie algorithmic learning techniques and 'deep learning' by way of what have become known as 'neural networks' owing to their conceptual similarity to nets of brain cells interconnected with and communicating among each other in adjustable ways. These are not new concepts (this author – VM – worked on them in the late 1980s and they were far from a new concept then), but the key change is that they have become *practically* applicable to real-world functions owing to increased processing speed and effectively limitless computer memory and storage, which were both in short supply in past decades.

Algorithmic learning serves as the cornerstone of AI, encompassing a spectrum of methodologies aimed at extracting actionable conclusions from vast datasets. In particular, 'deep learning' allows computational models that are composed of multiple processing layers (imagine a web of 'cells' connected to one another by connections the strength of which can be adjusted during a learning process) to learn representations of data with multiple levels of abstraction. As LeCun et al.[6] put it, it discovers intricate structure in large datasets by using an algorithm by which the internal connection strengths between 'cells' are adjusted to indicate how a machine should change its internal parameters, which are then used to compute the representation in each layer of cells from the representation in the immediately preceding layer. What one ends up with is a system which can associate input data with a corresponding output, for large amounts of data on which the system is 'trained', and can generalise such that it provides a meaningful output for data which it has not seen before, based on common features with data which it has encountered before.

There has been much discussion both within the Law and outside of AI systems such as 'ChatGPT'. ChatGPT functions through a combination of deep learning, natural language processing and large-scale machine learning techniques. It is pre-trained on a corpus of text data sourced from the internet, carried out by feeding the model a large amount of text and training it to predict the next word in a sequence. By doing so, the model learns the statistical patterns, syntactic structures, and semantic relationships present in the text data without having been told explicitly how to write any given language. Consider here the possibility of a ChatGPT-style system trained on case data augmented by some specifically algorithmic programming to enable it to appreciate types of legal document such as statements of case, rather than having been trained solely on the generality of text on the internet.

One key element is what the designers refer to as a 'self-attention mechanism', which allows the model to weigh the importance of each word in a sequence based on its context within the sequence. By attending to relevant words, the model can better understand the relationships between words and generate coherent responses. It can be fine-tuned on specific tasks or domains to improve its performance for particular applications, which involves further training the model on a smaller dataset that is specific to the target task, such as question answering or text generation. This allows ChatGPT to adapt its

6 Y. LeCun, Y. Bengio, and G. Hinton, Deep learning. Nature 521, 2015, pp. 436–444.

knowledge and skills to the requirements of different scenarios. Given the relative simplicity of how ChatGPT works, the performance it produces is impressive, although it has also been found sometimes to invent facts or even case law when applied to legal opinion writing, an area where improvement is needed, but which may prove to be less of an issue where the task at hand is not legal argument based on precedent but rather the use of rich text data exclusively taken from real cases which have passed through the justice system to reach outcomes whether by settlement or trial and where the facts and context, and positions of the parties, are more likely to be relevant to settlement.

A Conversation

In discussion with ChatGPT, I asked it to consider the feasibility of using real case data on a large scale to predict outcomes, and the conversation threw up the following:

> *VM*: Some people say that a model like Bing or Chat GPT would not be capable of reliably predicting a range of possible out-of-court settlements of disputes, based on a large dataset of actual disputes which were either settled out of court or reached a conclusion after a trial. Do you think such an approach is promising and why?
>
> *ChatGPT*: The feasibility and reliability of using a model like Bing or ChatGPT to predict a range of possible out-of-court settlements of disputes based on a large dataset of actual disputes is a topic of debate. While there are challenges and limitations, there are also promising aspects to consider:
>
> Data availability and quality: One promising aspect is the availability of large datasets containing information about actual disputes, including those settled out of court and those resolved through trial. These datasets can provide valuable insights into factors that influence settlement outcomes, such as case details, legal arguments, parties involved, and settlement terms.
>
> Pattern recognition: AI models like ChatGPT excel at recognizing patterns and relationships within large datasets. By analyzing historical data on dispute resolution outcomes, these models can potentially identify recurring patterns and factors that correlate with successful out-of-court settlements.
>
> Efficiency and cost savings: Predictive models have the potential to streamline the dispute resolution process by providing parties with estimates of likely settlement outcomes early in the proceedings. This could lead to more efficient negotiations, reduced legal costs, and faster resolution of disputes, benefiting both parties and the legal system as a whole.
>
> Iterative improvement: AI models can be trained iteratively, continuously learning from new data and refining their predictive capabilities over time. As more data become available and the model is exposed to a broader range of dispute scenarios, its accuracy and reliability in predicting settlement outcomes may improve.
>
> Supplementing human expertise: While AI models can provide valuable insights and predictions, they are not meant to replace human judgment.

A Testable Hypothesis and One Which can Practicably be Done

Such a tool as that envisaged above if created, would be experimentally testable because it could proffer a *prediction* at the start whilst parties were in negotiation, and the outcome could be compared with the prediction as a form of validation of the tool, and to continue to train it across a vast array of case data where cases fail to settle out of court, such that – if the experiment is a 'success' at least – a system could say something like:

> In cases of this type with the following key features [...], across a sample of 102,000 decided cases and 523,000 out of court settlements the typical settlement at this stage achieved costs saving of £*x* relative to a trial of a similar value claim, and a time saving of *y* months in enforcement. Settlement ranges adjusted for the data in this case spanned a range from £A to £B with a 95% degree of confidence. Forms of settlement typically included the following features in addition to or instead of immediate payment of money.

Such is not a 'judgment' but it is a rational conclusion from data obtained from large numbers of real cases derived from the cradle to grave model suggested in section 12.1. Indeed if experimental testing showed sufficient reliability of prediction between 'prediction' and outcome at trial one could in the somewhat further future consider whether a party who fails to 'beat the dealer' so to speak is automatically liable for costs if he or she goes to trial against the prediction: a form of 'Part 36' or Calderbank offer made by a system which is coldly based on real examples of decisions across the range of judges in the country and settlements which proved acceptable to parties in disputes. Further, one could even consider that the output of such systems, if constructed to provide a set of reasons for the decision, could inform and shape submissions in the event a matter goes to court and make available to the parties a rationally based starting point from which to argue, incorporating, to an extent, effective research and pre-reading which no human lawyer or judge could conceivably carry out.

All this is plainly an idea but it is an *objectively testable* one: a rare thing in the law. I suggest that this is a necessary endeavour because if such systems can be achieved even in just one area of court claim such as family divorce money cases, for example, the savings to the public and the saving of court and judicial resources would be immense. Conversely, being a testable system, little harm arises from failure, since at least having confirmed the null hypothesis, namely that the complexities of life and law are beyond computational learning, we would know that the focus must be on greater levels of human mediation and resourcing. One may find regions of predictability in categories of court or case: either way, knowing the answer is vital if we are not to face the stark reality that even with thousands of human mediators, justice backlogs, whether in the UK or globally, will be beyond reasonable management with consequent impacts on the prosperity of people who can ill afford their businesses or lives to hit the financial rocks merely because disputes over rights remain mired in procedural mud.

12.3 THE ROLE AND IMPLICATIONS OF DIGITALISATION IN FINDING A ROUTE TO REDUCE THE NATIONAL CASE BACKLOG IN THE CIVIL JUSTICE SYSTEM

How Can the 'Backlog' in Civil Justice be Defined?

The first issue to consider is what the backlog is and how it can be measured? In short, a backlog arises when demand for the resolution of disputes exceeds the supply of the means of resolution, for example, the trial and the judges to deliver judgment.

On 28 August 1846, Queen Victoria gave Royal Assent to an Act colloquially called the Small Debts Act 1846, which brought into being the modern County Court system. The Act was to provide 'for the more easy recovery of small debts and demands in England'.[7]

Why Was this Change Needed?

During the late 18th and early 19th centuries, the population of the UK began to move to industrial cities in search of work. As they did so, the pressure of work on the existing county courts overwhelmed their limited resources, and modernisation was required to address the new demand for a just and efficient system of dispute resolution for money claims. In all, 500 new county courts were created, which were highly efficient. Such was their success that they began to attract more work of different types during the second half of the 19th century, which included bankruptcy and personal injury claims.[8]

In the 20th century, the Common Law and the UK Parliament created new rights (thereby bringing about claims to enforce those rights) with the growth of different tortious claims (especially the modern law of negligence) giving rise to workplace claims and personal injury claims of all kinds. By 1994, the tendency to ossification that characterises English and Welsh civil procedure led the Government to commission Lord Woolf to undertake an inquiry

---

[7] Small Debts Act 1846, Preamble.

[8] Patrick Polden *A History of the County Court* (Cambridge University Press 1999).

into Access to Justice. He identified that 'The key problems facing civil justice today are cost, delay and complexity'.[9] These structural weaknesses were exacerbated by mis-management of the system with various attempts at reform since the mid-1960s which recommended much but changed little.

By 2024 the question of the backlog had dominated civil justice policy for decades. Backlog clearance continues to dominate civil justice thinking. This is because the backlog bites and blights the good operation of the courts that enable the exercise of civil rights. As emphasised by Sir Edward Coke:

> And therefore, every Subject of this Realme, for injury done to him in bonis, terris, vel persona [in goods, in lands, or in person], by any other Subject … may take his remedy by the course of the Law, and have justice, and right for the injury done to him, freely without sale, fully without any deniall, and speedily without delay. Hereby it appeareth, that Justice must have three qualities, it must be Libera, quia nihil iniquius venali Justitia; Plena, quia Justitia non debet claudicare; & Celeris, quia dilatio est quaedam negatio [Trans: Free, because nothing is more iniquitous than saleable justice; full, because justice ought not to limp; and speedy, because delay is in effect a denial]; and then it is both Justice and Right.[10]

For definitional purposes therefore, for a justice system to experience a 'backlog' of civil justice cases is to have an accumulation of cases that cannot be resolved by the courts with appropriate procedures at reasonable cost and with reasonable speed.[11]

Is There a Backlog in the Civil Justice System?

In December 2019, waiting times to first hearing in the Small Claims Track (SCT, for cases claiming less than £10,000) were 37.1 weeks.[12] This was the worst delay for a decade; in 2009, the average waiting time was only 30.5 weeks. The warning signs were clear: too few judges working in poor-quality buildings using paper systems which caused the case file to become lost too frequently. As the Justice Committee of the House of Commons noted in its Report entitled 'Court Capacity' published on 27 April 2022:

---

9 The Right Honourable The Lord Woolf, Master of the Rolls *Access to Justice Interim Report*, chapter 3 (HMSO 1995).

10 See, Edward Coke, *Part 2 Institutes of the Laws of England* (first published 1642, 1809) 55–56 in reference to the Magna Carta. Most recently cited with approval by the UK Supreme Court in *R (on the application of UNISON) v Lord Chancellor* [2017] UKSC 51 [75] (Lord Reed).

11 On the requirements of a modern Civil justice system see Lord Woolf, 'Access to Justice: Final Report', July 1996, section 1, para 1.

12 See, Table 1.5 of the MoJ's Civil Justice Statistics: https://www.gov.uk/government/statistics/Civil-justice-statistics-quarterly-january-to-march-2020.

> To enhance the capacity of the civil and family courts, it is vital to address each of the core elements of court capacity: judicial, staff, digital and physical. As the Lord Chief Justice explained, digital and physical capacity have a significant bearing on the ability to recruit judges and expand judicial capacity. (para 33)

The coronavirus (COVID-19) pandemic that affected the UK from the first quarter of 2020 led the Government to close the physical Court Estate: the buildings in which courts and the administrators of justice are housed. Immediate and important steps were taken by the Ministry of Justice (MoJ) and Senior Judiciary to mitigate the effect of such closure, which enabled the wheels of justice to keep turning. Nevertheless, the system, already creaking, was driven to near collapse within the space of a year.

By December 2020 the average waiting time to first hearing was 45.3 weeks. Statistics on waiting times show that, in February 2024, the average waiting time for a first hearing in the SCT was 50.5 weeks (see Figure 12.2).[13]

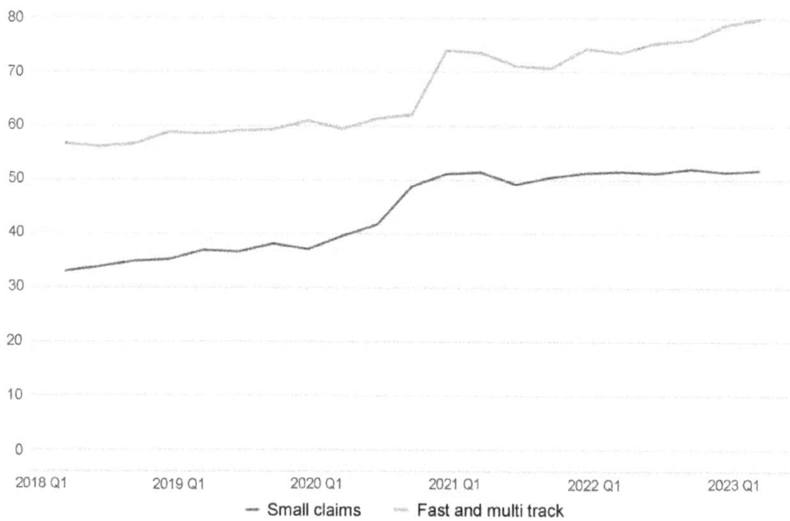

Source: Ministry of Justice UK Civil Justice Statistics Summary published 1 June 2023.

Figure 12.2 *Weeks to first hearing*

[13] HMCTS management information – February 2024 https://www.gov.uk/government/statistical-data-sets/hmcts-management-information-february-2024 (www.gov.uk).

At the time of the first lockdown, the challenge of the backlog began to preoccupy civil justice policy makers. As the then Lord Chief Justice Burnett of Maldon explained to the Justice Committee of the House of Commons:

> temporary court venues are most likely to be used in civil, family and tribunal proceedings … If we don't think about it now and only start thinking about it months ahead when things have got no better, we will be building up a backlog of cases which will take a very long time to clear.[14]

In an effort to understand the scale of the issue (which had never been quantified), DisputesEfiling.com Limited (DEF, of which Tony Guise is Director and a co-author of this chapter) undertook empirical-based research to explore the scale of the civil justice backlog. Unless one can quantify a problem, one cannot solve it.

DEF published its findings as a White Paper on 20 June 2020 entitled: 'Breaking the Backlog and overcoming the Tsunami of Civil litigation in E&W – An empirical view of the Civil justice response to the Lockdown'[15] (the White Paper). DEF identified the following contributory factors:

(a) 'to the pre-Pandemic cases that were backlogged there are added cases backlogged on account of the Pandemic itself', White Paper, p. 13.
(b) 'A rolling programme of Staff cuts [combined with] the Reform Programme being incomplete caused a backlog to accumulate even before the Pandemic struck', as Table 12.1 shows.
(c) '[Staff cuts are] also reflected in the time taken to process applications at the CCMCC[16] in Salford according to HMCTS' performance data for the CCMCC where the delay as at 1 June 2020 in the total processing (working) days from receipt of an interlocutory application to an order or comment being typed is 53 days; almost 11 working weeks or 3 working months' (HMCTS Civil Business Centres Performance Information[17]).

---

14 The Law Society Gazette, 22 May 2020.

15 The White Paper with its appendices is available by request to tonyguise@disputesefiling.com.

16 CCMCC = County Court Money Claims Centre, a centralised handling centre for all correspondence and applications to the County Courts. It has been closed and functions transferred elsewhere.

17 See, HMCTS, Civil Business Centres Performance Information https://www.gov.uk/government/publications/hmcts-civil-business-centres-performance-information/weekly-performance-national-business-centres-updated-5-december-2022 accessed 6 June 2025.

(d) 'A similar, if not worse, picture appears in the Tribunals system. In the Employment Tribunals (where high levels of claims may be expected post-Lockdown) the Backlog is even greater with disposals at almost 6,000 for 2019–2020 with new cases at just over 10,000.'[18]

Table 12.1 *Average time between issue and trial in weeks*

Year (as at December)	Small claims track	Fast track and multi-track
2015	31.6	53.9
2016	30.4	52.9
2017	32.2	58.2
2018	35.2	58.8
2019	37.1	60.9

Source: Ministry of Justice Civil Justice Statistics.

Since publishing the White Paper over five years ago, DEF has continued to monitor the growth of the backlog and the lengthening waiting times for first hearings. DEF's latest work in this area was published on 3 April 2024 and confirmed that:

> By the end of Q1 2023 the waiting time to first hearing in the SCT (for cases up to £10,000 by claim value) was 51.9 weeks though by September 2023 it had hit 55.4 weeks. In the higher value Tracks (Fast (FT) and Multi (MT), the Intermediate Track did not come into being until October 2023) the delay was even worse, 80 weeks. Please bear in mind that for most cases first hearings are adjourned for want of the paper file or a Judge, or both.
>
> This means waiting times are actually far, far worse than the MoJ's averages suggest, and those averages are bad. There are also wide variations between regions as found in a survey undertaken by Express Solicitors. If the trial court is in the wrong postcode parties may wait over 120 weeks for a hearing.
>
> With every passing year since the Pandemic wait times have grown 4 weeks longer.
>
> If the Civil justice system is left to its own devices DEF has estimated that by September 2025 the wait time for a first hearing in the SCT will be ca 70 weeks and in the FT/MT ca 90 weeks.

18 Georgina Sturge, *Court Statistics for E&W.* Parliamentary Briefing (13 September 2024 House of Commons Library).

> In human terms this represents millions of lives and livelihoods blighted by the Backlog.

In the White Paper DEF argued that:

> Without ADR firmly in the centre of the Civil justice system and managed online the Civil courts will be overwhelmed. The Tsunami [of litigation] will begin to interrupt the Civil justice system from September 2020 with successive waves arriving from that month onwards as Lockdown measures concerned with Civil justice are progressively removed. (DEF, White Paper, 42 para 114(a))

Regrettably DEF's June 2020 forecast proved prescient. This unhappy situation arises because of a combination of crises: firstly, the failure to complete the digitisation of Civil, Family and Tribunals justice in 2020 as planned; secondly, the recruitment crisis affecting the ranks of the Judiciary and especially amongst the District Bench, which handles most of the cases in the Civil Courts; and thirdly, because no prompt steps have yet been taken to introduce mandatory alternative dispute resolution (ADR) into Civil, Family and Tribunal proceedings. However, during 2024, positive steps have been taken in that direction, as we explain below.

The Civil Justice Council's Approach

The CJC is established under s.6(3) of the Civil Procedure Act, 1997 with functions that include keeping the Civil Justice system under review and making proposals for research. The Council is an Advisory Public Body operating under the aegis of the Ministry of Justice(MoJ), administratively supported by the MoJ and funded through the MoJ's budget.

As part of its statutory remit, the Council established an inquiry in 2021 to review the operation of a set of guides or protocols which regulate the steps parties and their lawyers take before issuing proceedings. These guides came to be known as Pre-Action Protocols (PAPs) and emanated from Recommendations 97–102 of Lord Woolf's Access to Justice Final Report. Recommendation 99 said that the PAPs were to 'set out codes of sensible practice which parties are expected to follow when faced with the prospect of litigation'.

In the 25 years that followed Lord Woolf's recommendation some 18 PAPs[19] had been written and the CJC judged that the time had come to review their operation. The Working Group that was established included amongst its

[19] The full list of 17 PAPs and a PAP Practice Direction is available here: Pre-Action Protocols – Civil Procedure Rules (justice.gov.uk).

members Professor Masood Ahmed, co-Editor of this book. The Terms of Reference for the Review included this:

> Should there be any changes to PAPs as a result of the HMCTS reform programme and the digitisation of the Civil justice system generally? To what extent are PAPs already online? Should there be further digitisation of PAP steps and guidance?[20]

An Interim Report was published in November 2021 and the Working Group's Final Report (Part 1) was published on 21 August 2023.[21] The CJC published Part 2 in November 2024.

Of the 29 Recommendations made in the Working Group's Final Report, we need only consider three because those are the most relevant to backlog clearance:

> 9.3 Compliance with pre-action protocols be made formally mandatory.
>
> 9.12 The WG recommends that governance of pre-action portals be allocated to the OPRC.
>
> 9.15 … there should be a formal certification process for private portals that are marketed to prospective parties as being compliant with pre-action protocols applying to the parties' dispute – and therefore 'court ready'.

The reference to OPRC in Recommendation 9.12 is an abbreviation of Online Procedure Rule Committee, which is a body constituted under the Judicial Review and Courts Act 2022. Formally launched in November 2023, its statutory duties require the OPRC to make rules:

> for the transfer by electronic means of information held for the purposes of an online dispute-resolution service to a court or tribunal. (s.24(1)(a))

Section 24(4) defines online dispute resolution service as:

> a service accessible by electronic means for facilitating the resolution of disputes without legal proceedings.

All PAPs contain an obligation to engage in an ADR process, such as mediation, before commencing court action.

---

20 Civil Justice Council Working Group on Pre-Action Protocols Final Report (Part 1) Annex 1, Terms of Reference no. 10, August 2023.

21 Civil Justice Council publishes final report on Pre-Action Protocols – Courts and Tribunals Judiciary.

Drawing all these points together, the plan going forward (assuming the Working Group's Recommendations are accepted) is that the OPRC will make rules to deliver the following:

- Before beginning any court action in the Civil or Family Courts or before any Tribunal in E&W the parties must engage in the pre-action steps specified in the appropriate PAP.
- Those steps will involve engaging in a form of ADR.
- All steps should be conducted through an online platform provided by the private sector that meets requirements specified by the OPRC; these are called online dispute management platforms (ODMs).
- Providers of ADR services will provide their services through an ODM.

The consequences of this approach are significant:

- The action in litigation will now be in pre-action.
- According to the Biennial Mediation Audit published in 2023 by the Centre for Effective Dispute Resolution, private sector mediators in 2022 settled 92% of all disputes either on the day of the mediation or shortly afterwards.[22]
- In consequence, over time, the backlog in the civil courts will be eradicated.
- This new regime upends the business models of litigation practitioners. Law firms and barristers have traditionally run dispute resolution cases on a business model that involves managing claims to trial, assuming settlement may happen at some point as one draws near the trial itself.

The delivery of access to justice in the 21st century has been profoundly hampered by the mismanagement of digitisation, making waiting times before the first hearing longer than when the Reform Programme began in 2016. This is a perverse outcome few, if any, could have imagined when work on that programme commenced.

The State remains obliged to provide an effective means of resolving differences between its citizens, whether individuals or businesses. At a time of economic and social challenge for the UK, it is vitally important to begin effective measures to reduce the backlog and, in doing so, unlock ca £53bn of cash flow tied up in disputes involving small to medium-sized enterprises, according to

---

[22] https://www.cedr.com/wp-content/uploads/2023/02/Tenth-CEDR-Mediation-Audit-2023.pdf on p. 7.

a report published by the Federation of Small Businesses in 2016 and allowing for inflation for the figure the Federation estimated then (£40bn).[23]

The quickest and easiest way to do that is to make engaging with ADR a mandatory obligation in pre-action and to have those processes managed online. This approach is finally being introduced in E&W. The steps taken so far are:

(a) mandatory ADR introduced for a limited class of claims for less than £10,000 on 22 May 2024;
(b) this was rolled out to nearly all claims for less than £10,000 in November 2024;
(c) power for the Courts to order ADR in all other post-issue cases began on 1 October 2024;
(d) the next phase would be the introduction of mandatory ADR in the pre-court phase; and
(e) the final phase will offer an OPRC-designed accreditation scheme for those online platforms wishing to connect to Court portals via APIs.

The great opportunities that open up are all have the same aim: creating systems that enable enduring change and finally get away from the anecdote and knee-jerk reform approach that has beset civil justice since the early 19th century. The three great pillars of enduring change are:

(a) analysis of and research into very rich data to inform reform;
(b) the use of AI both to manage mass dispute resolution through ADR processes and to propose solutions based on data from those settlements; and
(c) ADR service providers supporting the development of further reforms such as an effective online entry point with appropriate resources and signposting routes to resolution, funded under a Justice Infrastructure Levy akin to the Theatre Restoration Levy and many other such schemes.

These are the near horizons of digital dispute resolution. The plan to introduce a mandatory requirement to engage in ADR could be completed by 2026 or 2027. Yet many serious issues remain to be addressed, and we touch on some of those in the next section of this chapter.

23 Federation of Small Businesses, *Tied Up* 2016.

12.4 HOW IS THE PRIVATE SECTOR TO BE FUNDED ON A SUSTAINABLE BASIS TO DELIVER THIS PEOPLE-INTENSIVE, OFTEN MEDIATION-BASED, SERVICE ENABLED BY SOPHISTICATED TECHNOLOGY?

The most recent explanation of the new marketplace for ADR services in pre-court came from the Deputy Head of Civil Justice, Lord Justice Birss, in his speech on the occasion of the 24th Competition Law Association Burrell Lecture: 'Is a focus on data the way to improve access to justice in a multi-faceted world?', given on 30 November 2023.[24] In this speech, His Lordship observed:

> Imagine a person going to a site run by a provider of legal advice and assistance, could be a lawyer or in the third sector. They explain their problem by answering questions online – even just entering their basic details. … The resulting advice may be to try an online mediation service. Options for such services are presented and the person invited to select one. They do so and their details are sent directly to the online mediation provider. We all hope for success at that stage, but let's say … the matter is not resolved.
>
> The vision is that the provider's system will … then be able to refer them on, this next stage may then involve further advice and/or bringing a civil, family or tribunal claim into the courts and tribunals system. The person selects the option to start a court action. The system has the information to do this for them, and they can then immediately see their claim on the court's system – maybe OCMC [Online Civil Money Claims – a Court portal] if it is a small money claim. (paras 48 and 49)

His Lordship concluded with remarks (in para 72) indicating he saw the pre-action space (indeed the entire civil justice system) as a type of public/private partnership.

The Law Society of England and Wales (LSEW) launched a Working Group to consider options and make proposals for '21st Century Justice'. In October 2023 the LSEW published a Green Paper[25] that addressed the need for the kind of system described by Lord Justice Birss. The proposals in the Green Paper relied heavily on the building of a diagnostic tool which the Working Group calls the Solutions Explorer. This was an idea originally developed by the CJC's Online Dispute Resolution Working Group chaired by Professor Richard Susskind which reported in 2015. It was supported by the civil justice

---

24 Judiciary.uk, 'Speech by Lord Justice Colin Birss: Is a Focus on Data the Way to Improve Access to Justice in a Multifaceted World?' (judiciary.uk, 30 November 2023) https://www.judiciary.uk/speech-by-lord-justice-colin-birss-is-a-focus-on-data-the-way-to-improve-access-to-justice-in-a-multifaceted-world/.

25 Fresh ideas for twenty-first century justice | The Law Society.

lobby group, Justice, and adopted by Lord Briggs in his Final Report on the Civil Courts Structure in 2016.

So far as the authors are aware, neither the OPRC, the LSEW, the FSB nor anyone else has addressed the question of how the 'accredited online mediation provider' is to be paid for this service sufficient to enable that provider to deliver a sustainable service.

Pre-action ADR is going to become, in effect, a mandatory requirement, a condition to be fulfilled before the Court allows Court proceedings to be issued. This has been done overseas, in particular in Türkiye, with 64% of cases settled in pre-action for labour, commercial and some property disputes. Their scheme has been running since January 2018, beginning with labour disputes.[26]

In the course of a 2017 UK Supreme Court decision, it was held that:

> In the County Court, on the other hand, fees for small claims are graduated according to the value of the claim. … The fee structure has thus been designed in a way which is likely to have a less deterrent effect on the bringing of small claims. *R (on the application of UNISON) v Lord Chancellor* [2017] UKSC 51 [20] (Lord Reed)

When determining how to create a sustainable public/private partnership in pre-court using private sector ADR Service Providers, the authors consider regard must be had, as to pricing level, to the Supreme Court's decision in the UNISON case.

The OPRC will probably have to set a scale of fees as has been done in Türkiye. An approach may be to tie the fees to be charged for mediation, for example, to the scale charged by HMCTS for issuing a court action, i.e. claim value dependent. In the authors' view, such an approach would be proportionate and consistent with the Supreme Court's decision in UNISON.

A further nuance concerning funding involves the long-standing State subsidy of court fees for those citizens who, through poor financial circumstances, qualify for remission of their fees. This is called 'Help with Fees'.[27] It strikes the authors that if Help with Fees is made available to alleviate hardship

---

[26] Statistics published by the Mediation Directorate of the Türkiye Ministry of Justice state that out of the 751,549 labour dispute cases that were mediated between 2 January 2018 and 31 December 2019, 64% of cases settled. See, https://pomeps.org/the-case-of-turkish-labor-mediation-disenfranchising-the-workers#:~:text=Statistics%20published%20by%20the%20Mediation,of%20cases%20were%20settled%20amicably.

[27] How to apply for help with fees: EX160A – https://www.gov.uk/government/publications/apply-for-help-with-court-and-tribunal-fees/how-to-apply-for-help-with-fees-ex160a-for-applications-made-or-fees-paid-on-or-after-27-november-2023 (www.gov.uk).

for qualifying citizens when they seek to exercise their right to issue court proceedings, then, logically, that should also be made available if the State requires ADR processes to be undertaken before issuing proceedings.

The authors also ask, and other than rhetorically, whether the telephone and support services currently provided by HMCTS through its outsourced providers We Are Group and Law for Life (Advicenow) should be expanded to support citizens in pre-action.

These are the authors' preliminary ideas about a complex subject. However, in the detail of this lies the success (or failure) of the entire pre-action ADR project about which there appears to be universal support from Senior Judiciary to the LSEW, FSB and many others.

The important thing to recognise and act upon is that the new pre-action regime is multi-faceted and complex. To make it work requires careful planning and a phased approach, for example, by starting with mandatory mediation (or other ADR process) in pre-action first and then developing digital requirements as experience and funding allowed. It is also the case that ideas which seem, at a distance, to be simple often become complex the closer they are examined.

The need for careful consideration and collaboration with all the players in the would-be system cannot be understated. To successfully deliver the plan for integrating ADR into the civil, family and tribunal justice systems in E&W the need for wide engagement with the community of stakeholders in the broadest sense cannot be over-emphasised.

Index